Camping with the Corps of Engineers

Sergeant Major Spurgeon L. Hinkle
United States Marine Corps, Retired
7th Edition

Cottage Publications, Inc.
P.O. Box 2832
Elkhart, IN 46515-2832
1.800.272.5518 (not for reservations)
website: www.cottagepub.com
e-mail: info@cottagepub.com

Camping with the Corps of Engineers

Sergeant Major Spurgeon L. Hinkle
United States Marine Corps, Retired
7th Edition

Copyright ©2007 by Sgt. Major Spurgeon L. Hinkle, USMC (Ret.)

Printed in the United States of America

Camping with the Corps of Engineers 7th Edition

ISBN 0-937877-50-6

Cottage Publications, Inc.
P.O. Box 2832
Elkhart, IN 46515-2832
1.800.272.5518
website: www.cottagepub.com
e-mail: info@cottagepub.com

— CONTENTS —

Introduction

The information in this book is derived from many sources, the bulk of information being provided by district and project office in put. Some from personal visits, camping and people who have used the facilities. Additional information was procured from web sites. I wish to thank those U. S. Army Corps of Engineers personnel and other individuals who have contributed to making this book a success. Included herein are listings on more than 200 projects and over 850 campgrounds.

The Corps of Engineers is a Corps of the United States Army under the Department of Defense. As such it operates much the same as any other government agency - in constant change. This is due to many factors, including but not limited to the following: Size of the Corps, direction from congress and higher U. S. army commands, leeway granted the project officers by the District Officer, size of the area utilized, budget concerns, safety, weather, and other uses in the area, to name a few.

When using this book, please be advised that facilities are subject to change at anytime. Camp grounds may be closed due to flooding, low flow augmentation releases, excessive soil erosion, insufficient usage or personnel to supervise usage and other sufficient reasons. New campgrounds may be opened without notice. Additionally, free areas which require a fee part of the year may not have some amenities such as water or electric available during the free season. Therefore, particularly when you are going to be traveling some distance, it is imperative that you call the campground or project office prior to departure for information necessary for your needs. Prices change, free parks may be closed or converted to fee parks, or parks may be consigned to other agencies (State, County, City, etc.) or leased to concessionaires.

In addition to the project addresses provided at the start of each project, a listing of districts are in the book for your use. Last known fees are listed and subject to change without notice. Fees may be collected by roving patrol, ranger, gate attendant or self deposit (honor system). Abbreviations have been held to a minimum. I also want to mention that the symbols for some amenities, such as electric and water hookups, do not mean that all sites have these amenities, but rather that at least some are available. Other symbols for amenities such as golf courses, laundry facilities, marina's, etc., may be there as an indication that they are nearby.

Your interest and assistance in providing me with updated information will be appreciated. Please forward to S. L. Hinkle, c/o Cottage Publications, P. O. Box 2832, Elkhart, IN 46515-2832. 1-800-272-5518. I have always found that the majority of Corps of Engineers Campgrounds are well maintained and administered. Hoping you will find them the same and get lots of use from this publication. May see you along the road - Happy Camping.

General Information

The U. S. Army Corps of Engineers is the nation's leading federal provider in outdoor recreation opportunities for the public. The Corps operates more than 2,500 recreation areas and leases an additional 1,800 sites. The Corps hosts 360 million visits a year at its lakes, beaches and other areas with estimates that 25 million Americans visit a Corps project at least once a year.

General regulations for the Corps of Engineers recreational facilities are contained in Title 36, U. S. Code. You may procure a copy at most Corps facilities.

Unless otherwise noted, for information on group camping areas and pavilion rentals, contact the project office.

Most projects will accept payment by personal check requiring such information as telephone number, driver's license number and address. Many, including the National Recreation Reservation Service, accept Master/Visa cards, American Express and Discover cards.

Many campgrounds and projects have much to offer that is not listed under the camping information. The listed information is taken from that received from the districts and projects, some more detailed than others. Common amenities not listed are fire rings, lampposts, tables, grills, and public telephones. Contact the project you will be visiting to obtain a complete listing. You may want to visit the district web sites listed on the address page.

America the Beautiful Senior Pass (formerly called the Golden Age Passport) is a lifetime pass issued to citizens/permanent residents of the U.S. who are 62 years of age and older. It may be used for a 50% discount on federal use fees charged for camping, use of dumping station facilities, boat launching fees, parking fees, day-use fees and annual passes and as an entrance pass for national parks, historic sites, national museums, recreation areas and wildlife areas. To obtain a pass, you must appear in person, show proof of age (driver's license, birth certificate or similar document establishing age, citizenship or permanent resident status), and pay a $10 one-time fee.

America the Beautiful Access Pass (formerly Golden Access Pass) is issued to citizens/permanent residents who are blind or medically determined to be permanently disabled and as a result are eligible to receive benefits under federal law. They have the same benefits as the Senior Pass. To obtain a pass, you must appear in person, show proof of being blind or permanently medically disabled and eligible to receive benefits under federal law. There is no charge for this card, and age is not a factor.

These discounts for entry and camping apply to the cardholder and those accompanying them in a private noncommercial vehicle, which includes recreational vehicles.

Concessionaires normally do not offer the discount - some honor them. Ask! Some state parks do honor the passes - most don't.

Passes may be obtained from National Forest supervisors' offices, most Forest Service ranger station offices, all National Park Service areas where entrance fees are charged, Bureau of Land Management state and district offices, Tennessee Valley Authority recreational areas where fees are charged, all National Fish and Wildlife Service regional offices and National Wildlife Refuges where entrance fees are charged, Bureau of Reclamation offices and at Hoover Dam. However, the U.S. Army Corps of Engineers offices are not permitted by law to distribute America the Beautiful passes due to an oversight in Congress when the legislation was approved.

All America the Beautiful passes are accepted at Corps-operated facilities where fees are charged, including at campgrounds, boat ramps and designated swimming beaches. Holders of the Senior Pass or Access Pass receive 50% discounts on fees. A valid camping permit entitles the holder to use day-use facilities without charge.

Pets - Pets are permitted at most Corps campgrounds. They must be in the camper, vehicle, pen or on a leash no longer than 6'. Owners are requested to clean up after their pets. They are not allowed on beach areas where swimming is designated nor in rest rooms/showers, etc. Additional pet requirements and restrictions may apply at individual campgrounds and parks.

For the National Recreation Reservation Service (NRRS), call toll free, 1-877-444-6777, TDD 877-833-6777, or use the web site, www.ReserveUSA.com. Have the following information available when you call to place the reservation: Name of campground and project (lake, river, etc.), camp site number if possible or the type of site desired, arrival and departure dates, name, address and phone number, vehicles, trailers, tents and other equipment you will be bringing, license numbers of all vehicles you will be bringing, Golden Age/Access Passport Number (if you have one), and your credit card number (Master, Visa, American Express or Discover) to pay for the reservation stay. Many campground reservations required a 3 day minimum stay on weekends. Additionally, many projects require a cancellation fee when making the reservation.

Some campers may desire to contract as a gate attendant. Contact the district in the area you desire. Additionally, the Corps of Engineers has a volunteer program available for those who wish to help in many different areas. Call 1-800-865-8337, or visit the web site, www.orn.usace.army.mil/volunteer/

Symbols

1. Archery range
2. Ball field
3. Bath house/showers
4. Basketball court
5. Bike trails
6. Billiards
7. Boating
8. Boat launch
9. Campfire areas
10. Campfire programs
11. Canoeing
12. Comfort station/toilets
13. Drinking water
14. Dump station
15. Electric hookups
16. Equestrian trail
17. First-aid station
18. Fishing
19. Golf nearby
20. Handicap site
21. Handicap facilities
22. Handicap fishing pier
23. Hiking or nature trail
24. Laundry in camp or nearby
25. LP-gas nearby
26. Marina
27. Visa/Mastercard
28. Model airplane field
29. Motorbike trail
30. Multi-use court
31. No swimming
32. Off-road/all terrain vehicle area
33. Pets on leash
34. Picnic/public use area
35. Pier/dock
36. Playground
37. Rockhounding
38. Rowboats only NO MOTORS
39. Sailing
40. Shooting range
41. Skiing trail
42. Snowmobiling trail
43. Swimming beach
44. Swimming pool
45. Tennis court
46. Tent camping only/no RVs
47. Tenting
48. Volleyball court
49. Water hookups
50. Water skiing

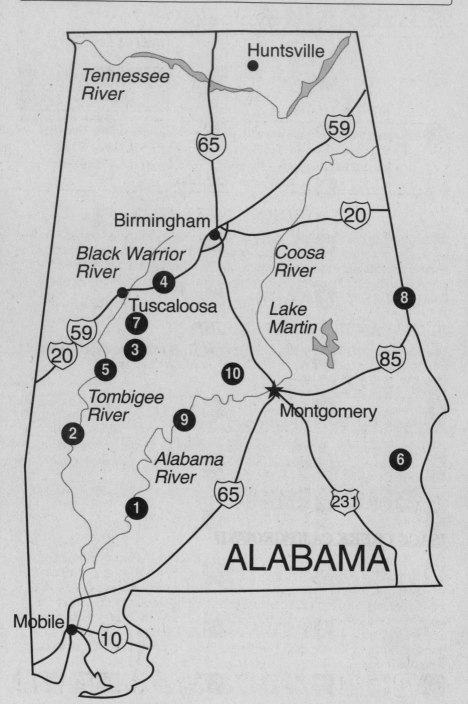

ALABAMA

STATE CAPITAL:
Montgomery
NICKNAME:
Yellowhammer State

22nd State - 1819

Site reservation, National Recreation Reservation Service (NRRS), toll free, 1-877-444-6777; TDD 877-833-6777, www.recreation.gov, (Master, Visa, American Express & Discover cards).

CLAIBORNE LAKE (MB) 1

A 5,900 acre surface area lake with over 60 miles of shoreline is located 3 miles northwest of Claiborne off United States Route 84, on the Alabama River, northeast of Mobile in southwest Alabama. Alcohol is prohibited at these campgrounds. Site Manager, Alabama River Lakes, 1226 Powerhouse Road, Camden, AL 36726. (334) 682-4244.

BELLS LANDING CAMPGROUND

From Hybart, go 3 miles south on State Road 41. 14 primitive sites. All sites are free. Recreational vehicle maximum length is 20'. Open all year.

HAINES ISLAND CAMPGROUND

From Monroeville, go 8 miles north on State Road 41, 10 miles west on County Road 17 (signs). Picnic shelter. 12 primitive sites. All sites are free. Recreational vehicle maximum length is 40'. Open all year.

ISACC CREEK CAMPGROUND

From Monroeville, go 8 miles north on State Road 41, 5 miles northwest on County Road 17 (signs) to Wainwright, 5 miles west to Finchburg, 4 miles southwest (left) on Lock & Dam Road, 0.6 mile left to campground. An extra vehicle fee may be charged. There is a fish cleaning station and picnic shelter available and a convenience store is nearby. 61 sites with 50 ampere service, 17 handicap sites, 4 pull through sites. Sites with 50 ampere service are $14; premium sites with 50 ampere service are $16. Recreational vehicle maximum length is in excess of 65'. Open all year. (334) 282-4254. NRRS.

SILVER CREEK CAMPGROUND

From Claiborne, go 8 miles northwest on United States Route 84 (signs). 8 primitive sites. All sites are free. Recreational vehicle maximum length is 20'. Open all year.

WEST BANK CAMPGROUND

From Claiborne, go northwest on State Road 48. 2 primitive sites. All sites are free. Open all year.

COFFEEVILLE LAKE (MB) 2

An 8,800 acre surface area lake, 97 miles in length, located 3 miles southwest of Coffeeville off United States Route 84, north of Mobile in west-central Alabama near the Mississippi state line. Demopolis Site Office, Black Warrior-Tombigbee River Lakes, 384 Resource Management Drive, Demopolis, AL 37632. (334) 289-3540.

SERVICE PARK CAMPGROUND

From Coffeeville, go 4 miles west on United States Route 84 across bridge, access right (signs). Off the road vehicles are prohibited. 32 sites with water and electdic, 10 pull through sites, 2 tent only sites, 1 handicap pull through site. Tent sites with water and electric and premium sites with water and electric hookups are $16; sites with water and electric are $14. Recreational vehicle maximum length is in excess of 65'. This campground requires a 2 night minimum stay on weekends and a 3 night minimum on holiday weekends. Open all year. (251) 754-9338. NRRS.

DEMOPOLIS LAKE (MB) 3

A 10,000 acre surface area lake located just north of Demopolis, west of United States Route 43, south of Tuscaloosa, in west-central Alabama. Checkout time is 3 p.m. Demopolis Site Office, Demopolis Lake, 384 Resource Management Drive, Demopolis, AL 36732. (334) 289-3540.

FORKLAND/MCCONNICO CREEK CAMPGROUND

From Demopolis, go 9 miles north on United States Route 43, at Forkland, 1 mile southwest (left) on county road (signs). Group camping for up to 50 people and 2 vehicles and a picnic shelter are available. Off the road vehicles are prohibited. 42 sites with water and electric, 13 pull through sites. Sites with water and electric hookups are $14; premium sites with water and electric hookups are $16. Recreational vehicle maximum length is in excess of 65'. This campground requires a 2 night minimum stay on weekends and a 3 night stay on holiday weekends. Open all year. (334) 289-5530. NRRS.

FOSCUE CAMPGROUND

From Demopolis go 3 miles west on United States Route 80 (signs), 2 miles north (right) on Maria Avenue. Group camping, amphitheater and a picnic shelter are available. 54 sites with water and 50 ampere service, 49 full hookups, 2 pull through sites, 9 handicap sites with full hookups. Sites with water and 50 ampere service are $16; premium sites with full hookups are $18. Recreational maximum vehicle length is in excess of 65'. (Some sites may be closed for renovation). This campground requires a 2 night minimum stay on weekends and a 3 night stay on holiday weekends. Open all year. (334) 289-5535. NRRS.

HOLT LAKE (MB) 4

A 3,200 acre surface area lake located 6 miles northeast of Tuscaloosa northwest of Peterson. Off the road vehicles are prohibited. Resource Manager, Holt Lake, P. O. Box 295, Peterson, AL 35478. (205) 553-9373/554-1684.

BLUE CREEK CAMPGROUND

From Tuscaloosa, go 13 miles north on State Road 69, 10 miles east on County Road 38, 2.5 miles on Blue Creek Road. 18 sites. All sites are free. Open all year.

BURCHFIELD BRANCH CAMPGROUND (Old Lock 16)

From Tuscaloosa, I-20/59, exit 86, take County Road 59 to Brookwood, 0.8 mile east on State Road 216, 16.6 miles northwest on County Road 59, veer left 0.1

mile on Ground Hog Road, 1.2 miles left at stop sign on Lock 17 Road, 3.9 miles left at Grocery store to park. A picnic shelter for up to 100 people is $30, tubing is available and a convenience store is nearby. 37 sites with water and electric, 1 tent only site, 36 - 50 ampere, 2 pull through sites, 24 handicap sites. A tent only site is $12; sites with water and 50 ampere service are $18. Recreational vehicle maximum length is in excess of 65'. This campground requires a 2 day minimum stay on weekends and a 3 day stay on holiday weekends. Open all year. (205) 497-9828. NRRS.

DEERLICK CREEK CAMPGROUND

From Tuscaloosa, I-20/59, exit 73, go 4.2 miles west on United States Route 82 (McFarland Boulevard), 14 miles northeast on Rice Mine Road (County Road 30), 3.6 miles on County Road 87 (New Watermelon Road), 3.5 miles on County Road 42 (Lake Nicol Road), 3.2 miles left on County Road 89 (Deerlick Road). A picnic shelter is $30, horseshoe pits, paved bicycle trail, and an amphitheater are available. 46 sites, 40 with water and electric, 6 primitive tent only sites, 90 pull through sites, 1 handicap site with water and electric. Primitive tent sites are $10; sites with water and electric hookups are $16; premium sites with water and electric hookups are $18. Recreational vehicle maximum length is 40'. Open from March 1st to November 19th. (205) 759-1591. NRRS.

TENNESSEE-TOMBIGBEE WATERWAY (MB) 5

The Tennessee-Tombigbee Waterway is a navigable link between the lower Tennessee Valley and the Gulf of Mexico. Stretching 234 miles from Demopolis, AL to Pickwick Lake in the northeast corner of MS, this man-made channel has a series of ten locks and dams forming ten pools. Off the road vehicles are prohibited. The Tom Bevill visitor center, Pickensville, AL, (205) 373-8705 (open daily except on some federal holidays) is an 1830-1850 era "antebellum" style center with a restored 1926 sternwheeler "United States Snagboat", interpretive exhibits, artifacts, group tours. Checkout time is 3 p.m., visitors fee is $3 to 9 p.m., and a fee of $3 for the 3rd and 4th vehicle is charged. Resource Manager, Waterway Management Center, 3606 west Plymouth Road, Columbus, MS 39701. (662) 327-2142.

COCHRANE CAMPGROUND

From Aliceville, go 10 miles south on State Road 17 (signs), 2 miles west of Huyck Bridge (signs), turn right 2 miles on access road. A picnic shelter is available, an emergency night exit is provided and there is an accessible handicap fishing area. 60 sites with water and electric, 3 handicap sites. Sites with water and electric hookups are $12; premium sites with water and electric hookups are $14. Recreational vehicle maximum length is in excess of 65'. This campground requires a 2 night minimum stay on weekends and a 3 night stay on holiday weekends. Open from March 1st to December 31st. (205) 373-8806. NRRS (March 1st to September 15th.

PICKENSVILLE CAMPGROUND

From Pickensville/Junction State Road 14, at caution light go 2.6 miles west on State Road 86 across waterway bridge, on right. A fish cleaning station and picnic shelters are available. A night time emergency exit is available and there is a handicap accessible fishing area. 176 sites with water and electric, 29 full hookups, 4 handicap sites with water and electric, 1 handicap site with full hookups. Sites with water and electric hookups are $16; premium sites with water and electric hookups and sites with full hookup are $18; premium sites with full hookups are $20. Recreational vehicle maximum length is in excess of 65'. This campground required a 2 night minimum stay on weekends and a 3 night stay on holiday weekends. Open all year. (205) 373-6328. NRRS (1 March to 15 September).

WALTER F. GEORGE LAKE (MB) 6

A 45,000 acre surface area lake located on the Chattahoochee River, Alabama/ Georgia state line, adjacent to Ft. Gaines, GA, west of Albany, GA, north of Dothan. Checkout time is 3 p.m. Visitor vehicle to 9:30 p.m., a fee is charged. Off the road vehicles and golf carts are prohibited. Picnic shelters are available, for reservation call (334) 585-6537. Resource Manager, Walter F. George Lake, Rt. 1, Box 176, Ft. Gaines, GA 31751-9722. (229) 768-2516/(334) 585-6537. See GA listing.

BLUFF CREEK CAMPGROUND

From Phenix City, go 3 miles south on United States Route 431, 18 miles south (left) on State Road 165, east (left at signs) across railroad, on right. A picnic shelter and fish cleaning station are available. 88 sites with water and electric, 6 pull through sites. Sites with water and electric hookups are $20. Recreational vehicle maximum length is 40'. This campground requires a 2 night minimum stay on weekends and a 3 night stay on holiday weekends. Open from February 28th to October 28th. (256) 855-2746. NRRS.

HARDRIDGE CREEK CAMPGROUND

From Ft. Gaines, GA, go 3 miles west across river, 1 mile west on State Road 46, 3 miles north on State Road 97, east at sign. A picnic shelter is available. There are restaurants and a convenience store located nearby. 77 sites with water and electric, 19 pull through sites, 20 full hookups, 3 buddy sites. Sites with water and electric are $20; sites with full hookups are $22. Recreational vehicle maximum length is 30'. This campground requires a 2 night minimum stay on weekends and a 3 night stay on holiday weekends. Open from March 2nd to December 3rd. (334) 585-5945. NRRS.

WHITE OAK CREEK CAMPGROUND

From Eufaula, go 8 miles south on United States Route 431, 2 miles southeast (left) on State Road 95, east (left) at sign prior to the White Oak Creek bridge. A picnic shelter and a fish cleaning station are available. there is a convenience store located nearby. 130 sites with water and electric, 5 pull through sites. Sites with water and electric hookups are $20. Recreational vehicle maximum length is 40'. This campground requires a 2 night minimum stay on weekends and a 3 night stay on holiday weekends. Open all year. (334) 687-3101. NRRS.

WARRIOR LAKE (MB) 7

A 7,800 acre surface area lake located 6 miles southeast of Eutaw off State Road 14, southwest of Tuscaloosa. Public use areas. Demopolis Site Office, Demopolis Lake, 384 Resource Management Drive, Demopolis, AL 36732. (334) 289-3540.

JENNINGS FERRY/ROEBUCK LANDING CAMPGROUND

From Eutaw, go 5.7 miles east on State Road 14, across Warrior River Bridge. A fish cleaning station is available. 52 sites with water and electric, 8 pull through sites. Sites with water and electric hookups are $16. Recreational vehicle maximum length is 65'. This campground requires a 2 night minimum stay on weekends and a 3 night stay on holiday weekends. Open all year.

WEST POINT LAKE (MB) 8

A 25,900 acre surface area lake 35 miles along the Chattahoochee River located southwest of Atlanta and I-85 on the Alabama/Georgia state line near West Point, GA, northeast of Montgomery. Resource Manager, West Point Lake, 500 Resource Manager Drive, West Point, GA 31833-9517. (706) 645-2937. See GA listing.

AMITY CAMPGROUND

From Lanett, go 7 miles north on County Road 212, 0.5 mile east on County Road 393 (signs). An amphitheater is available. 96 sites, 93 with water and electric, 3 tent only sites. Primitive tent only sites are $16; sites with water and electric hookups are $22. This campground requires a 2 night minimum stay on weekends and a 3 night stay on holiday weekends. Recreational vehicle maximum length is 20'. Open from March 16th to September 8th. (334) 499-2404. NRRS.

WILLIAM 'BILL' DANNELLY LAKE (MB) 9

A 24 square mile lake encompassing 105 miles of the Alabama river starting northwest of Camden, 1 mile below the Lee Long Bridge, State Road 10/28 southwest of Selma on United States Route 41 in southwest Alabama. Crappie and Bass tournaments are held during the year as well as civil war enactments. An excellent bow hunting area for deer and turkey. An extra vehicle/visitor fee is charged to 9:30 p.m. Resource Manager, William B. Dannelly Lake, 1226 Powerhouse Road, Camden, AL 36726-9109. (334) 682-4244.

CHILATCHEE CREEK CAMPGROUND

From Alberta, go 11 miles southeast on County Road 29 (signs), left on Chilatchee Road. A picnic shelter and fish cleaning station are available. 53 sites, 47 with water and electric, 28 - 50 ampere, 3 pull through sites, 5 handicap sites with water and 50 ampere. Sites without electric hookups are

$8; sites with water and electric hookups and sites with water and 50 ampere are $14; premium sites with water and electric hookups and premium sites with water and 50 ampere are $16. Recreational vehicle maximum length is 65'. Open from January 1st to November 11th. (334) 573-2562. NRRS.

ELM BLUFF

From Camden, go 15.5 miles northeast on State Road 41. 10 primitive sites. All sites are free. Open all year.

MILLERS FERRY/EAST BANK CAMPGROUND

From Camden, go 11 miles northwest on State Road 28, right before Lee Long Bridge (signs). A picnic shelter is available, a fee is charged for each vehicle over 2 and there is a convenience store is located nearby. 66 sites with water and electric, 52 - 50 ampere service, 12 handicap sites, 6 pull through sites. Sites with water and electric hookups and sites with water and 50 ampere service are $14; premium sites with water and 50 ampere service are $16. Recreational vehicle maximum length is in excess of 65'. Open all year. (334) 682-4191. NRRS.

SIX MILE CREEK CAMPGROUND

From Selma/Junction United States Route 80, go 9 miles south on State Road 41, 1.6 miles west (right) on County Road 139 (signs), 0.7 miles north on County Road 77. Two picnic shelters are available. 31 sites with water and electric, 3 handicap sites. Sites with water and electric hookups are $14; premium sites with water and electric hookups are $16. Recreational vehicle maximum length is in excess of 65'. Open all year. (334) 875-6228. NRRS (April 1st to September 13th).

WOODRUFF LAKE (MB) 10

A 20 square mile lake southeast of Selma off United States Route 80, 5 miles north of Benton, 8 miles west of Montgomery. A fee may be charge for visitors. Site Manager, Alabama River Lakes, 8493 United States Route 80 west, Hayneville, AL 36040. (334) 872-9554/8210.

GUNTER HILL CAMPGROUND

From Montgomery, I-65, exit 167, go 9 miles west on State Road 80, 4 miles north (right) on County Road 7 (signs). A picnic shelter is available to campers only and a convenience store is nearby. 146 sites with water and electric, 10 handicap sites. Sites with water and electric hookups are $16. Some primitive camping is available - contact the office for information. Recreational vehicle maximum length is in excess of 65'. Open all year. (334) 269-1053. NRRS.

PRAIRIE CREEK CAMPGROUND

From Montgomery, go 25 miles west on State Road 80, 5 miles north on County Road 23 (signs), 3 miles west on County Road 40. A picnic shelter is available to campers only. 62 sites with water and electric, 7 tent only sites, 2 pull through sites, 2 handicap sites. Tent only sites are $12; sites with water and electric hookups are $14; premium sites with water and electric hookups are $16. Recreational vehicle maximum length is 35'. Open all year. (334) 418-4916. NRRS.

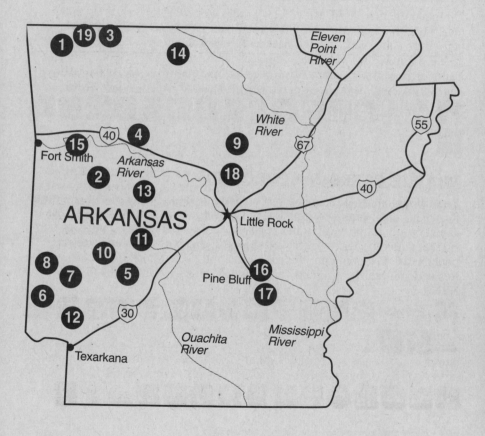

ARKANSAS

STATE CAPITAL:
Little Rock
NICKNAME:
The Natural State

25th State - 1836

Site reservation, National Recreation Reservation Service (NRRS), toll free, 1-877-444-6777; TDD 877-833-6777, www.recreation.gov, (Master, Visa, American Express & Discover cards).

Little Rock District - A fee may be charged for use of the dump station by non-campers. An extra fee may be charged for sites with water hookups.

BEAVER LAKE (LR) 1

A 28,000 acre surface area lake with 487 miles of shoreline is located 9 miles northwest of Eureka Springs on United States Route 62, 186 miles northwest of Little Rock in northwest Arkansas. Trout fishing, scuba diving and river rafting are located nearby, checkout time is 3 p.m., and alcohol is prohibited at these parks. Free sites in winter may have reduced amenities. Resource Manager, Beaver Lake, 2260 North 2nd Street, Rogers, AR 72756. (479)636-1210/253-5866.

DAM SITE LAKE CAMPGROUND

From Eureka Springs, go 4.5 miles west on United States Route 62 (signs), 3 miles south (left) on State Road 187 (signs). A picnic shelter is $60 and a change shelter is available. 48 sites with water and electric, 36 - 50 ampere. Sites with water and electric hookups are $16; sites with water and 50 ampere service are $17. Open from April 1st to October 31st. (479) 253-5828.

DAM SITE RIVER CAMPGROUND

From Eureka Springs, go 4.3 miles west on United States Route 62 (signs), 2.5 miles south (left) on State Road 187 across and below the dam (signs). River rafting trips are available nearby. 55 sites with electric. Sites with electric hookups are $16. Recreational vehicle maximum length is in excess of 65'. This campground requires a 2 night minimum stay on weekends and a 3 night stay on holiday weekends. Open April 1st to October 28th. (479) 253-9865. NRRS (May 15th to September 15th).

HICKORY CREEK CAMPGROUND

From Springdale/Junction United States Route 412, go 1 mile north on United States Route 71, 4.5 miles east on State Road 264, 1 mile north (right) on Cow Face Road (County Road 6602, signs), east (left) on Hickory Creek Road. Two picnic shelters are $75 and are reserve able and available all year. 61 sites with electric, 19 - 50 ampere, 1 full hookup, 1 handicap site. From April 1st to October 31st, sites with electdric hookups are $16; premium sites with 50 ampere service are $17; a full hookup site is $22; from November 1st to March 31st, sites are $12. Recreational vehicle maximum length is 50'. This campground requires a 2 night minimum stay on weekends and a 3 night stay on holiday weekends. Open all year. (479) 750-2943. NRRS (May 19th to September 16th).

HORSESHOE BEND EAST CAMPGROUND

From Rogers/Junction United States Route 71, go 5 miles east on State Road 94 (signs). Two picnic shelters, GPA for up to 100 people and 10 vehicles and DUA for up to 100 people and 15 vehicles are $75 and are reserve able available all year. 63 sites with electric, 3 tent only sites, 6 double sites. Tent sites are $10; sites with electric hookups are $16; double sites with electric hookups are $34. Recreational vehicle maximum length is in excess of 65'. This campground requires a 2 night stay on weekends and a 3 night stay on holiday weekends. Open April 1st to October 31st. (479) 925-7195. NRRS (May 12th to September 19th).

HORSESHOE BEND WEST CAMPGROUND

From Rogers/Junction United States Route 71, go 5 miles east on State Road 94 (signs). A picnic shelter for up to 100 people and 75 vehicles is $75 and is available all year. 125 sites with electric, 8 double sites, 1 handicap site. From April 1st to October 31st, sites with electric hookups are $16; double sites with electric hookups are are $32; from November 1st to March 31st, sites with electric hookups are $12. Recreational vehicle maximum length is in excess of 65'. This campground requires a 2 night minimum stay on weekends and a 3 night stay on holiday weekends. Open all year. (479) 935-7195. NRRS (May 12th to September 19th).

INDIAN CREEK CAMPGROUND

From Gateway, go 5 miles east, 4 miles south (right) on Indian Creek Road (signs, County Road 89). A picnic shelter is available. 33 sites with electric. Sites with electric hookups are $16. Open 1 May to September 6th. (479) 656-3145.

LOST BRIDGE NORTH CAMPGROUND

From Garfield/Junction State Road 62, go 6 miles southeast on State Road 127 (signs), turn on 127 Spur, left on Marina Road. Group camping area for up to 40 people and 6 vehicles(for Scout groups, etc., only, open all year, NRRS) is $40. 48 sites with electric, 1 handicap site, 9 pull through sites. Sites with electric hookups are $16. Recreational vehicle maximum length is 60'. This campground requires a 2 night minimum stay on weekends and a 3 night stay on holiday weekends. Open from May 1st to September 29th. (479) 359-3312. NRRS (May 19th to September 15th).

LOST BRIDGE SOUTH CAMPGROUND

From Garfield/Junction State Road 62, go 5 miles southeast (right) on State Road 127 (signs), left on Marina Road. A picnic shelter is $60. 38 sites with 50 ampere. Sites with electric hookups are $16; premium sites with electric hookups are $17. Recreational vehicle maximum length is 55'. This campground requires a 2 night minimum stay on weekends and a 3 night stay on holiday weekends. Open from 1 May to September 27th. (479) 359-3755. NRRS (May 19th to September 15th).

PRAIRIE CREEK CAMPGROUND

From Rogers/Junction United States Route 71 (signs), go 4 miles east on State Road 12, 1 mile north on North Park Road. Two picnic shelters are reserve able all year, East and West for up to 100 people and 75 vehicles are $75. 112 sites with electric, 15 - 50 ampere, 1 tent only site, 3 pull through sites, 6 double sites, 1 full hookup. From April 1st to October 31st, a tent only site with electric, sites with electric hookups and premium sites with electric hookups are $16; sites with 50 ampere service are $17; sites with water and 50 ampere service are $19; a full hookup site is $22; double sites with electric hookups are $32; from November 1st to March 31st, sites with electric hookups are $12;

sites with water and 50 ampere service are $16. Recreational vehicle maximum length is in excess of 65'. This campground requires a 2 night minimum stay on weekends and a 3 night stay on holiday weekends. Open all year. (479) 925-3957. NRRS (May 19th to September 15th).

ROCKY BRANCH CAMPGROUND

From Rogers/Junction United States Route 71 (signs), go 11 miles east on State Road 12 (signs), 4.5 miles northeast on State Road 303 (signs) on left. Two picnic shelters are $60k call the office for reservations. 44 sites with electric, some double sites. From May 1st to October 31st, sites with electric hookups are $16. From November 1st to April 30th, sites 3 through 25 with electric hookups are $12. Open all year. (479) 925-2526.

STARKEY CAMPGROUND

From Eureka Springs, go 4 miles west on United States Route 62 (signs), 4 miles southwest on State Road 187, 4.3 miles west (right) on County Road 2176 (Mundell Road, signs). A picnic shelter, call the office for reservations, and a change shelter are available. 23 sites with electric. Sites with electric hookups are $16. Open from May 1st to September 8th. (479) 253-5866.

WAR EAGLE CAMPGROUND

From Springdale/Junction United States Route 71, go 10 miles east on State Road 412 (signs), 3 miles northwest on County Road 95. A picnic shelter, for reservations call the office, is $60. 26 sites with electric. From May 1st to October 31st, sites with electric hookups are $16; premium sites with electric hookups are $17; from November 1st to April 30th, sites with electric hookups are $12. Open all year. (479) 750-4722.

BLUE MOUNTAIN LAKE (LR) 2

A 2,910 acre surface area lake located 1.5 miles southwest of Waveland on State Road 309 off State Road 10, 5 miles east of Blue Mountain, 101 miles northwest of Little Rock. A day use fee may be charged in free camping areas. Park Manager, Rt. 1, Box 173AA, Blue Mountain Lake, Waveland, AR 72842-9600. (479) 947-2372.

OUTLET AREA CAMPGROUND

From Waveland/Junction State Road 10, go 1.8 miles south (right) on State Road 309 across & below dam on Petit Jean River(signs). A fish cleaning station is available. 41 sites with water and electric, 3 double sites, 4 pull through sites. From March 1st to October 31st, sites with water and electric hookups are $14; double sites with water and electric hookups are $28; from November 1st to February 28th, sites with water and electric hookups are $12; double sites with water and electric hookups are $24. Recreational vehicle maximum length is in excess of 65'. This campground requires a 2 night minimum stay on weekends and a 3 night stay on holiday weekends. Open all year. (479) 947-2101. NRRS (May 1st to September 15th).

WAVELAND CAMPGROUND

From Waveland, go 0.9 mile south (signs), go 0.9 mile west. A picnic shelter, fish cleaning station, amphitheater and a change shelter are available. 51 sites with water and electric. From March 1st to October 31st, sites with water and electric hookups are $14; double sites with water and electric hookups are $25; from November 1st to February 28th, sites with water and electric hookups are $12; double sites with water and electric are $24. Recreational vehicle maximum length is 40'. This campground requires a 2 night minimum stay on weekends and a 3 night stay on holiday weekends. Open March 1st to October 31st. (479) 947-2102. NRRS (May 18th to September 14th).

BULL SHOALS LAKE (LR) 3

A 45,440 acre surface area lake located 15 miles west of Mountain Home on State Road 178 in north-central Arkansas, southeast of Branson, Missouri. Off the road vehicles are prohibited and checkout time is 3 p.m. For information call (870) 425-2700. Resource Manager, Bull Shoals Lake, P. O. Box 2070, Mountain Home, AR 72654-2070. See MO listing.

BUCK CREEK CAMPGROUND

From Protem (sign), MO., go 5.5 miles southeast on State Road 125 (signs). A picnic shelter for up to 50 people and 10 vehicles is $40, and a marine dump station and change shelter are available. 38 sites, 36 with electric, 1 double site. Sites without electric hookups are $12; sites with electric hookups are $16; a double site with electric is $32. Recreational vehicle maximum length is 40'. This campground requires a 2 night minimum stay on weekends and a 3 night stay on holiday weekends. Open from April 1st to September 30th. (417) 785-4313. NRRS (May 16th to September 12th).

DAM SITE CAMPGROUND

From Bull Shoals, go 1 mile southwest on State Road 178 (signs). A picnic shelter for up to 50 people and 2 vehicles is $40. 35 sites with electric. Sites with electric hookups are $16. Recreational vehicle maximum length is 40'. This campground requires a 2 night minimum stay on weekends and a 3 night stay on holiday weekends. Open from April 1st to September 30th. (870) 445-7166. NRRS (May 16th to September 12th).

HIGHWAY 125 CAMPGROUND

From Peel, go 5.1 miles north on State Road 125. A picnic shelter for up to 50 people and 20 vehicles is $40 and a marine dump station is available. 38 sites with electric. Sites with electric hookups are $16. Recreational vehicle maximum length is 45'. This campground requires a 2 night minimum stay on weekends and a 3 night stay on holiday weekends. Open from April 1st to October 31st. (870) 436-5711. NRRS (May 16th to September 12th).

LAKEVIEW CAMPGROUND

From Mountain Home/Junction United States Route 62, go 6 miles northwest to Midway on State Road 5, 7.1 miles southwest on State Road 178 (signs), north on Boat Dock Road. A group camping area is available and two picnic shelters, GS1 for up to 50 people and 10 vehicles is $50 and GS2 for up to 25 people and 10 vehicles are $40. A convenience store is located nearby. 88 sites, 72 with electric, 2 - 50 ampere, 6 double sites, 1 tent only site. A tent only site is $8; sites without electric hookups are $12; sites with electric hookups are $16; premium sites with water and electric hookups and sites with water and electric, 2nd price, are $17; sites with water and 50 ampere service are $18; double sites with electric are $32; double sites with electric, 2nd price, and premium double sites with water and electric are $34, a triple site is $48. Recreational vehicle maximum length is 40'. This campground requires a 2 night minimum stay on weekends and a 3 night stay on holiday weekends. Open from April 1st to October 31st. (870) 431-8116. NRRS (May 17th to September 13th).

LEAD HILL CAMPGROUND

From Lead Hill/Junction State Road 14, go 3.5 miles north through Diamond City on State Road 7 (signs). Picnic shelters, GS2 for up to 50 people and 15 vehicles is $40 and GS11 for up to 100 people and 20 vehicles is $50, and a marine dump station and change shelter are available. 75 sites with electric, 1 double site, 1 handicap site with electric, 4 pull through sites. Sites with water and electric hookups are $16; a double site with water and electric hookups is $32. Recreational vehicle maximum length is 40'. This campground requires a 2 night minimum stay on weekends and a 3 night stay on holiday weekends. Open from April 1st to October 31st. (870) 422-7555. NRRS (May 17th to September 12th).

OAKLAND/OZARK ISLE CAMPGROUND

From Oakland, go 4 miles west on State Road 202. A picnic shelter for up to 36 people and 10 vehicles is $40 and a change shelter is available. 83 sites, 46 sites with electic, 1 - 50 ampere, 1 handicap site with electric. Sites with water and electric hookups are $16. Recreational vehicle maximum length is 40'. This campground requires a 2 night minimum stay on weekends and a 3 night stay on holiday weekends. Open from April 1st to October 31st. (870) 431-5744. NRRS (May 16th to September 12th).

TUCKER HOLLOW CAMPGROUND

From Lead Hill/Junction State Road 7, go 7 miles northwest on State Road 14 (sign), 3 miles north on State Road 281, go east. Two picnic shelters, GPR1 for up to 25 people and 10 vehicles is $40 and GRP2 for up to 50 people and 25 vehicles is $50, and a change shelter is available. 30 sites with electric, 1 double site, 1 triple site, 1 handicap site, 2 pull through sites. Sites with electric hookups are $16, a double site with electric hookups is $32; a triple site without electric hookups is $48. Recreational vehicle maximum length is 40'. This campground requires a 2 night minimum stay on weekends and a 3 night stay on holiday weekends. Open from April 1st to October 31st. (870) 436-5622. NRRS on double and triple sites only (May 17th to September 13th).

DARDANELLE LAKE (LR) 4

A 34,300 acre surface area lake with 315 miles of shoreline is adjacent to southwest side of Russellville, east of Fort Smith and north of Dardanelle on State Road 22. Resource Manager, Dardanelle Lake, 1598 Lock and Dam Road, Russellville, AR 72802-1087. (479) 968-5008.

DELAWARE CAMPGROUND

From Subiaco/Junction State Road 22, go 3 miles north on State Road 197, 2.5 miles northeast on State Road 393. A picnic shelter, 1/2 day - $25, 1 day - $40. 13 tent only sites. All sites are $6. Open from May 1st to Labor Day.

OLD POST ROAD CAMPGROUND

From Russellville/Junction United States Route 64, go 2.2 miles south on State Road 7, 1 mile west on Lock & Dam Road (signs). Eight picnic shelters (Madrch 1st to October 31st), 1/2 day - $35, 1 day - $50, and a soccer field, tennis court and soft ball field are available (a fee is charged for these). 41 sites with water and electric. Sites with water and electric hookups are $18. Recreational vehicle maximum length is in excess of 65'. This campground requires a 2 night minimum stay on weekends and a 3 night stay on holiday weekends. Open alll year. (479) 968-7962. NRRS (March 1st to October 31st)).

PINEY BAY CAMPGROUND

From London, go 4 miles east on United States Route 64, 3 miles north on State Road 359 (signs). A picnic shelter (March 1st to October 31st) for 1/2 day is $35 and 1 day is $50, and an amphitheater is available. 91 sites, 85 with electric, 3 handicap sites with water and electric, 1 handicap site with electric, 1 pull through site. Sites without electric hookups are $10; sites with electric hookups are $16; sites with water and electric hookups are $18. Recreational vehicle maximum length is in excess of 65'. This campground requires a 2 night minimum stay on weekends and a 3 night stay on holiday weekends. Open all year. (479) 885-3029. NRRS (March 1st to October 31st_).

RIVER VIEW CAMPGROUND

From Russellville/Junction United States Route 64, go 4.5 miles south on State Road 7 across outlet, go northwest, below dam. A picnic shelter, 1/2 day - $35, 1 day - $50. 18 sites, 8 with water and electric. All sites are $12. Open from March 1st to October 31st.

SHOAL BAY CAMPGROUND

From New Blaine/Junction State Road 22, go 1.6 miles northwest on State Road 197 (signs). Two picnic shelters, 1/2 day - $35, 1 day - $50, and an amphitheater is available. 82 sites with electric, 2 pull through sites, 1 handicap site with water and electric. Sites with water and electric hookups are $16; premium sites with water and electric hookups are $18. Recreational vehicle maximum length is 50'. This campground requires a 2 night minimum stay on weekends and a 3 night stay on holiday weekends. Open all year. (479) 938-7335. NRRS (March 1st to October 31st)).

SPADRA CAMPGROUND

From Clarksville/Junction United States Route 64, go 2 miles south through Jamestown on State Road 103. A picnic shelter, 1/2 day - $35, 1 day - $50. 29 sites with electric, 1 full hookup, 5 tent only sites. Sites with electric hookups are $13; sites with water and electric hookups are $15; a site with full hookups is $16. Open all year. (479) 754-6438.

SWEEDEN ISLAND CAMPGROUND

From Atkins/Junction State Road 324, go 15 miles southwest through Wilson on State Road 105, Lock & Dam #9. A picnic shelter, 1/2 day - $35, 1 day - $50. 28 sites, 22 with electric. Tent only sites are $10; sites with electric hookups are $16. Open all year. (479)641-7500.

DEGRAY LAKE (VK) 5

A 13,500 acre surface area lake with 207 miles of shoreline is located 8 miles northwest of Arkadelphia, west of I-30, exit 78, off State Road 7, 67 miles southwest of Little Rock. Resource Manager, DeGray Lake, 729 Channel Avenue, Arkadelphia, AR 71923. (870) 246-5501.

ALPINE RIDGE CAMPGROUND

From Alpine/Junction State Road 8, go 10 miles east through Fendley on State Road 346. 49 sites with electric, 1 handicap site. From November 1st to February 28th, sites with electric hookups are $10; from March 1st to October 31st, sites with electric hookups are $10; premium sites with electric hookups are $16. Recreational vehicle maximum length is 40'. This campground requires a 2 night minimum stay on weekends and a 3 night stay on holiday weekends. Open all year. NRRS.

ARLIE MOORE CAMPGROUND

From Bismarck, go 2.2 miles southeast on State Road 7, 2 miles west on Arlie Moore Road. A picnic shelter and an amphitheater are available. A camper store is located nearby. 87 sites with electric, 1 handicap site. From November 1st to February 28th, all sites are $10; from March 1st to October 31st, sites with electric hookups are $10; premium sites with electric hookups are $16. Recreational vehicle maximum length is 30'. This campground requires a 2 night minimum stay on weekends and a 3 night stay on holiday weekends. Open all year. NRRS.

CADDO DRIVE CAMPGROUND

From Bismarck, go 3.5 miles southeast on State Road 7, 2.7 miles west on Edgewood Road (gravel). A picnic shelter for up to 100 people and 15 vehicles is available. 72 sites with electric, 27 tent only sites, 2 pull through sites. Sites with electric hookups are $10. Recreational vehicle maximum length is 40'. This campground requires a 2 night minimum stay on weekends and a 3 night stay on holiday weekends. Open from March 1st to October 31st. NRRS.

EDGEWOOD CAMPGROUND

From Bismarck, go 4.8 miles southeast, 3 miles west on Edgewood Road(south of Caddo Drive Park). Boat rentals are available nearby. 49 sites with electric, 4 tent only sites, 2 double sites, 9 pull through sites, 1 handicap site. From November 1st to February 28th, sites are $10; double sites are $20; from March 1st to October 31st, tent only sites with electric and sites with electric hookups are $10; premium sites with electric hookups are 16; a double site with electric hookups is $28; a premium double site with electric hookups is $32. Recreational vehicle maximum length is 30'. This campground requires a 2 night minimum stay on weekends and a 3 night stay on holiday weekends. Open all year. NRRS.

IRON MOUNTAIN CAMPGROUND

From I-30, exit 78, go 2.5 miles north on State Road 7, 2.5 miles west across dam on Skyline Drive, north on Iron Mountain Road. 69 sites with electric, 5 tent only sites, 1 pull through site. From November 1st to February 28th, sites are $10; from March 1st to October 31st, tent only sites with electric and sites with electric hookups are $10; premium sites with electric hookups are $16. Recreational vehicle maximum length is 30'. This campground requires a 2 night minimum stay on weekends and a 3 night stay on holiday weekends. Open all year. NRRS.

LENOX MARCUS

From Lambert/Junction State Road 84, go 0.8 mile southwest, 2.2 miles south on gravel road. 200 acres of remote camping is free. Open all year.

OAK BOWER

Group use cabin area with showers and dining hall, reservation through the field office [(870) 246-5501, ext. 4005], $250 minimum. Contact office for additional information. Open all year.

OZAN POINT CAMPGROUND

From Alpine Community, go 6.8 miles northeast through Fendley on State Road 346, 1.5 miles east on gravel road. 50 sites. All sites are $6. Open from March 1st to November 30th.

POINT CEDAR CAMPGROUND

From Point Cedar/Junction State Road 84, go 3.5 miles southwest. 62 sites. All sites are $6. Recreational vehicle maximum length is 40'. Open from March 1st to November 30th.

SHOUSE FORD CAMPGROUND

From Point Cedar/Junction State Road 84, go 3.5 miles southeast, go east. 100 sites with electric, 1 tent only site, 1 full hookup, 1 handicap site. From November 1st to February 28th, sites are $10; from March 1st to October 31st, a tent only site with electric and sites with electric hookups are $10; premium sites with electric hookups are $16. Recreational vehicle maximum length is 40'. This campground requires a 2 night minimum stay on weekends and a 3 night stay on holiday weekends. Open all year. NRRS.

DEQUEEN LAKE (LR) 6

A 1,680 acre surface area lake located 4 miles northwest of De Queen, off United States Route 71, 96 miles southwest of Hot Springs, north of Texarkana near the Oklahoma state line. A fee is charged for the use of the dump station by non campers. Resource Manager, DeQueen Lake, 706 DeQueen Lake Road, DeQueen, AR 71832. (870) 584-4161.

BELLAH MINE CAMPGROUND

From De Queen, go 7 miles north on United States Route 71, 5.3 miles west on Bellah Mine Road (signs). A convenience store is located nearby and a fish cleaning station is available. 20 sites with water and electric. From November 1st to February 28th, sites are $10; from March 1st to October 31st, sites with water and electric hookups are $13; premium sites with water and electric hookups are $15. Recreational vehicle maximum length is in excess of 65'. This campground requires a 2 night minimum stay on weekends and a 3 night stay on holiday weekends. Open all year. (870) 386-7511. NRRS (May 16th to September 13th).

OAK GROVE CAMPGROUND

From De Queen, go 3 miles north on United States Route 71, 5.5 miles west on DeQueen Lake Road, 0.3 mile north (signs). A picnic shelter with water and electric for up to 150 people and 50 vehicles is $25, an amphitheater is available, and a convenience store is located nearby. 36 sites with water and electric, 7 pull through sites, 1 handicap site. From November 1st to February 28th, sites are $10; from March 1st to October 31st, sites with water and electric hookups are from $13; premium sites with water and electric are $15. Recreational vehicle maximum length is in excess of 65'. This campground requires a 2 night minimum stay on weekends and a 3 night stay on holiday weekends. Open all year. (870) 642-6111. NRRS (March 1st to September 30th).

PINE RIDGE CAMPGROUND

From De Queen, go 3 miles north on United States Route 71, 5.5 miles west on DeQueen Creek Road, 1.5 miles west on County Road (signs), go north. Group camping for up to 120 people and 1 vehicle is $25 to $30 and a fish cleaning station is available. A small store is located nearby. 46 sites, 17 with water and electric, 4 pull through sites. From November 1st to February 28th, sites without electric are $6; sites with electric hookups are $10; from March 1st to October 31st, sites without electric hookups are $9; sites with water and electric hookups are $13; premium sites with water and electric hookups are $15. Recreational vehicle maximum length is in excess of 65'. This campground requires a 2 night minimum stay on weekends and a 3 night stay on holiday weekends. Open all year. NRRS.

DIERKS LAKE (LR) 7

A 1,360 acre surface area lake located 72 miles southwest of Hot Springs, north of Texarkana, east of DeQueen, 5 miles northwest of Dierks in southwest Arkansas. Resource Manager, Dierks Lake, P. O. Box 8, Dierks, AR 71833. (870) 286-3214/2346.

BLUE RIDGE CAMPGROUND

From Dierks, go 3 miles northeast on United States Route 70, 4 miles northwest on State Road 4, 2.6 miles west on County Road (signs). Group camping area is $35, and a fish cleaning station is available. 22 sites, 17 with water and electric. Sites without electric hookups are $8; sites with water and electric hookups are $13. Open all year.

HORSESHOE BEND CAMPGROUND

From Dierks, go 3 miles west on United States Route 70, 3.5 miles northwest on Lake Road (signs), below dam. A picnic shelter for up to 100 people and 1 vehicle, 1/2 day - $25, 1 day - $40, and a change shelter is available. 11 sites with water and electric. Sites with water and electric hookups are $11. Open all year. (870) 286-3214).

JEFFERSON RIDGE CAMPGROUND

From Dierks, go 5 miles west on United States Route 70, 5 miles northwest on Green Chapel Road (signs), access east on the west side of the dam. An amphitheater and a fish cleaning station are available, and a picnic shelter, 1/2 day - $25, 1 day - $40. 84 sites with water and electric, 38 handicap sites, 41 pull through sites. From November 1st to February 28, sites with water and electric hookups are $12; premium sites with water and electric hookups are $14; from March 1st to October 31st, sites with water and electric hookups are $13; premium sites with water and electric hookups are $15. Recreational vehicle maximum length is in excess of 65'. Open all year. NRRS.

GILLHAM LAKE (LR) 8

A 1,370 acre surface area lake located 6 miles northeast of Gillham, 15 miles north of DeQueen, east of United States Route 71, southwest of Little Rock near the Oklahoma state line. A fee is charged for use of dump station by non campers. Resource Manager, Gillham Lake, 706 DeQueen Lake Road, DeQueen, AR 71852. (870) 584-4162.

BIG COON CREEK CAMPGROUND

From Project Office, go 0.5 mile northeast to dam, l mile northwest, access northeast. A fish cleaning station and an amphitheater are available. 31 sites with water and electric, 2 pull through sites. Sites with water and electric hookups are $13; premium sites with water and electric hookups are $15. Recreational vehicle maximum length is in excess of 65'. This campground requires a 3 night minimum stay on weekends and on holiday. Open March 1st to September 30th. (870) 385-7126. NRRS (May 17th to September 13th).

COSSATOT REEFS CAMPGROUND

From Gillham, go 6 miles northeast past project office near dam. A picnic shelter for up to 100 people and 1 vehicle is $25, and an amphitheater and fish cleaning station are available. 27 sites, 25 sites with water and electric, 2 tent only sites. Tent only sites are $9; sites with water and electric hookups are $13; premium sites with water and electric hookups are $15. Recreational vehicle maximum length is in excess of 65'. This campground requires a 3 night minimum stay on holidays. Open March 1st to September 30th. (870) 386-7261. NRRS (May 13th to September 17th).

LITTLE COON CREEK CAMPGROUND

From Gillham, go 6 miles northeast past project office, 1 mile northwest past Coon Creek Park on County Road. 10 sites with water and electric. Sites with water and electric hookups are $13. Open all year.

GREERS FERRY LAKE (LR) 9

A 31,500 acre surface area lake located north of Heber Springs on State Road 25, 65 miles north of Little Rock. Checkout time is 4 p.m. There is a Visitor Center by the project office near the dam. Project Office, Greers Ferry Lake, P. O. Box 1088, Heber Springs, AR 72543-9022. (501) 362-2416.

CHEROKEE CAMPGROUND

From Drasco, go 7.5 miles west to Brownsville on State Road 92 (signs), 4.5 miles south. 33 sites, 16 with electric. Sites without electric hookups are $12; sites with electic hookups are $14; premium sites with electric hookups are $16. Open from May 15th to September 15th.

CHOCTAW CAMPGROUND

From Clinton, go 5 miles south to Choctaw (sign) on United States Route 65, 3.8 miles east on State Road 330 (signs). A picnic shelter is available. 146 sites, 91 with electric, multiple family sites, overflow area. Sites without electric hookups are $14; sites with electric hookups are $19; premium sites with electric hookups are $17. Recreational vehicle maximum length is in excess of 65'. Open from April 1st to October 31st. NRRS (May 15th to September 15th).

COVE CREEK CAMPGROUND

From Heber Springs, go 6.3 miles southwest on State Road 25, 3 miles northwest on State Road 16, 1.2 miles northeast (signs). A picnic shelter is available. 65 sites, 31 with electric, multiple family sites, over flow area (no fee after all camp sites are full). Sites without electric hookups are $14; sites with electric hookups are $17; premium sites with electric hookups are $19.

Recreational vehicle maximum length is in excess of 65'. Open April 1st to October 31st. NRRS (May 15th to September 15th).

DAM SITE CAMPGROUND

From Heber Springs, go 3.4 miles north on State Road 25B (signs), west side of dam. Picnic shelters are $30 to $150, and a marine dump station is available. Golf carts, all terrain and off the road vehicles are prohibited. 252 sites, 158 with electric, 49 handicap sites, 49 - 50 ampere, multiple family sites. Sites without electric hookups are $14; sites with electric hookups are $17; premium sites with electric hookups are $19; sites with water and electric hookups are $20. Recreational vehicle maximum length is in excess of 65'. Open from April 1st to ctober 31st. NRRS (May 15th to September 5th).

DEVILS FORK CAMPGROUND

From Greers Ferry/Junction State Road 92, go 0.5 mile north on State Road 16, west side (signs). A picnic shelter is available. 55 sites with electric. Sites with electric hookups are $17; premium sites with electric hookups are $19. Recreational vehicle maximum length is in excess of 65'. Open all year. NRRS (May 15th to September 5th).

HEBER SPRINGS PARK

From Heber Springs, go 2 miles west on State Road 110, 0.5 mile north (signs). A picnic shelter, 1/2 day $25, 1 day $40. 142 sites, 106 with electric, multiple family sites. Sites without electric hookups are $14; sites with electric hookups are $17; premium sites with electric hookups are $19. Recreational vehicle maximum length is in excess of 65'. Open from April 1st to October 31st. NRRS (May 15th to September 5th).

HILL CREEK CAMPGROUND

From Drasco, go 12 miles west past Brownsville (sign) on State Road 92, 3 miles northwest on State Road 225 (signs), 2 miles south. A picnic shelter is, 1/2 day - $25, 1 day - $40. 41 sites, 25 with electric, multiple family sites and overflow camping. Sites without electric hookups are $14; sites with electric hookups are $17. Recreational vehicle maximum length is in excess of 65'. Open from April 1st to September 15th. NRRS (May 15th to September 5th).

JOHN F. KENNEDY CAMPGROUND

From Heber Springs, go 4.4 miles north on State Road 25, 1 mile east across dam, south side (signs), below dam on the Little Red River (a trout stream). A picnic shelter is, 1/2 day - $35, 1 day - $50. 74 sites with electric, mutiple family sites. Sites with electric hookups are $17; premium sites with electric hookups are $19; premium sites with water and electric hookups are $20. Recreational vehicle maximum length is in excess of 65'. Open all year. NRRS (April 15th to September 5th).

MILL CREEK CAMPGROUND

From Bee Branch, go 13.2 miles northeast on State Road 92 (signs), 3 miles north. A picnic shelter is free. 39 sites. All sites are free. Open from May 15th to September 15th.

NARROWS CAMPGROUND

From Greers Ferry, go 2.5 miles southwest on State Road 16, across bridge, north side (signs). Picnic shelters are, 1/2 day $25, 1 day - $40. 60 sites with electric, overflow area. Sites with electric hookups are $17; premium sites with electric hookups are $19. Recreational vehicle maximum length is in excess of 65'. Open from April 1st to October 31st. NRRS (May 15th to September 5th).

OLD HIGHWAY 25 CAMPGROUND

From Heber Springs, go 6.2 miles north on State Road 25, 2.8 miles west on old State Road 25 (signs). Picnic shelters are available (call the office) and a group camping area with 16 sites for up to 128 people and 48 vehicles is $150. 125 sites, 89 with electric, multiple family sites. Sites without electric hookups are $14; sites with electric hookups are $17; premium sites with electric hookups are $19. Recreational vehicle maximum length is in excess of 65'. Open from April 1st to October 31st. NRRS (May 15th to September 5th).

SHILOH CAMPGROUND

From Greers Ferry/Junction State Road 92, go 3.5 miles southeast on State
Road 110 (signs). A picnic shelter is, 1/2 day - $25, 1 day - $40 (call the office),
a group camping area with 17 sites for up to 204 people and 12 vehicles is
$150, and a marine dump station is available. 116 sites, 60 with electric. Sites
without electric hookups are $14; sites with electric hookups are $17; premium
sites with electric hookups are $19. Recreational vehicle maximum length
is in excess of 65'. Open from April 1st to October 31st. NRRS (May 15th to
September 5th).

SUGAR LOAF CAMPGROUND

From Bee Branch, go 12 miles northeast on State Road 92 (signs), 1.5 miles
west on State Road 337. A picnic shelter is, 1/2 day - $25, 1 day - $40 (call the
office). 95 sites, 56 with electric. Sites without electric hookups are $14; sites
with electic hookups are $17; premium sites with electric hookups are $19.
Recreational vehicle maximum length is in excess of 65'. Open from April 1st to
October 31st. NRRS (May 15th to September 5th).

LAKE GREESON (VK) 10

A 7,260 acre surface area lake 12 miles long located 6 miles north of
Murfreesboro on State Road 19, 69 miles northeast of Texarkana. Visitors to
10 p.m., and a 31 mile cycle trail is available. Free sites in the winter may have
reduced amenities. Resource Manager, Lake Greeson Field Office, 155 Dynamite
Hill Road, Murfreesboro, AR 71958. (870) 285-2151.

ARROWHEAD POINT CAMPGROUND

From east of Newhope/Junction State Road 369, go 0.5 mile east on United
States Route 70, southeast to campground. 23 sites, 12 tent only sites. From
March 1st to October 31st, sites are $6; from November 1st to February 28,
some sites are available and are free. Recreational vehicle maximum length is
35'. Open all year.

BEAR CREEK CAMPGROUND

From Kirby/Junction United States Route 70, go 0.5 mile south on State Road
27, 1.4 miles west. 18 sites, 5 tent only sites. From March 1st to October 31st,

sites are $5; from November 1st to February 28th, some sites are available and are free. Recreational vehicle maximum length is 30'. Open all year.

BUCKHORN CAMPGROUND

From Murfreesboro/Junction State Road 27, go 6 miles north on State Road 19, 3 miles northwest of dam, 2 miles east on gravel road (signs). 9 sites, 2 tent only sites. From March 1st to October 31st, sites are $5; from November 1st to February 28th, some sites are available and are free. Recreational vehicle maximum length is 30'. Open all year.

COWHIDE COVE CAMPGROUND

From Kirby/Junction United States Route 70, go 5.9 miles south on State Road 27, 2.7 miles west. Off the road vehicles are prohibited. 50 sites, 48 sites with electric, 2 tent only sites, 2 pull through sites, 1 handicap site. From November 1st to February 28th, sites are $6 (no showers); from March 1st to October 31st, tent only sites are $10; sites with electric hookups are $13; premium sites with electric hookups are $15. Recreational vehicle maximum length is 40'. This campground requires a 2 night minimum stay on weekends and a 3 night stay on holiday weekends. Open all year. NRRS (May 1st to September 30th).

KIRBY LANDING CAMPGROUND

From Kirby/Junction State Road 27, go 2.2 miles southwest on United States Route 70, 1.2 miles south. Off the road vehicles are prohibited. 87 sites with electric, 6 pull through sites, 1 handicap pull through site. From November 1st to February 28, sites with electric are $10; from March 1st to October 31st, sites with electric hookups are $13; premium sites with electric hookups are $16. Recreational vehicle maximum length is 45'. This campground requires a 2 night minimum stay on weekends and a 3 night stay on holiday weekends. Open all year. NRRS (May 1st to September 30th).

LAUREL CREEK CAMPGROUND

From Kirby/Junction United States Route 70, go 2.4 miles south on State Road 27, 3.4 miles southwest on gravel road. 12 sites, 3 tent only sites. From March

1st to October 31st, sites are $5; from November 1st to February 28th, some sites are available and are free. Recreational vehicle maximum length is 20'. Open all year.

NARROWS DAM AREA CAMPGROUND

At the dam on the east side. A picnic shelter for up to 50 people and 26 vehicles is available (contact the office). Off the road vehicles are prohibited. 24 sites, 18 with electric, 2 full hookups, 1 handicap site. From November 1st to February 28th, sites with electric hookups are $10; from March 1st to October 31st, sites without electric hookups are $10, sites with electric hookups are $13. Recreational vehicle maximum length is 60'. This campground requires a 2 night minimum stay on weekends and a 3 night stay on holiday weekends. Open all year. (There is a possibility this campground may be closed, call for information) NRRS (May 1st to September 30th).

PARKER CREEK CAMPGROUND

From the dam, go 1.7 miles northwest on gravel road. 57 sites, 46 with electric, 3 tent only sites, 2 full hookups. Off the road vehicles are prohibited. From November 1st to November 30th, sites without electric hookups are $10; from March 1st to October 31st, sites without electric hookups are $10; sites with electric hookups are $13; premium sites with electric hookups are $15. Recreational vehicle maximum length is 35'. This campground requires a 2 night minimum stay on weekends and a 3 night stay on holiday weekends. Open from March 1st to November 30th. NRRS (May 1st to September 30th).

PIKEVILLE CAMPGROUND

From dam, go 1.5 miles northwest of Parker Creek Park. 12 sites, 1 tent only site. From March 1st to October 31st, sites are $5; from November 1st to March 31st, some sites are available and are free. Recreational vehicle maximum length is 30'. Open all year.

ROCK CREEK

From dam, 6.7 miles northwest around west side of dam on gravel roads (signs). 9 sites. All sites are free. Open all year.

SELF CREEK/JIM WYLIE CAMPGROUND

From Daisy/Junction United States Route 70, go 1 mile west across bridge on United States Route 70. A picnic shelter for up to 60 people and 41 vehicles. 72 sites, 41 with electric, 9 tent only sites, 23 pull through sites, 1 full hookup. From November 1st to February 28, sites without electric hookups are $10; from March 1st to October 31st, tent only sites and sites without electric hookups are $10; tent sites with electric and sites with electric hookups are $13; premium sites with electric hookups are $15. Recreational vehicle maximum length is 45'. This campground requires a 2 night minimum stay on weekends and a 3 night stay on holiday weekends. Open all year. NRRS (May 1st to September 30th).

STAR OF THE WEST CAMPGROUND

From Junction State Road 369, go 4 mile west on United States Route 70, go southwest. 20 sites, 8 tent only sites, some pull through sites. From March 1st to October 31st, sites are $6; from November 1st to February 28th, some sites are available and are free. Recreational vehicle maximum length is 50'. Open all year.

LAKE OUACHITA (VK) 11

A 40,060 acre surface area lake located 13 miles northwest of Hot Springs on United States Route 270 and State Road 277, 67 miles southwest of Little Rock. Visitors to 10 p.m., and off the road vehicles are prohibited. Resource Manager, Lake Ouachita Field Office, 1201 Blakely Dam Road, Royal, AR 71968-9493. (501) 767-2108/2101.

BIG FIR CAMPGROUND

From Mt. Ida/Junction United States Route 270, go 5.1 miles northeast on State Road 27, 6.5 miles east on State Road 188, 4.5 miles east on gravel road. 29 sites. Sites are $10; premium sites are $13. Recreational vehicle maximum length is 20'. Open from March 1st to October 31st.

BRADY MOUNTAIN CAMPGROUND

From Royal/Junction United States Route 270, go 4 miles north through Bear. A picnic shelter and a fish cleaning station are available. 74 sites, 57 with electric, 17 tent only sites, 1 handicap site with electric. Tent only sites are $10; premium tent only sites are $12; sites with electric hookups are $14; premium sites with electric hookups are $16. Recreational vehicle maximum length is 55'. This campground requires a 2 night minimum stay on weekends and a 3 night stay on holiday weekends. Open all year. (501) 760-1146. NRRS (May 1st to September 30th).

BUCKVILLE CAMPGROUND

From Blue Springs/Junction State Road 7, go 16 miles west on State Road 298, south through Avant, 3.6 miles on gravel road. 5 sites. All sites are free. Recreational vehicle maximum length is 20'. Open all year.

CRYSTAL SPRINGS CAMPGROUND

From Crystal Springs/Junction United States Route 270, go 2.9 miles north. A picnic shelter for up to 125 people and 21 vehicles, and a fish cleaning station and change shelter are available. 74 sites, 63 with water and electric, 15 - 50 ampere, 11 tent only sites, 2 handicap sites with water and electric, 6 pull through sites. Tent only sites are $10; premium tent only sites asre $12; sites with water and electric hookups are $16; premium sites with water and electric hookups and sites with water and 50 ampere service are $17. Recreational vehicle maximum length is 55'. This campground requires a 2 night minimum stay on weekends and a 3 night stay on holiday weekends. Open all year. (501) 991-3390. NRRS (May 1st to September 30th).

DENBY POINT CAMPGROUND

From Silver, go 0.7 mile east on United States Route 270, 0.8 mile north. Two group camping areas for up to 125 people and 12 vehicles, Loop A, $55 and Loop B, $55 to $60, and a fish cleaning station is available. Boat rentals are located nearby. 67 sites, 60 with electric, 7 tent only sites. Tent sites are $10; premium tent sites are $12; sites with electric hookups are $14; premium sites with electric hookups are $16. Recreational vehicle maximum length is 55'. This campground requires a 2 night minimum stay on weekends and a 3 night stay on holiday weekends. Open all year. (501) 867-4475. NRRS (May 1st to September 30th).

IRONS FORK

From Story/Junction State Road 27, 8.3 miles east on State Road 298, 1.3 miles southeast on gravel road. 45 sites. All sites are free. Open all year.

JOPLIN CAMPGROUND

From Joplin/Junction United States Route 270, go 2.4 miles north. A fish cleaning station is available. Boat rentals and restaurants are located nearby. Area for small recreational vehicles and pop ups, slide outs not recommended. 65 sites, 62 with electric, 32 tent only sites. Tent only sites are $10; premium tent only sites with electric are $12; sites with electric hookups are $14; premium sites with electric hookups are $16. Recreational vehicle maximum length is 35'. This campground requires a 2 night minimum stay on weekends and a 3 night stay on holiday weekends. Open all year. NRRS (May 1st to September 30th).

LENA LANDING CAMPGROUND

From Lena/Junction State Road 298, go 1.1 miles south on gravel road. Restaurants are located nearby. 10 sites. Sites are $11; premium sites are $15. Recreational vehicle maximum length is 35'. Open from March 1st to October 31st.

LITTLE FIR CAMPGROUND

From Junction State Road 27, through Rubie, go 3 miles east on State Road 188, 2.2 miles north. 29 sites. Sites are $11; premium sites are $13. Recreational vehicle maximum length is 55'. Open from March 1st to October 31st.

STEPHENS PARK

From Mountain Pine, go 1 mile west, below the dam. A picnic shelter is available. 9 sites. From November 1st to February 28th, sites are $8; from March 1st to October 31st, sites are $10; sites with electric hookups are $14. Recreational vehicle maximum length is 35'. Open all year.

SPILLWAY GROUP CAMPGROUND

Below dam. Group camping area with 6 sites. The group camping fee is $30. Call the office for information.

TOMPKINS BEND CAMPGROUND

From Joplin, go 1 mile west on United States Route 270, 2.4 miles north. An amphitheater and a fish cleaning station are available. 77 sites, 63 with electric, 14 tent only sites. Tent only sites are $10; premium tent only sites are $12; sites with electric hookups are $12; premium sites with electric hookups and sites with water and electric hookups are $15; premium sites with water and electric hookups are $17. Recreational vehicle maximum length is 55'. This campground requires a 2 night minimum stay on weekends and a 3 night stay on holiday weekends. Open all year. (501) 867-4476. NRRS (May 1st to September 30th).

TWIN CREEK CAMPGROUND

From Silver, go 1 mile northwest on gravel road. Boat rentals and restaurants are located nearby. 15 sites. Sites are $10; premium sites are $14. Overflow camping is available on major holidays only. Recreational vehicle maximum length is 20'. Open from March 1st to October 31st.

MILLWOOD LAKE (LR) 12

A 29,000 acre surface area lake located 9 miles east of Ashdown on State Road 32, 28 miles north of Texarkana. For lake level information call (870) 898-4533/1-888-687-9830. Project Manager, Millwood Tri Lakes Office, 1528 Highway 32 east, Ashdown, AR 71822. (870) 898-3343, extension 3.

BEARD'S BLUFF CAMPGROUND

From Saratoga, go 3 miles south on State Road 32, between the road & lake (signs). A group camping area is available, a picnic shelter is $25 and an outdoor wedding chapel is $25. For shelter and chapel reservations, call (870) 388-9556. 29 sites, 28 with water and electric, 3 full hookups, 1 double site, 5 handicap sites. From November 1st to February 28th, a site without hookups is $10; sites with water and electric hookups are $11; sites with full hookups are $13; from March 1st to October 31st, a site without electric hookups is $10, sites with water and electric hookups are $13; premium sites with water and electric hookups and sites with full hookups are $15. Open all year. (870) 388-9556.

BEARD'S LAKE CAMPGROUND

From Saratoga, go 4 miles south on State Road 32, below the dam. 8 sites, 3 tent only sites. From November 1st to February 28, sites without electric hookups are $8; sites with electric hookups are $9; from March 1st to October 31st, sites without electic hookups are $9; sites with water and electric hookup are $13. Open all year.

COTTONSHED LANDING CAMPGROUND

From Schaal, go 2 miles south. A picnic shelter is $25 (for reservations, call (870) 287-71189), and fish cleaning station is available. 46 sites with water and electric. From November 1st to February 28, sites are $11; from March 1st to October 31st, sites with water and electric hookups are $13; premium sites with water and electric hookups are $15. Open all year. (870)287-7118.

PARALOMA LANDING CAMPGROUND

From Brownstown/Junction State Road 317, go 4 miles southeast through Paraloma on State Road 234. A fish cleaning station is available. 34 sites with water and electric, some pull through sites. From November 1st to February 28, sites with water and electric hookups are $8; from March 1st to October 31st, sites with water and electric hookups are $11. Open all year.

RIVER RUN EAST CAMPGROUND

From Ashdown, go 12 miles east on State Road 32, below the dam. 8 sites. All sites are $5. Open all year.

RIVER RUN WEST CAMPGROUND

From Ashdown, 10 miles east on State Road 32, below dam, west side of Little River. 4 sites. All sites are $5. Open all year.

SARATOGA LANDING CAMPGROUND

From Saratoga, go 1 mile south on State Road 32, 1 mile west on access road. A picnic shelter is available. 17 sites. Sites are $5. Open all year.

WHITE CLIFFS CAMPGROUND

From Brownstown/Junction State Road 234, go 4 miles south on State Road 317, gravel road. Group camping is $10 and there is an off the road vehicle area on adjacent property. 18 sites. All sites are $5. Open all year.

NIMROD LAKE (LR) 13

A 3,550 acre surface area lake located 8.3 miles southeast of Ola on State Road 7, 66 miles northwest of Little Rock in north-central Arkansas. Off the road vehicles are prohibited and checkout time is 1 p.m. Project Office, Nimrod Lake, 3 Highway 7 south, Plainview, AR 72857-9600. (479) 272-4324.

CARTER COVE CAMPGROUND

From Plainview, go 3.4 miles southeast on State Road 60 (signs), 0.8 mile south. Three picnic shelters for up to 50 people and 26 vehicles and a fish cleaning station are available. 34 sites with water and electric, 3 double sites, 1 pull through site. Sites with water and electric hookups are $14; double sites with water and electric hookups are $28. Recreational vehicle maximum length is 30'. This campground requires a 2 night minimum stay on weekends and a 3 night stay on holiday weekends. Open all year. (479) 272-4983. NRRS (May 15th to October 25th).

COUNTY LINE CAMPGROUND

From Fourche Junction at dam, go 1.7 miles west on State Road 60, south of road (signs). A fish cleaning station is available. 20 sites with water and electric. Sites with water and electric hookups are $14. Recreational vehicle maximum length is 30'. This campground requires a 2 night minimum stay on weekends and a 3 night stay on holiday weekends. Open from March 1st to October 31st. (479) 272-4945. NRRS (May 19th to September 15th).

QUARRY COVE CAMPGROUND

From Ola, go 9 miles southeast on State Road 7, 0.5 mile west on State Road 60 to access road. A picnic shelter, fish cleaning station and an amphitheater are available. 31 sites with water and electric, 1 double site. Sites with water and electric hookups are $14; a double site with water and electric hookups is $28. Showers are closed in the winter. Recreational vehicle maximum length is 30'. This campground requires a 2 night minimum stay on weekends and a 3 night stay on holiday weekends. Open all year. (479) 272-4233.

RIVER ROAD CAMPGROUND

From Ola, go 9 miles southeast on State Road 7, 0.3 mile on River Road below dam on the Fourche Lefave River. A picnic shelter is available. 21 sites with electric, 4 - 50 ampere, 2 double sites, 2 pull through sites. Sites with electric hookups are $13; sites with water and electric hookup are $14; double sites with water and electric hookups are $28. Recreational vehicle maximum length is 30'. This campground requires a 2 night minimum stay on weekends and a 3 night stay on holiday weekends. Open all year. (479) 272-4835. NRRS (March 15th to October 25th).

SUNLIGHT BAY CAMPGROUND

From Plainview/Junction State Road 28, go 3.5 miles south on Sunlight Bay Road. Three picnic shelters and a fish cleaning station are available. Showers are closed in the winter. 28 sites with water and electric, 4 - 50 ampere, 4 double sites. Sites with water and electric are $14; double sites with water and electric are $28. No showers available from November 1st to February 28th.Recreational vehicle maximum length is 30'. This campground requires a 2 night minimum stay on weekends and a 3 night stay on holiday weekends. Open all year. (479) 272-4234. NRRS (March 15th to October 25th).

NORFORK LAKE (LR) 14

A 22,000 acre surface area lake located 4 miles northeast of Norfork on State Road 177, near the Missouri state line, southeast of Branson, Missouri. Off the road vehicles are prohibited and checkout time is 3 p.m. Free sites in winter may have reduced amenities. Resource Manager, Norfolk Lake, P. O. Box 2070, Mountain Home, AR 72654-2070. (870) 425-2700. See MO listing.

BIDWELL POINT CAMPGROUND

From Mountain Home/Junction State Road 201, go 9 miles northeast on United States Route 62, 2 miles north across bridge on State Road 101, northeast side (right). A picnic shelter for up to 200 people and 50 vehicles is $50. 48 sites, 46 with electric, 1 handicap site with water and electric. Sites without electric are $12; sites with electric hookups are $16; premium sites with electric hookups are $17. Recreation vehicle maximum length is 40'. This campground requires a 2 night minimum stay on weekends and a 3 night stay on holiday weekends. Open from April 1st to September 30th. (870) 467-5375. NRRS (May 16th to September 15th).

CRANFIELD CAMPGROUND

From Mountain Home/Junction State Road 201, go 5.5 miles east on United States Route 62 (signs), 1.6 miles north (left) on County Road 34. An amphitheater and change shelter are available, and two picnic shelters, CF1 and CF2 for up to 60 people and 20 vehicles are $50. there is a handicap accessible fishing area. 67 sites with electric, 6 pull through sites, 2 handicap sites with electric. Sites with electric hookups are $16. Recreational vehicle maximum length is 35'. This campground requires a 2 night minimum stay on weekends and a 3 night stay on holiday weekends. Open from April 1st to October 31st. (870) 492-4191. NRRS (May 16th to September 15th).

GAMALIEL CAMPGROUND

From Mountain Home, go 9 miles northeast on United States Route 62, 4.5 miles north on State Road 101, 3 miles southeast on County Road 42. A picnic shelter for up to 100 people and 20 vehicles is $40. 64 sites with electric, 3 pull through sites, 3 handicap sites. Sites with electric hookups are $11; premium sites with electric hookups are $15. Recreational vehicle maximum length is 40'. This campground requires a 2 night minimum stay on weekends and a 3 night stay on holiday weekends. Open from April 1st to September 30th. (870) 467-5680. NRRS (May 16th to September 15th).

HENDERSON CAMPGROUND

From Mountain Home/Junction State Road 201, go 10 miles east on United States Route 62, cross lake bridge, east side (left, signs). A picnic shelter is

$40 (NRRS), and a marine dump station is available. 38 sites with electric, 4 pull through sites. Sites with electric hookups are $14. Recreational vehicle maximum length is 30'. This campground requires a 2 night minimum stay on weekends and a 3 night stay on holiday weekends. Open from April 1st to September 30th. (870) 488-5282.

JORDAN CAMPGROUND

From Jordan, go 2.5 miles north on County Road 64. A picnic shelter, JS1 for up to 36 people and 20 vehicles is $40 (NRRS). 40 sites, 33 with electric, 7 tent only sites, 1 handicap site with electric. From April 1st to September 30th, tent only sites are $7; sites with electric hookups are $15; from October 1st to March 31st, some sites are available and are free. Recreational vehicle maximum length is 30'. This campground requires a 2 night minimum stay on weekends and a 3 night stay on holiday weekends. Open all year. (870) 499-7223.

PANTHER BAY CAMPGROUND

From Mountain Home/Junction State Road 201, go 8.6 miles east on United States Route 62, 1 mile north on State Road 101, right on 1st access road (signs). A picnic shelter and marine dump station are available. 28 sites, 15 with electric. Sites without electric hookups are $9; sites with electric hookups are $14. Open from April 1st to September 30th. (870) 492-4544.

QUARRY COVE/DAM SITE A CAMPGROUND

From Norfork, go 2.9 miles northeast to Salesville on State Road 5, 2 miles east of State Road 177 (signs). Group camping walk-in area for up to 150 people is $60, picnic shelters are $40 to $50 and there is a handicap accessible fishing area. 68 sites with electric, 24 - 50 ampere, 2 pull through sites, 1 tent handicap site with electric. Sites with electric hookups are $16; premium sites with 50 ampere service are $18. Recreational vehicle maximum length is 60'. This campground requires a 2 night minimum stay on weekends and a 3 night stay on holiday weekends. Open all year. (870) 499-7216. NRRS (May 16th to September 15th).

ROBINSON POINT CAMPGROUND

From Mountain Home/Junction State Road 201, go 9 miles east on United States Route 62, 2.5 miles south (right) on County Road 279 (signs). An amphitheater is available and a picnic shelter, RBS1 for up to 36 people and 20 vehicles is $40. 102 sites with electric, 3 pull through sites, 4 - 50 ampere, 1 handicap site with electric, 1 pull through handicap site. Sites with electric hookups are $16; sites with 50 ampere service are $17. This campground requires a 2 night minimum stay on weekends and a 3 night stay on holiday weekends. Recreational vehicle maximum length is 40'. Open from April 1st to October 31st. (870) 492-6853. NRRS (May 16th to September 15th).

OZARK LAKE (LR) 15

A 10,600 acre surface area lake with 173 miles of shoreline is located southeast of Ozark, 39 miles east of Ft. Smith. Checkout time is 2 p.m., and alcohol is prohibited. Park Manager, Ozark Lake, 6042 Lock and Dam Road, Ozark, AR 7294. (479) 667-1100/2129/1-800-844-2129.

AUX ARC CAMPGROUND

From Ozark, go 1.3 miles south on State Road 23, 1 mile east on Highway 309, left at Aux Arc access road. Three picnic shelters are, 1/2 day - $35, 1 day - $50 (contact the office). A convenience store is located nearby. 64 sites, 60 with water and electric, 7 - 50 ampere, 1 full hookup with 50 ampere. Sites without electric hookups are $9; sites with electric hookups are $13; sites with water and electric hookups are $15; premium sites with water and electric hookups are $17; sites with water and 50 ampere service are $18. Recreational vehicle maximum length is in excess of 65'. This campground requires a 2 night minimum stay on weekends and a 3 night stay on holiday weekends. Open all year. (479) 667-1100. NRRS (March 1st to October 31st)).

CITADEL BLUFF CAMPGROUND

From Cecil, go 1.6 miles north on Highway 41. A picnic shelter is available. 25 sites. All sites are $6. Open all year.

CLEAR CREEK CAMPGROUND

From Alma, go 5.2 miles south on highway 162 (signs), 3.6 miles east (left) on Clear Creek Road. A picnic shelter is, 1/2 day - $35, 1 day - $50. 41 sites, 25 with electric, 4 pull through sites. Sites without electric hookups are $9; sites with electric hookups are $16. Recreational vehicle maximum length is in excess of 65'. This campground requires a 2 night minimum stay on weekends and a 3 night stay on holidays. Open from March 1st to October 31st. (479) 632-4882. NRRS (May 19th to September 15th).

RIVER RIDGE CAMPGROUND

From Cecil, go 12 miles west on Highway 96, 1.2 miles northeast on Hoover's Ferry Road. 18 sites. All sites are free. Open from March 1st to September 30th.

SPRINGHILL CAMPGROUND

From Ft. Smith/Junction I-540, exit 3, go 7.3 miles south on Highway 59 (signs). A group camping area is available and six picnic shelters, GCA01 and GC1 for up to 30 people and 10 vehicles, PS02, PS05, SA5 and SA2 for up to 50 people and 5 vehicles are, for 1/2 day are $35, for 1 day are $50. 44 sites with electric, 27 - 50 ampere, 1 full hookup. Sites without electric hookups are $9; sites with electric hookups and sites with 50 ampere service are $17; sites with water and 50 ampere service are $18. Recreational vehicle maximum length is in excess of 65'. This campground requires a 2 night minimum stay on weekends and a 3 night stay on holidays. Open all year. (479) 452-4598. NRRS (May 19th to September 15th).

RIVER AREA (LR)
ARKANSAS POST TO PINE BLUFF 16

Pine Bluff Project Office, P. O. Box 7835, Pine Bluff, AR 71611. (870) 534-0451.

MERRISACH LAKE CAMPGROUND LOCK #2

From Tichnor/Junction State Road 44, go 8.2 miles south, exit northwest near project office (signs). Four picnic shelters, GS1 for up to 75 people and 10 vehicles and GS2 for up to 75 people and 22 vehicles with electric are $40, GS3 for up to 75 people and 22 vehicles and GS4 for up to 75 people and 10 vehicles without electric are $30, and there is a convenience store and restaurants are located nearby. 65 sites, 59 with electric, 3 - 50 ampere. Sites with electric hookups are $11; sites with water hookups are $12; sites with water and electric hookups are $16; premium sites with water and electric hookups are $18; sites with water and 50 ampere service are $19. Recreational vehicle maximum length is in excess of 65'. Open all year. NRRS.

NOTREBES BEND CAMPGROUND

From Tichnor/Junction State Road 44, go 8.2 miles south across canal west of project office, 5.5 miles west, on the east side of the dam. Checkout time is 2 p.m., and there is a combination gate lock provided for late entry by registered campers. Restaurants are located nearby. 30 sites with water 50 ampere service. Sites with water and 50 ampere service are $17. Recreational vehicle maximum length is 50'. Open from March 2th to October 31st. NRRS.

PENDLETON BEND CAMPGROUND

From Dumas, go 9 miles north on United States Route 65, 2 miles east on State Road 212 (signs). A picnic shelter for up to 75 people and 12 vehicles is $40, there is a combination gate lock for late entry by registered camperes and checkout time is 2 p.m. 31 sites with water and electric, 18 - 50 ampere, 2 pull through sites, 3 handicap sites with water and electric. Sites with water and electric hookups are $16; premium sites with water and electric hookups are $18; sites with water and 50 ampere service are $18. Recreational vehicle maximum length is 40'. Open all year. (870) 479-3292. NRRS.

WILBUR D. MILLS CAMPGROUND

From Dumas, go 9 miles north on United States Route 65, 2 miles east on State Road 212 (signs), go through Pendleton Bend campground. Checkout time is 2 p.m. 21 sites with water and electric, 1 handicap site. Sites with water and electric hookups are $14. Recreational vehicle maximum length is 60'. Open from March 2nd to October 31st. NRRS.

RIVER AREA - PINE BLUFF TO
LITTLE ROCK (LR) 17

Pine Bluff Resident Office, P. O. Box 7835, Pine Bluff, AR 71611. (870) 534-0451.

RISING STAR CAMPGROUND

From Linwood/Junction United States Route 65, go 3.6 miles east on Blankinship Road. A picnic shelter is $60 and a convenience store is located nearby. 25 sites with water and 50 ampere service. Sites with water and 50 ampere service are $19. Recreational vehicle maximum length is 40'. Open from March 1st to October 31st. NRRS (May 16th to September 12th).

TAR CAMP CAMPGROUND

From Redfield/Junction United States Route 65/State Road 46, go 5.8 miles east (signs). Two picnic shelters, SO1 and SO2 for up to 60 people and 20 vehicles are $60. 48 sites, 45 - 50 ampere. All sites are $19. This campground requires a 2 night minimum stay on weekends and a 3 night stay on holiday weekends. Recreational vehicle maximum length is 40'. Open all year.. NRRS (May 19th to September 15th).

WILLOW BEACH CAMPGROUND

From From north of Little Rock on I-440, go east 2.5 miles on United States Route 165, south on Colonel Manard road, 1 mile west on Blue Heron (signs). Two picnic shelters for up to 60 people and 20 vehicles are $50 to $60, and there is a handicap accessible fishing area. 21 sites with 50 ampere. Sites with water and 50 ampere service are $19. Recreational vehicle maximum length is 40'. Open all year. (501) 961-1332. NRRS (May 16th to September 17th).

RIVER AREA - LITTLE ROCK TO DARDANELLE (LR)
TOAD SUCK FERRY - MURRAY L&D 18

Checkout time is 2 p.m. Resource Manager, Toad Suck Ferry, Rt. 5, Box 199, Conway, AR 72032. (501) 329-2986.

CHEROKEE L&D #9 CAMPGROUND

From Morrilton, go 0.7 mile south on Cherokee Street, 0.8 mile south on Quincy Road (signs). Two picnic shelters are available all year (for reservations, call the office), 1/2 day - $35, 1 day - $50. 33 sites with electric. Sites with water and electric hookups are $14; sites with water and 50 ampere service are $20.

Open from March 1st to October 31st. (501) 354-9155.

CYPRESS CREEK CAMPGROUND

From Houston/Junction State Road 216, go 2 miles north on State Road 113. 9 sites. All sites are free. Recreational vehicle maximum length is 40'. Open from March 1st to October 31st.

MAUMELLE CAMPGROUND

From Junction I-430, go 4 miles west on State Road 10 (Cantrell Road), 4 miles north on Pinnacle Valley Road (signs). Eight picnic shelters are, 1/2 day - $35, 1 day - $50. 129 sites with water and electric, 3 pull through sites, 24 - 50 ampere, 1 handicap site with water and electric. Sites with water and electric hookups are $18; sites with water and 50 ampere service are $20. Recreational vehicle maximum length is in excess of 65'. This campground requires a 2 night minimum stay on weekends and a 3 night stay on holiday weekends. Open all year. (501) 868-9477. NRRS (March 1st to October 31st).

POINT REMOVE CAMPGROUND

From Morriton, go 0.7 mile south on Cherokee Street. 16 sites. All sites are free. Open from March 1st to October 31st.

SEQUOYA CAMPGROUND

From Morriton, go 4 miles south on State Road 9, 2 miles west on River View Road. A picnic shelter is $35 for 1/2 day and $50 for a day. 14 sites with electric. Sites with electric hookups are $14. Open all year.

TOAD SUCK FERRY CAMPGROUND

From Conway, I-40, exit 129, go 7 miles west on State Road 60 (signs), 0.5 mile east on access road. Five picnic shelters, S1a, S4a and S5c for up to 50 people, and S2c and S3a for up to 100 people are, 1/2 day - $35, 1 day - $50, and checkout time is 3 p.m.. 48 sites with water and electric, 33 -50 ampere, 1 handicap site with water and 50 ampere. Sites with water and electric hookups are $18; sites with water and 50 ampere service are $20. Recreational vehicle maximum length is in excess of 65'. This campground requires a 2 night minimum stay on weekends and a 3 night stay on holiday weekends. Open all year. (501) 759-2005. NRRS (March 1st to October 31st).

TABLE ROCK LAKE (LR) 19

Located in north-central Arkansas, south of Branson, Missouri, on State Road 165, west of United States Route 65. Exhibits, auditorium and audio-visual presentations are available. Resource Manager, Upper White River Project Office, 4600 State Road 165 Ste. A, Branson, MO 65616-8976. (417) 344-4101. See MO listing.

CRICKET CREEK CAMPGROUND

From Ridgedale, MO., go 5.3 miles southwest on State Road 14 (signs). 36 sites, 28 with electric, 3 tent only sites, 4 pull through sites. Tent sites are $12; sites with electric hookups are $16; sites with water and electric hookups are $17. Recreational vehicle maximum length is in excess of 65'. This campground requires a 2 night minimum stay on weekends and a 3 night stay on holiday weekends. Open from April 1st to September 28th. (870) 426-3331. NRRS (April 1st to September 29th).

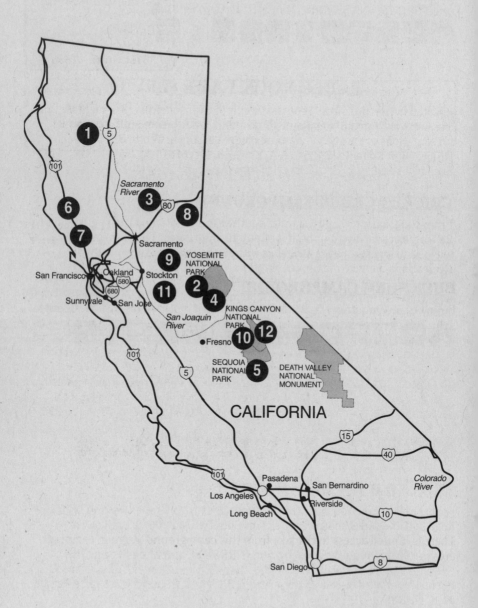

CALIFORNIA

STATE CAPITAL:
Sacramento
NICKNAME:
Golden State

31st State - 1850

Site reservation, National Recreation Reservation Service
(NRRS), toll free, 1-877-444-6777; TDD 877-833-6777,
www.recreation.gov, (Master, Visa, American Express
& Discover cards).

BLACK BUTTE LAKE (SAC) 1

A 4,460 acre surface area lake with 40 miles of shoreline located 8 miles west of
Orland and I-5, 100 miles northwest of Sacramento in north-central California.
For dam tours and ranger programs, call the office for scheduling. Off the road
vehicles and all terrain vehicles are prohibited. Park Manager, Black Butte Lake,
19225 Newville Road, Orland, CA 95963-8901. (530) 865-4781.

BUCKHORN CAMPGROUND

From Orland/Junction I-5, Black Butte Lake exit, go 14 miles west on County
Road 200 (Newville Road, signs) past dam, 0.5 mile southwest of junction with
Black Butte Road. A group camping area for up to 80 people is $90 to $105 and
requires a reservation (NRRS) and an amphitheater and fish cleaning station
are available. Picnic shelters for up to 80 people and 40 vehicles are $110. 85
sites, 5 tent only walk-in sites, 28 pull through sites. From November 1st to
February 28th, sites are $10; from March 1st to October 31st, sites are $15.
Recreational vehicle maximum length is in excess of 65'. Open all year. NRRS
(April 1st to September 30th).

ORLAND BUTTES CAMPGROUND

From Orland/Junction I-5, Black Butte Lake exit, go 6 miles west on County
Road 200, 3.3 miles southwest (left) on County Road 206, 0.5 mile west.
There is limited access to the lake from this campground. A group camping
area is $90 and requires a reservation (NRRS), an amphitheater and fish
cleaning station are available. 35 sites, 18 pull through sites. All sites are $15.
Recreational vehicle maximum length is 35'. Open from April 1st to September
10th. NRRS.

EASTMAN LAKE (SAC) 2

A 1,780 acre surface area lake located 25 miles northeast of Chowchilla, 55 miles north of Fresno. Park Manager, Eastman Lake, P. O. Box 67, Raymond, CA 93653-0067. (559) 689-3255.

CODORNIZ CAMPGROUND

From Raymond, on Highway 99, go east on 26th Avenue, north on Route 29 (signs). Four group camping areas, North A, North B, South and Equestrian (see listings below), and a picnic shelter, amphitheater and fish cleaning station are available. All group areas and loops listed below are within the Cordorniz campground. 65 sites, 14 with electric, 14 pull through sites, 5 full hookups, 2 handicap sites with water and electric. Primitive equestrian sites with water hookups are $10 (May be reserved by equestrian groups and nonprofit organizations through the office); standard sites with water hookups and family horse sites are $14; premium sites with water hookups are $16; premium sites with water and electric hookups are $20; sites with full hookups are $22. Recreational vehicle maximum length is in excess of 65'. Open all year. NRRS.

EQUESTRIAN/MULTI PURPOSE AREA

Group camping, amphitheater, corral and hitching posts. Limited to equestrian groups of up to 60 people and 30 vehicles is $25. Contact park headquarters for details. Sites are primitive. All sites are $8. Open all year. NRRS.

NORTH GROUP SECTION A CAMPGROUND

Group camping for up to 40 people and 15 vehicles is $55. Open all year. NRRS.

NORTH GROUP SECTION B CAMPGROUND

Group camping for up to 100 people and 25 vehicles is $55. Open all year. NRRS.

SOUTH GROUP CAMPGROUND

Group camping for up to 160 people and 50 vehicles is $75. Open all year. NRRS.

WILDCAT GROUP CAMPGROUND

On east side of lake. For Scouts and non-profit groups and overflow only. Call office to reserve. 19 sites with water, 7 pull through sites, 3 horse sites.

ENGLEBRIGHT LAKE (SAC) 3

An 815 acre surface area lake located 21 miles east of Marysville on State Road 20, 75 miles northeast of Sacramento. Group tours and ranger programs are scheduled through the office. Park Manager, Englebright Lake, P. O. Box 6, Smartville, CA 95977-0006. (530) 432-6427.

BOAT IN CAMPING

Boat-in only. 100 primitive sites. From May 1st to September 30th, sites are $10; from October 1st to April 30th, some sites are available and are free. Open all year. Contact park manager for details.

POINT DEFIANCE GROUP CAMPGROUND

Group camping area for up to 50 people is $50 to $75. Picnic shelters from Sunday through Thursday are $50 and for Friday and Saturday they are $75 with a reservation required. Contact office for information and reservation.

HENSLEY LAKE (SAC) 4

A 1,500 acre surface area lake located 17 miles northeast of Madera on State Road 400, north of Fresno. Multi-use trails are available. Contact the office for tours and ranger programs. Resource Manager, Hensley Lake, P. O. Box 85, Raymond, CA 93653. (559) 673-5151.

HIDDEN VIEW CAMPGROUND

From Chowchilla/Junction Highway 99, take Avenue 26 (signs). Two group camping areas for up to 50 people are $50 with a reservation required, picnic shelters are $25, a fish cleaning station is available and there is an amphitheater with evening shows on Friday and Saturday. 55 sites, 15 with water and electric, 17 pull through sites, 1 handicap site with water and electric(call the office for reservation). Sites without hookups are $14; premium sites with water and electric hookups are $20. Maximum recreational vehicle length is in excess of 65'. This campground requires a 3 day minimum stay on holiday weekends. Open all year. NRRS.

WAKALUMI

Primitive area. Groups may reserve by contacting the office.

KAWEAH LAKE (SAC) 5

A 1,945 acre surface area lake located 3 miles northeast of Lemoncove on State Road 198, southeast of Fresno, 21 miles east of Visalia. There is a visitor center at Lemon Hill Park and swimming is permitted unless otherwise posted. There is a fee for non-camper use of showers or dump station. Contact office for scheduling group tours and ranger programs. Resource Manager, Kaweah Lake, P. O. Box 44270, Lemoncove, CA 93244-4270. (559) 597-2301.

HORSE CREEK CAMPGROUND

From dam, go 3 miles east on State Road 198, left side (signs), located 10 miles from Sequoia National Park. Evening programs are offered at the amphitheater from Memorial Day through Labor Day, a fish cleaning station is available, checkout time is 2 p.m., and camp fire programs are held from memorial day through labor day. A convenience store and restaurants are located nearby. 80 sites, 35 pull through sites, 1 handicap site. All sites are $16. Overflow area is open on major holidays. Recreational vehicle maximum length is 35'. This campground requires a 3 day minimum stay on holiday weekends. This campground may be closed from mid April to mid July due to fooding. Open all year. (559) 561-3155. NRRS.

LAKE MENDOCINO (SF) 6

A 1,822 acre surface area lake located 2 miles northeast of Ukiah on Lake Mendocino Drive off United States Route 101, 1.5 miles east of Calpella off State Road 20, 120 miles north of San Francisco. There is an equestrian trail at the south end of the lake, off the road vehicles are prohibited and checkout time is 11 a.m. There are over 300 sites. Park Manager, Lake Mendocino, 1160 Lake Mendocino Drive, Ukiah, CA 95482-9404. (707) 462-7581.

BU-SHAY CAMPGROUND

From Ukiah, go 5 miles north on United States Route 101, 2.7 miles east on State Road 20, after crossing the Russian River bridge turn left 1 mile. Three group camping areas are Deer Creek accommodating up to 80 people and 20 vehicles, Little Bear accommodating up to 120 people and Tata accommodating up to 104 people, from $140 to $200 (NRRS), picnic shelters are available, coin operated showers, no 3rd vehicle permitted and an amphitheater with summer evening shows on Friday and Saturday. 164 sites. All sites are $20. Recreational vehicle maximum length is 40'. Open from May 15th to September 26th. NRRS.

CHE-KA-KA CAMPGROUND

From Ukiah, go 2 miles north on United States Route 101, Lake Mendocino exit, north (left) at North State Street, east (right) to Lake Mendocino Drive, top of hill on right (signs). Two picnic shelters, OVR for up to 50 people and 25 vehicles and JOR for up to 50 people and 20 vehicles are $35. An 18 hole golf course is available (Disc Golf). A 3rd vehicle is not permitted inside the campground. 22 sites. All sites are $16. Recreational vehicle maximum length is 43'. Open from April 13th to September 26th. NRRS (Reservations may not be available, call for information).

KAWEYO STAGING AREA

By permit only.

KY-EN CAMPGROUND

From Ukiah, go 5 miles north on United States Route 101, 1 mile east (right) on Highway 20, 0.8 mile east on Marina Drive. Pomo Visitor's Center, an amphitheater is available, coin operated showers and a 3rd vehicle is not permitted. Four picnic shelters, PSA and PSC without electric for up to 50 people and 20 vehicles are $30, and PSB and OAKG with electric for up to 50 people and 20 vehicles are $35. 101 sites, 3 with water and electric, 2 full hookups, 2 pull through sites. Sites are $20; premium sites are $22; 2d vehicle is $8 to $9. Recreational vehicle maximum length is 35'. On premium sites this campground requires a 2 day minimum stay on weekends and a 3 day stay on holiday weekends. Open from April 1st to September 30th. NRRS (Reservations may not be available, call for information).

MITI PARK

Accessible by boat-in only on the east side of the dam. 10 sites. All sites are $8. Open from May 1st to September 30th.

LAKE SONOMA (SF) 7

A 2700 acre surface area lake located 3 miles west of Geyserville, Canyon Road exit off United States Route 101, north of San Francisco. Visitor center. Group tours and ranger programs may be scheduled by calling the project office. More than 40 miles of trails for hikers, horseback riders and mountain bikers, and checkout time is noon. A fish hatchery is located at the dam and is operated by the state. Park Manager, Lake Sonoma, 3333 Skaggs Springs Road, Geyserville, CA 95441-9644. (707) 433-9483.

LIBERTY GLEN CAMPGROUND

From Healdsburg/Junction United States Route 101, Dry Creek Road exit, go 15 miles west (signs). A group camping area for up to 150 people and 51 vehicles is $80, and an amphitheater is available. Firewood sales are available during the summer months, there is no shoreline on this campground, sites are limited to 1 vehicle and a fee is charges for a 2nd vehicle. 97 sites, 16 double sites, 7 handicap sites. All sites are $16; double sites $32. Recreational vehicle maximum length is 46'. Open all year. Call before going to this campground due to a water outage.

BOAT-IN-SITES

15 campgrounds, includes two group camping areas, Broken Bridge and Island View, which are $40 from October 1st to March 31st and $56 from April 1st to September 30th, accessed by boat-in or hike-in only. 115 primitive sites. All sites are $10. Camper must register for the site at the visitor center. Open all year. NRRS.

MARTIS CREEK LAKE (SAC) 8

A 770 acre surface area lake located 6 miles southeast of Truckee on State Road 267, 32 miles southwest of Reno, Nevada on I-80. Contact the office for group tours/ranger programs and reservations for handicap sites (530) 639-2342. Motorized (gas or electric) boats are prohibited. Resource Manager, Martis Creek Lake, P. O. Box 6, Smartville, CA 95977-0006.

ALPINE MEADOWS CAMPGROUND

North side of dam, 0.3 mile northeast of State Road 267. Amphitheater. 25 sites, 6 pull through sites, 2 handicap sites. All sites are $14. Open from May 25th to October 15th. Recreational vehicle maximum length is 30'.

NEW HOGAN LAKE (SAC) 9

A 4,400 acre surface area lake with 50 miles of shoreline located 30 miles northeast of Stockton off State Road 26, 1 mile south on Hogan Dam Road, east of San Francisco, southeast of Sacramento. Nature Walk and ranger progams may be scheduled through the office. Coin operated showers and checkout time is 2 p.m. Park Manager, New Hogan Lake, 2713 Hogan Dam Road, Valley Springs, CA 95252-9510. (209) 772-1343.

ACORN CAMP EAST CAMPGROUND

From Valley Springs, go 0.5 mile south on State Road 26, 1 mile south (left) on Hogan Dam Road (signs), 0.7 mile east on Hogan Parkway. Campfire programs at the amphitheater on weekends, fish cleaning stations and a group camping area are available. There is a shower fee of $.50 for 5 minutes. 128 sites, 3 handicap sites, 30 pull through sites. From October 1st to March 31st, sites are $8; from April 1st to September 30th, on Friday, Saturday and the day preceding a holiday, sites are $16; on Sunday through Thursday, sites are $12. There is an $8 fee for each vehicle parked in the interior parking lot. Recreational vehicle maximum length is in excess of 65'. This campground requires a 2 day minimum stay on weekends and a 3 day stay on holiday weekends. Open all year. NRRS (April 1st to September 30th).

COYOTE POINT GROUP CAMPGROUND

Access to this campground is through Oak Knoll campground. A combination lock is provided on the gate for late entry by registered campers. This is a group area for up to 50 people and is $100. A shower fee of $.50 for 5 minutes is charged in adjoining campground, an amphitheater and a fish cleaning station are available. This campground requires a 2 night minimum stay on weekends and a 3 night stay on holiday weekends. Open from April 1st to October 31st.

DEER FLAT PARK

Accessible by boat-in only on the east side of the lake. Register at Acorn West. 30 primitive sites and on board camping. All sites and on board camping are $8. Open from April 1st to September 30th.

OAK KNOLL CAMPGROUND

From Valley Springs, go 0.5 mile south on State Road 26, 1 mile south on Hogan Dam Road, 0.7 mile east on Hogan Parkway, 1.1 miles north on South Petersburg Road. An amphitheater is available, a group camping area is $100, on board camping (houseboats) are $8, and a fish cleaning station in Acorn East. There is a shower fee of $.50 for 5 minutes. 50 primitive sites, 8 pull through sites. All sites are $10. Recreational vehicle maximum length is in excess of 65'. This campground requires a 2 day minimum stay on weekends and a 3 day stay on holiday weekends. Open from May 1st to September 3rd. NRRS.

PINE FLAT LAKE (SAC) 10

A 13,000 acre surface area lake with 67 miles of shoreline located 1 mile east of Piedra, 35 miles east of Fresno. Checkout time is 2 p.m. Dam tours, ranger programs and group/handicap sites, for scheduling and reservation, call (559) 787-2589. Park Manager, Pine Flat Lake, P. O. Box 117, Piedra, CA 93649-0117.

ISLAND PARK CAMPGROUND

From Piedra, go 9.5 miles northeast on Trimmer Springs Road, go south (signs). A fish cleaning station and an amphitheater are available, two group camping areas, Buck and Blue Oak, each accommodating up to 75 people and

20 vehicles are $75 and coin operated showers. Some sites may be closed from May 1st to August 31st due to high water. 97 sites, includes 60 overflow, 23 tent only sites, 1 handicap site. All sites are $16. No 3rd vehicles permitted. Recreational vehicle maximum length is in excess of 65'. Open all year. NRRS.

STANISLAUS RIVER PARKS (SAC) 11

The parks are located below the Melones Dam on the Stanislaus River, east of San Francisco, off State Road 99. From Modesto turn on State Road 108/120, 12 miles east of Oakdale turn north on Kennedy Road, north on Sonora Road, cross Stanislaus River and the Knights Ferry Information Center is on the right. Fishing and white-water rafting and canoeing area. All camping is by reservation only with camping permits issued at Information Center. For reservations (1 to 2 weeks in advance) call (209) 881-3517. Park Manager, Stanislaus River Parks, 17968 Covered Bridge Road, Oakdake, CA 95361-9510.

HORSESHOE ROAD

From Knights Ferry, west on Sonoroa & Orange Blossom Roads to Horseshoe Road. Boat-in, walk-in or bike-in only for individual sites. Group camping is $38. 16 sites. All sites are $8. Open all year.

MC HENRY AVENUE

From Modesto, 6 miles north on McHenry Avenue across Stanislaus river, 1 mile west on River Road, left at park sign. Boat-in, walk-in or bike-in only for individual sites. Group camping is $38. 4 sites. All sites are $8. Open from January 1st to October 31st.

VALLEY OAK

From Oakdale, 1.5 miles north on State Road 120, left on Orange Blossom Road, 3 miles east on Rodden Road, turn left. Boat-in, walk-in or bike-in only for individual sites. Group camping is $38. 10 sites. All sites are $8. Open all year.

SUCCESS LAKE (SAC) 12

A 2,450 acre surface area lake located 8 miles east of Porterville on State Road 190 (Sierra Nevada Foothills), north of Bakersfield. Swimming permitted. Off the road vehicles are prohibited. For 24 hour camping information, call (559) 783/9200. Resource Manager, Success Lake, P. O. Box 1072, Porterville, CA 93258. (559) 784-0215.

TULE RECREATION AREA

From dam, go 2 miles east on State Road 190, go north (signs). A picnic shelter, amphitheater, and fish cleaning station are available,and campfire programs on Saturdays from Memorial Day to Labor Day. A convenience store is located nearby. 103 sites, 7 with water and electric, 27 pull through sites, 2 handicap sites. Sites without electric hookups are $16; sites with water and electric hookups are $21. No 3rd vehicle is permitted. Recreational vehicle maximum length is in excess of 65'. This campground requires a 3 day minimum stay on holiday weekends. Open all year. NRRS.

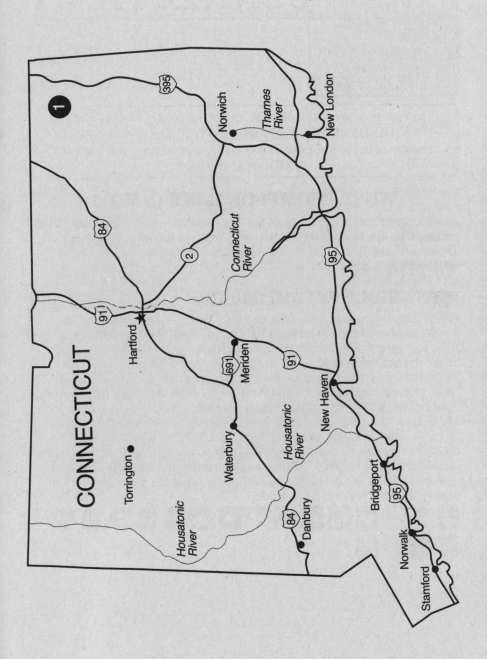

CONNECTICUT

STATE CAPITAL:
Hartford
NICKNAME:
Constitution State

5th State - 1788

Site reservation, National Recreation Reservation Service
(NRRS), toll free, 1-877-444-6777; TDD 877-833-6777,
www.recreation.gov, (Master, Visa, American Express
& Discover cards).

WEST THOMPSON LAKE (NAE) 1

A 200 acre surface area lake located northeast of Putnam off State Road 12 in
northeast Connecticut. Field dog trial area location. Resource Manager, West
Thompson Lake, RFD 1, 449 Reardon Road, North Grosvernordale, CT 06255-
9801. (860) 923-2982.

WEST THOMPSON CAMPGROUND

From North Grosvenordale/I-395, exit 99, go 1 mile east on State Road 200,
2 miles south (right) on State Road 193 (signs), cross State Road 12 at traffic
light, first right 0.5 mile on Reardon Road, left 0.2 mile on recreation road.
Picnic shelters for up to 75 people are $50, for reservations call 1-860-923-
2982), horseshoe pits, amphitheater, alcohol is prohibited, checkout time is
noon, no swimming permitted and there are no waterfront sites. A convenience
store and restaurants are located nearby. 24 sites, 1 handicap site with water
and electric. Sites without electric hookups are $15; 2 adirondack shelters are
$20; premium sites with water and electric hookups are $30. There is a $5 fee
for each person over 4, maximum of 6. Firewood available for a fee. Recreational
vehicle maximum length 45'. This campground requires a 2 night minimum
stay on weekends and a 3 night stay on Holiday weekends. Open May 18th to
September 9th. (860) 923-3121. NRRS.

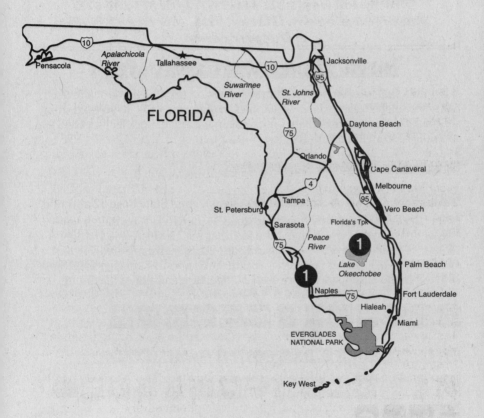

FLORIDA

STATE CAPITAL:
Tallahassee
NICKNAME:
Sunshine State

27th State - 1845

Site reservation, National Recreation Reservation Service (NRRS), toll free, 1-877-444-6777, TDD 877-833-6777, www.recreation.gov, (Master, Visa, American Express & Discover cards).

OKEECHOBEE WATERWAY (JX) 1

A 154 mile waterway stretching from Ft. Myers on the Gulf of Mexico through Lake Okeechobee (approximately 30 miles in diameter, 467,000 acres), exiting at Stuart on the Atlantic Ocean. Checkout time is noon. Lock facility tours are scheduled through the Park Rangers. Visitor Center in Alva (239) 694-2582 and St. Lucie (772) 219-4575. South Florida Operations Office, 525 Ridgelawn Road, Clewiston, FL 33440-5399. (863) 983-8101.

ORTONA LOCK & DAM SOUTH

From Labelle, go 8 miles east on State Road 80, north (left) on Dalton Lane (signs). A picnic shelter with handicap facilities for 2 to 40 people and 15 vehicles is available, and there is a handicap accessible fishing area. 51 sites with water and 50 ampere service, 4 pull through sites, 4 handicap sites. Sites with water and 50 ampere service are $24. Recreational vehicle maximum length is 45'. Open all year. (863) 675-8400. NRRS.

ST. LUCIE LOCK & DAM SOUTH CAMPGROUND

From Junction I-95, exit 101, go 0.5 mile west on State Road 76, right on Locks Road (signs). A picnic shelter for up to 20 people is $35, call (772) 287-1382. 12 sites, 9 with water and electric, 3 primitive tent only sites, 1 handicap site, plus 8 sleep-on boat sites with hookups. Tent only sites are $20; sites with water and electric hookups and boat sites with water and electric hookups are $24. Recreational vehicle maximum length is 45'. Open all year. (772) 287-1382. NRRS.

W. P. FRANKLIN LOCK & DAM NORTH CAMPGROUND

North of Fort Myers/JCT I-75, exit 25, go 10 miles east on US 80, 4 miles north on State Road 31, 3 miles east on State Road 78, north on North Franklin Road (signs). Two picnic shelters for up to 30 people and 1 vehicle are $35, and there is a handicap accessible fishing area. Shopping is available in nearby Ft. Myers. 30 sites with water and 50 ampere service, 1 pull through site, 1 handicap site, plus 8 sleep on boat sites with hookups. Sites with water and 50 ampere service and boat sites with water and electric hookups are $24. Recreational vehicle maximum length is 35'. Open all year. (239) 694-8770. NRRS.

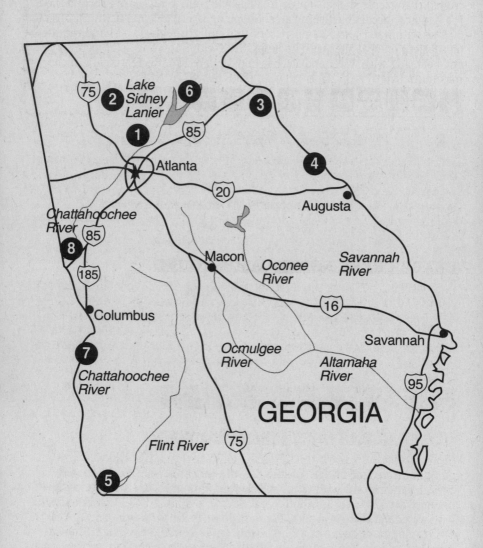

GEORGIA

STATE CAPITAL:
Atlanta
NICKNAME:
Peach State

4th State - 1788

Site reservation, National Recreation Reservation Service (NRRS), toll free, 1-877-444-6777; TDD 877-833-6777, www.recreation.gov, (Master, Visa, American Express & Discover cards).

ALLATOONA LAKE (MB) 1

A 12,000 acre surface area lake with 270 miles of shoreline is located 30 miles northwest of Atlanta off I-75, east of Cartersville in northwest Georgia. A fee is charged for visitors to 10:00 p.m., and off the road vehicles are prohibited. Master, Visa, Discover and American Express cards are accepted at all campgrounds. Operations Manager, Allatoona Lake, P. O. Box 487, Cartersville, GA 30120-0487. (678) 721-6700.

CLARK CREEK NORTH CAMPGROUND

From Atlanta, I-75 north, exit 278, go 2.3 miles north on Glade Road (signs) cross lake bridge, go left. 24 sites with water and electric, 8 - 50 ampere, 2 handicap sites, 5 pull through sites. Sites with water and electric hookups are $24; sites with water and 50 ampere service are $26. Recreational vehicle maximum length is 40'. This campground requires a 2 night stay on weekends and a 3 night stay on holiday weekends. Open from April 23th to September 3rd. NRRS.

CLARK CREEK SOUTH CAMPGROUND

From Atlanta, I-75 north, exit 278, go 2 miles north on Glade Road (signs), go right before lake bridge. 40 sites, 24 with water and electric, 5 tent only sites, 1 handicap site with water and electric. Tent only sites and sites without hookups are $14; sites with water and electric hookups are $20; premium sites with water and electric are $22. Recreational vehicle maximum length is 40'. This campground requires a 2 night stay on weekends and a 3 night stay on holiday weekends. Open from April 27th to September 3rd. This campground is temporary closed - contact the office for information. NRRS.

MCKASKEY CREEK CAMPGROUND

From Cartersville, I-75, exit 290, go 2 miles east (right) on State Road 20 (signs), 1.5 miles south on Spur 20, 1.5 miles east on County Road (McKaskey Creek Road). 51 sites, 32 with water and electric, 6 tent only sites, 2 handicap sites with water and electric, 5 pull through sites. Tent sites and sites without hookups are $16; sites with water and electric hookups are $20; premium sites with water and electric hookups are $24. Recreational vehicle maximum length is 40'. This campground requires a 2 night stay on weekends and a 3 night stay on holiday weekends. Open from March 30th to September 3rd. NRRS.

MCKINNEY CAMPGROUND

From Atlanta, I-75 north, exit 278, go 3 miles east on Glade Road past Clark Creek to 2nd 4 way stop sign (signs), 1 mile north (left) on King's Camp road, left at forks. 150 sites with water and electric, 8 handicap sites with 50 ampere service, 35 pull through sites. Sites with water and electric hookups are $20; sites with water and 50 ampere service are $22; premium sites with water and electric hookups are $24. Recreational vehicle maximum length is 40'. This campground requires a 2 night stay on weekends and a 3 night stay on holiday weekends. Open all year. NRRS.

OLD 41 #3 CAMPGROUND

From Atlanta, I-75 north, exit 283, go .07 mile west to stop light, .08 mile right on State Road 92 (Lake Acworth Drive) crossing the overpass, right to bottom of overpass, 2.5 miles left (signs). 55 sites with water and electric, 30 - 50 ampere, 1 full hookup, 6 double sites, 4 pull through sites. Sites with water and electric hookups are $20; premium sites with water and electric hookups are $24; premium sites with water and 50 ampere service are $26; double sites with water and 50 ampere service are $52. Recreational vehicle maximum length is 50'. This campground requires a 2 night stay on weekends and a 3 night stay on holiday weekends. Open from April 13th to September 3rd. NRRS.

PAYNE CAMPGROUND

From Atlanta, I-75 north, exit 277, go 2 miles east on State Road 92, north (left) on Old Alabama Road to dead end, 1.5 miles east (right) on Kellogg Creek Road (signs). 60 sites, 39 with water and electric, 23 - 50 ampere, 2 full hookups, 1 handicap site with water and electric, 1 double site, 9 pull through sites. Sites without hookups are $14; sites with water and electric hookups are $20;

premium sites with water and 50 ampere service are $22; sites with full hookup sites and premium sites with water and electric hookups are $24; premium sites with water and 50 ampere service are $26; a double site with water and 50 ampere service is $40. Recreational vehicle maximum length is 40'. This campground requires a 2 night stay on weekends and a 3 night stay on holiday weekends. March 30th to September 3rd. NRRS.

SWEETWATER CAMPGROUND

South of Canton/Junction State Road 5, go 5 miles west on State Road 20 across Knox Bridge, 2 miles south. A group camping area for up to 54 people has 9 sites with a picnic shelter and is $220. 151 sites, 118 with water and electric, 52 - 50 ampere, 1 handicap site with water, 1 handicap site with water and 50 ampere, 23 pull through sites, 1 full hookup, 1 double site with full hookups. Sites without hookups and sites with water hookups are $16; sites with water and electric hookups are $20; sites with water and 50 ampere service are $22; a site with full hookups and premium sites with water and electric hookups are $24; premium sites with water and 50 ampere service are $26; a double sites with full hookups is $44. Recreational vehicle maximum length is in excess of 65'. This campground requires a 2 night stay on weekends and a 3 night stay on holiday weekends. Open from March 30th to September 3rd. NRRS.

UPPER STAMP CREEK CAMPGROUND

From Cartersville, I-75, exit 290, go 4 miles east on State Road 20, 1.3 miles south on Wilderness Road (signs), dirt road to left. 20 sites, 18 with water and electric, 2 tent only sites, 2 handicap sites, 1 pull through site. Tent only sites are $14; sites with water and electric hookups are $20; premium sites with water and electric hookups are $22. Recreational vhicle maximum length is 30'. This campground requires a 2 night stay on weekends and a 3 night stay on holiday weekends. Open from April 27th to September 3rd. This campground is temporary closed - contact the office for information. NRRS.

VICTORIA CAMPGROUND

From Atlanta, I-75 north to I-575 north, exit 7, go 3 miles west on Old Alabama Road, 3.5 miles north (right) on Bells Ferry Road, 3 miles west (left) on Victoria Landing Drive. 74 sites with water and electric, 14 - 50 ampere, 2 full hookups, 2 handicap sites with water and electric, 27 pull through sites. Sites with water and electric hookups are $20; premium sites with water and electric hookups are $22; sites with full hookups and sites with water and 50 ampere service are

$24. Recreational vehicle maximum length is 65'. This campground requires a 2 night stay on weekends and a 3 night stay on holiday weekends. Open from March 30th to October 13th. NRRS.

CARTERS LAKE (MB) 2

A 3,200-acre surface area lake located 27 miles north of Cartersville on United States Route 411 north of junction with State Road 136, southwest of Ellijay in northwest Georgia. Site Manager, Carter Lake, P. O. Box 96, Oakman, GA 30732-0096. (706) 334-2248.

BOAT IN CAMPGROUND

From dam boat launch, go east. 12 primitive sites. All sites are free. Open all year.

DOLL MOUNTAIN CAMPGROUND

From Ellijay, go south on Old Highway 5, south on State Road 382, go west. CAUTION - Steep down grade to the campground. A picnic shelter and an amphitheater are available, and a night time emergency exit is provided. 66 sites, 39 with water and electric, 27 tent only sites, 5 pull through sites, 10 - 50 ampere, 1 handicap site. Tent only sites are $14; tent only sites with water and electric, sites with water and electric hookups and sites with water and 50 ampere service are $18; premium sites with water and 50 ampere service are $20. Recreational vehicle maximum length is 20'. This campground requires a 2 night stay on weekends and a 3 night stay on holiday weekends. Open from April 6th to October 27th. (706) 276-4413. NRRS.

HARRIS BRANCH CAMPGROUND

From Gordon, go 5.5 miles east on State Road 136, 0.7 mile east on State Road 382, go northwest. A group camping area is $50, plus a $5 reservation fee, contact the office for information and reservation. 10 sites. All sites are $14. Open from May 4th to September 30th. (706) 276-4545.

RIDGEWAY CAMPGROUND

From Ellijay, go approximately 5 miles west on State Route 282, access on the left. 20 primitive sites. All sites are $8. Open all year.

WOODRING BRANCH CAMPGROUND

From Ellijay, go 11 miles west on State Road 282/United States Route 76 (signs). A picnic shelter and an amphitheater are available. 42 sites, 31 with water and electric, 8 - 50 ampere, 11 tent only sites, 2 handicap sites. Tent only sites are $14; sites with water and electric hookups and sites with water and 50 ampere service are $18; premium sites with water and electric hookups are $20. This campground requires a 2 night stay on weekends and a 3 night stay on holiday weekends. Recreational vehicle maximum length is 40'. Open April 6th to October 27th.(706) 276-6050. NRRS.

HARTWELL LAKE (SV) 3

A 56,000 acre surface area lake with 962 miles of shoreline is located 5 miles north of Hartwell on United States Route 29, southwest of Greenville, SC on the state line. Guided tours of dam and powerplant are provided. Checkout time is 2 p.m., and public use of alcoholic beverages is prohibited. Off the road vehicle, golf carts and motorized scooters are prohibited. Project Manager, Hartwell Lake and Powerplant, P. O. Box 278, Hartwell, Ga. 30643-0278. (706) 856-0300/(888) 893-0678. See SC listing.

GEORGIA RIVER CAMPGROUND

From Hartwell, go 6.5 miles north on United States Route 29. 15 sites. From May 1st to September 9th, sites are $6; from March 1st to April 30th and September 10th to November 30th, some sites are available and are free. Open from March 1st to November 30th.

MILLTOWN CAMPGROUND

From Hartwell, go 4 miles north on State Road 51, 4 miles east on New Prospect Road, follow signs. Three group camping areas, loop A for up to 100 people and 30 vehicles and loop B for up to 70 people and 21 vehicles are $60, and loop C for up to 90 people and 27 vehicles is $50. 25 primitive sites, 1 pull

through site. All sites are $10. Recreational vehicle maximum length is 36'.
Open from May 9th to September 6th. NRRS.

PAYNES CREEK CAMPGROUND

From Hartwell, go 10 miles north on State Road 51 to Reed Creek, turn left
and follow signs. 44 sites with water and 50 ampere, 30 pull through sites. Sites
with water and 50 ampere service are $16; premium sites with water and 50
ampere service are $18. Recreational vehicle maximum length is 60'. Open from
May 1st to September 8th. NRRS.

WATSADLERS CAMPGROUND

From Hartwell, go 5.5 miles north on United States Route 29, follow signs. 49
lake front sites with water and 50 ampere, 2 double sites, 17 pull through sites.
From October 1st to March 31st, sites with water and 50 ampere service are
$18; double sites with water and 50 ampere service are $40; from April 1st to
September 30th, sites with water and 50 ampere serviceare $20; double sites
with water and 50 ampere service are $42. Recreational vehicle maximum
length is 50'. Open all year. NRRS.

J. STROM THURMOND LAKE (SV) 4

A 70,000 acre surface area lake with 1200 miles of shoreline is adjacent to
Clarks Hill, northwest of Augusta on South Carolina state line (United States
Route 221 crosses the top of dam). Exhibits on display at the visitor center.
Checkout time is 2 p.m. and public use of alcoholic beverages is prohibited.
Resource Manager, J. Strom Thurmond Lake, Route 1, Box 12, Clarks Hill, SC
29821-9701. (864) 333-1100/(800) 533-3478. See SC listing.

BIG HART CAMPGROUND

From Thomson, go 3 miles north on United States Route 78 past Junction with
State Road 43, 4 miles east (right) on Russell Landing Road (signs). A group
tent camping area for up to 30 people and 10 vehicles with a picnic shelter is
$75 and a fish cleaning station is available. 31 sites, 24 with water and electric,
25 pull through sites. Sites without electric hookups are $14; sites with electric
hookups are $16; premium sites with water and electric hookups are $18.
Recreational vehicle maximum length is 60'. This campground requires a 2
night stay on weekends and a 3 night stay on holiday weekends. Open from

April 1st to October 31st. During October walk in camping only is permitted. (706) 595-8613. NRRS.

BROAD RIVER CAMPGROUND

From I-85, exit 173, go 30 miles south on State Road 17, 11 miles towards Calhoun on State Road 72, 10 miles right on State Road 79 across the Broad River on the left. A fish cleaning station is available. 31 sites with water and electric, 2 triple sites, 7 double sites, 13 pull through sites, 1 handicap site. Sites with water and electric hookups are $16; premium sites with water and electric hookups are $18; double sites with water and electric hookups are $32; premium double sites with water and electric hookups are $36, triple sites with water and electric hookups are $48. A fee is charged for a 4th vehicle. Recreational vehilcle maximum length is in excess of 65'. This campground requires a 2 night stay on weekends and a 3 night stay on holiday weekends. Open from March 1st to September 4th. (706) 359-2053. NRRS (April 1st to September 4th.

BUSSY POINT CAMPGROUND

From Lincolnton, go south on State Road 47 to State Road 220 northeast, exit south at Kenna on gravel road. A picnic shelter is available. 14 primitive sites, 4 horse/horse trailer sites, 6 hike/bike/horseback/boat-in sites. All sites are $6. Open all year.

CLAY HILL CAMPGROUND

From Woodlawn, go 3 miles south on State Road 43, on the east side. 17 sites, 13 sites with water and electric, 4 primitive sites. Primitive sites are $10; sites with water and electric hookups are $14. Recreational vehicle maximum length is 25'. Open from April 1st to September 30th. (706) 359-7495.

HESTER'S FERRY CAMPGROUND

From Lincolnton/Junction United States Route 378, go 12 miles north on State Road 79, 2 miles east on highway 44 (signs). 26 sites, 16 with water and electric, 9 pull through sites, 10 primitive sites. Primitive sites are $14; sites with water and electric hookups are $16. There is a $3 fee for an extra vehicle. Recreational vehicle maximum length is 40'. This campground requires a 2 night stay on

weekends and a 3 night stay on holiday weekends. Open from April 1st to
October 31st. During October there is walk in camping only. (706) 359-2746.
NRRS (April 1st to September 29th).

PETERSBURG CAMPGROUND

From Pollards Corner, go 2 miles northeast on United States Route 221, go east.
A fish cleaning station, picnic shelters and a group camping area for up to 50
people and 1 vehicle are available. 93 sites, 85 with water and electric, 54 pull
through sites, 74 - 50 ampere, 2 handicap sites. Sites without electric hookups
are $14; sites with water and electric hookups are $16; premium sites with
water and electric hookups and sites with water and 50 ampere service are $18;
premium sites with water and 50 ampere service are $20. A $3 fee is charged
for 5th and 6th vehicle. Recreational vehicle maximum length is 45'. This
campground requires a 2 night stay on weekends and a 3 night stay on holiday
weekends. Open all year. (706) 541-9464. NRRS.

RAYSVILLE CAMPGROUND

From Woodlawn, to 7 miles south on State Road 43, go west. A fish cleaning
station and picnic shelters are available. 55 sites with water and 50 ampere, 32
pull through sites. Sites with water and 50 ampere service are $18; premium
sites with water and 50 ampere service are $20. Recreational vehicle maximum
length is 40'. This campground requires a 2 night stay on weekends and a 3
night stay on holiday weekends. Open from March 1st to October 30th. (706)
595-6759. NRRS.

RIDGE ROAD CAMPGROUND

From Highway 221 at Pollards Corner, go 4 miles northwest on State Road 47
toward Lincolnton, 5 miles northeast on Ridge Road to the campground. A fish
cleaning station is available. 69 sites with water and electric, 6 tent only sites,
27 pull through sites, 39 - 50 ampere. Sites without hookups are $14; sites
with water and electric hookups are $18; premium sites with water and electric
hookups and water and 50 ampere service are $20; double sites with water and
electric hookups are $36; double sites with water and 50 ampere service are
$40. There is a $3 fee for 5th and 6th vehicle. Recreational vehicle maximum
length is 50'. This campground requires a 2 night stay on weekends and a 3
night stay on holiday weekends. Open from April 1st to September 30th. (706)
541-0282. NRRS.

WINFIELD CAMPGROUND

From Pollards Corner, go 10 miles west on State Road 150, 5 miles north on Winfield Road. 80 premium sites with water and 50 ampere, 35 pull through sites. Premium sites with water and 50 ampere service are $20. There is a $3 fee for 5th and 6th vehicle. Recreational vehicle maximum length is 65'. This campground requires a 2 night stay on weekends and a 3 night stay on holiday weekends. Open from March 1st to September 30th. (706) 541-0147. NRRS.

LAKE SEMINOLE (MB) 5

A 37,500 acre surface area lake with 376 miles of shoreline is located north of Chattahoochee, Florida in southwest Georgia on the state line off United States Route 90. Checkout time is 3 p.m., alcohol is prohibited and visitors to 9:30 p.m., for a fee. Resource Site Manager, Lake Seminole, P. O. Box 96, Chattahoochee, FL 32324-0096. (229) 662-2001.

EAST BANK CAMPGROUND

From Chattahoochee, FL/Junction United States Route 90, go 1.5 miles north on Bolivar Street (Booster Club Road), left on East Bank Road. Horseshoe pits and a picnic shelter are available. 75 sites, 69 with water and electric, 38 - 50 ampere, 8 tent only sites, 1 double site with 50 ampere, 1 handicap site. Tent only sites are $12; sites with water and electric hookups are $16; a double site with water and 50 ampere service is $32. Recreational vehicle maximum length is in excess of 65'. Open all year. (229) 622-9273. NRRS.

FACEVILLE CAMPGROUND

From Bainbridge, go 14 miles south on State Road 97, go north. A picnic shelter is available. 7 sites, 4 tent only sites. All sites are $6. Recreational vehicle maximum length is 40'. Open all year.

HALES LANDING CAMPGROUND

From Bainbridge/Junction United States Route 84, go 3.8 miles southwest on State Road 253, 2 miles southwest on Ten Mile Still Road (sign), go south. A picnic shelter is available. 26 sites, 1 handicap site. All sites are $6. Open all year.

RIVER JUNCTION CAMPGROUND

From Chattahoochee, FL/Junction United States Route 90, go 2 miles north on Bolivar Street (Booster Club Road), left at sign. Group camping for scouts, reserve through Management Office. 16 sites. All sites are $6. Recreational vehicle maximum length is 40'. Open all year.

LAKE SIDNEY LANIER (MB) 6

A 38,000 acre surface area lake with 690 miles of shoreline is located west of I-985, exit 4, 35 miles northeast of Atlanta in north-central Georgia. Alcoholic beverages are prohibited, checkout time is 3 p.m., and visitors to 9:30 p.m., for a fee. Lanier Project Manager, Lake Sidney Lanier, P. O. Box 567, Buford, GA 30515-0567. (770) 945-9531.

BALD RIDGE CREEK CAMPGROUND

From Cumming, north on State Road 400, exit 16, right on Pilgrim Mill Road, right on Sinclair Shoals Road, left on Bald Ridge Road. A convenience store is nearby. 82 sites with water and electric, 9 pull throughs, 16 - 50 ampere, 2 full hookups, 3 handicap sites. Sites with water and electric hookups are $23; sites with water and 50 ampere service are $25. Recreational vehicle maximum length is in excess of 65'. This campground requires a 2 night stay on weekends and a 3 night stay on holiday weekends. Open from March 28th to October 28th. (770) 889-1591. NRRS.

BOLDING MILL CAMPGROUND

From Cumming, on State Road 400, exit 17, go northeast on State Road 306, right on highway 53, left on Old Sardis Road, left on Chestatee Road. A convenience store is nearby. 97 sites, 88 with water and electric, 9 tent only sites, 6 - 50 ampere, 36 handicap sites. Tent only sites are $15; sites with water and electric hookups are $23; sites with water and 50 ampere service are $25. Recreational vehicle maximum length is in excess of 65'. This campground requires a 2 night stay on weekends and a 3 night stay on holiday weekends. Open from April 26th to September 10th. This campground is temporary closed - contact the office for information. (770) 532-3650. NRRS.

CHESTNUT RIDGE CAMPGROUND

From Junction I-85, north on I-985, exit 4, left on Peachtree Industrial Boulevard, left on Gaines Ferry Road, left on Friendship Road, right on Chestnut Ridge Road. A convenience store is nearby. 84 sites, 51 with water and electric, 5 - 50 ampere, 7 pull through sites, 1 handicap site. Sites without electric hookups are $17; sites with water and electric hookups are $23; sites with water and 50 ampere service are $25. Recreational vehicle maximum length is in excess of 65'. This campground requires a 2 night stay on weekends and a 3 night stay on holiday weekends. Open from April 26th to September 10th. This campground is temporary closed - contact the office for information. (770) 967-6710. NRRS.

DUCKETT MILL CAMPGROUND

From Cumming/Junction State Road 400, go north to exit 17, right on Highway 306, right on Highway 53, right on Duckett Mill Road. A convenience store is nearby. 111 sites, 97 with water and electric, 14 tent only sites, 4 - 50 ampere, 1 handicap site. Tent only sites are $15; sites with water and electric hookups are $23; sites with water and 50 ampere service are $25. This campground requires a 2 night stay on weekends and a 3 night stay on holiday weekends. Open from April 25th to September 7th. (770) 532-9802. NRRS.

OLD FEDERAL CAMPGROUND

From I-985 north, exit 8, go left on State Road 347 (Friendship Road), right on Mc Ever Road, left on Jim Crow Road (signs). A picnic shelter is available and a convenience store is nearby. 83 sites, 59 with water and electric, 6 - 50 ampere, 1 handicap site, 1 tent only site. A tent only site and sites without hookups are $17; sites with water and electric hookups are $23; sites with water and 50 ampere service are $25. This campground requires a 2 night stay on weekends and a 3 night stay on holiday weekends. Open from March 28th to October 28th. (770) 967-6757. NRRS.

SAWNEE CAMPGROUND

From Cumming/Junction State Road 400 north, exit 14, go east (left) on Highway 20, left on Sanders Road, at 1st stop sign, 3.5 miles right on Buford dam road, on left. There is a convenience store nearby. 56 sites, 44 with water and electic. Sites without electric hookups are $17; sites with electric hookups are $23; sites with water and 50 ampere service are $25. Recreational vehicle maximum length is 40'. This campground requires a 2 night stay on weekends and a 3 night stay on holiday weekends. Open from April 25th to September 9th. (770) 887-0592. NRRS.

SHOAL CREEK CAMPGROUND

From Junction I-85, north on I-985, exit 4, go 3.2 miles west (left) on State Road 20, right on Peachtee Industrial Boulevard, left on Shadburn Ferry Road. Two group camping areas, group site 105 for up to 60 people and 24 vehicles is $170, and group site 106 for up to 50 people and 20 vehicles is $150, and a picnic shelter is available. 103 sites, 47 with water and electric, 31 pull through sites, 2 handicap sites. Sites without electric hookups are $17; sites with water and electric hookups are $23. This campground requires a 2 night stay on weekends and a 3 night stay on holiday weekends. Recreational vehicle maximum length is 65'. Open from April 25th to October 7th. (770) 945-9541. NRRS.

TOTO CREEK CAMPGROUND

From Cumming, go north on State Road 400, right on State Road 136, right at stop sign, left before crossing the bridge. 10 sites. All sites are $12. Open from April 27th to September 9th.

WALTER F. GEORGE LAKE (MB) 7

A 45,000 acre surface area lake with 640 miles of shoreline is located on the Chattahoochee River on the Alabama/Georgia state line, west of Albany, with the dam near Ft. Gaines off State Road 39. Visitors to 9:30 p.m., for a fee and checkout time is 3 p.m. Resource Site Manager, Walter F. George Lake, route. 1, Box 176, Ft. Gaines, GA 31751-9722. (229) 768-2516. See AL listing.

COTTON HILL CAMPGROUND

From Ft. Gaines, go 7 miles north on State Road 39, go west (signs). A picnic shelter and fish cleaning station are available. 104 sites, 94 with water and electric, 10 pull through sites, 10 tent only sites, 1 handicap site. Tent only sites are $18; sites with water and electric hookups are $20. Recreational vehicle maximum length is 40'. This campground requires a 2 night stay on weekends and a 3 night stay on holiday weekends. Open all year. (229) 768-3061. NRRS.

ROOD CREEK CAMPGROUND

From Georgetown/Junction United States Route 27, go 9.5 miles north on State Road 39, across Rood Creek, go west. Primitive camping area. All sites are free. Open from March 3rd to October 31st.

WEST POINT LAKE (MB) 8

A 25,900 acre surface area lake with 500 miles of shoreline located southwest of Atlanta, northwest of I-85 on the Georgia/Alabama state line north of West Point off United States Route 29. Power house visitor facility and dam tours available. Resource Manager, West Point Lake, 500 Resource Managers Drive, West Point, GA 31833-9517. (706) 883-6749/645-2937. See AL listing.

HOLIDAY CAMPGROUND

From La Grange, go 7 miles west on State Road 109 (follow signs), 2.3 miles south on Thompson Road. Two group camping areas, Running Deer with 5 RV sites and 5 tent sites for up to 80 people and 20 vehicles and Kee Kee with 14 RV sites and 5 tent sites for up to 80 people and 20 vehicles are $160, and an amphitheater is available. 143 sites, 92 with water and electric, 36 tent only sites, 2 double sites. Tent only sites and sites without hookups are $16; sites with water and electric hookups are $22; double sites are $44. Recreational vehicle maximum length is 65'. This campground requires a 2 night stay on weekends and a 3 night stay on holiday weekends. Open from February 23rd to September 23rd. (706) 884-6818. NRRS.

INDIAN SPRINGS GROUP CAMPGROUND

From La Grange, go 8 miles west on State Road 109, north side near Rock Mills Road. Contact the host at Whitetail campground at (706) 884-8972 for details. Four group tent camping areas, three areas for up to 48 people are $50 and one area for up to 120 people is $110, and a convenience store is located nearby.

This campground requires a 2 night stay on weekends and a 3 night stay on holiday weekends. Open from March 23rd to September 22nd. NRRS.

RINGER CAMPGROUND

From La Grange, go 8.7 miles north on United States Route 27, go west. 37 primitive sites. All sites are free. Recreational vehicle maximum length is 20'. Open all year.

R. SHAEFER HEARD CAMPGROUND

From West Point, go 4 miles north on United States Route 29 to dam road, left at signs. An amphitheater is available. 117 sites with water and electric, 10 sites with decks, 7 pull through sites, 10 double sites. Sites with water and electric hookups are $22; double sites with water and electric hookups are $44. Recreational vehicle maximum length is in excess of 65'. This campground requires a 2 night stay on weekends and a 3 night stay on holiday weekends. Open all year. (706) 645-2404. NRRS.

WHITETAIL RIDGE CAMPGROUND

From La Grange, go 7 miles west on State Road 109, 0.8 mile south on Thompson road, on left. Picnic shelters are available and a convenience store is located nearby. 58 sites with water and electric, 4 pull through sites, 3 double sites. Sites with water and electric hookups are $22; double sites with water and electric hookups are $44. Recreational vehicle maximum length is in excess of 65". This campground requires a 2 night stay on weekends and a 3 night stay on holiday weekends. Open from March 23rd to November 24th. (706) 882-8972. NRRS.

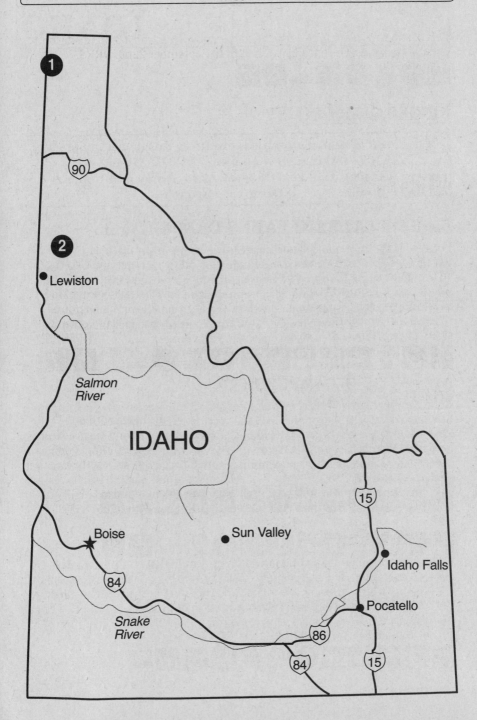

IDAHO

STATE CAPITAL:
Boise
NICKNAME:
Gem State

43rd State - 1890

Site reservation, National Recreation Reservation Service
(NRRS), toll free, 1-877-444-6777; TDD 877-833-6777,
www.recreation.gov, (Master, Visa, American Express
& Discover cards).

ALBENI FALLS DAM (SEA) 1

Located in the Panhandle of northwest Idaho across from Newport,
Washington, south of United States Route 2, 4 miles west of Priest River. 140+
sites in four campgrounds. A $7 fee is charged for a second vehicle overnight,
no unlicensed vehicles permitted, a fee is charged for showers and checkout
time is 2 p.m. The visitor center provides one hour powerhouse tours daily
from Memorial Day through Labor Day. For recorded campground status call
(208) 437-5517. Resource Manager, Albeni Falls Project, 2576 east Highway 2,
Oldtown, ID 83822-9243. (208) 437-3133.

ALBENI COVE CAMPGROUND

From Newport, go southeast on State Road 41, 3 miles east (left) on Fourth
Street (part gravel), stay on the dirt road veering left at the forks. A fee is
charged for firewood. Restaurants are located nearby. 14 sites, 4 walk-in tent
only sites, 2 pull through sites. Tent only sites and sites without hookups
are $15. Recreational vehicle maximum length 20'. Open from May 12th to
September 8th. NRRS.

PRIEST RIVER

From Priest River/Junction State Road 57, go 1 mile east on United States
Route 2, turn right. A picnic shelter is $35 (for information and reservation call
the office), an amphitheater is available and there is a bicycle camping area. 25
sites, 5 bike-in only sites, 8 pull through sites. Bike-in sites are $3; sites without
hookups are $15. Recreational vehicle maximum length is 60'. Open from May
12th to September 8th. NRRS.

RILEY CREEK CAMPGROUND

From Priest River/Priest River Park, go 9 miles east on United States Route 2 to LaClede, 1 mile south on Riley Creek road. Two picnic shelters are $35 (call the office for information and reservation), and an amphitheater and horseshoe pits are available. 67 sites with water and 50 ampere service. Sites with water and 50 ampere service are $15. Recreational vehicle maximum length is 40'. Open from May 12th to September 29th. NRRS.

SPRINGY POINT CAMPGROUND

From Sandpoint/Junction United States Route 2, go south on United States Route 95 across long bridge, 3 miles west on Lakeshore Drive, north of road. 38 sites, 1 walk-in tent only site, 7 pull through sites. All sites are $15. Open from May 12th to October 7th. NRRS.

DWORSHAK RESERVOIR (WW) 2

A 54 mile long lake located 5 miles northeast of Orofino on State Road 7, east of Lewiston, north of United States Route 12, in northwest Idaho. Noted for Kokanee Salmon, Rainbow Trout and Small Mouth Bass. Guided group tours, audio-visual programs, displays and a visitor center. For reservoir information call 1-800-321-3198. Resource Manager, P. O. Box 48, Ahsahka, ID 83520-0048. (208) 476-1255/1261/1-800-321-3198.

CANYON CREEK CAMPGROUND

From Orofino, go 11 miles northeast off Elk River, Wells Bench & Eureka Ridge Roads (gravel, signs). 17 primitive sites. All sites are free. Recreational vehicle maximum length 22'. Open from spring through the fall months.

COLD SPRINGS GROUP CAMPGROUND

Contact Office for information. Boat-in or hiking access only. Primitive area. All sites are free. Open from spring through the fall months.

DENT ACRES CAMPGROUND

From Orofino, go 20 miles northeast on Elk River Road via the Wells Bench Road (signs). A picnic shelter for up to 100 people and 26 vehicles is $25, a fish cleaning station (closed in winter), marine dump station, ice and firewood for a fee. 50 full hookup sites, 49 pull through sites, 1 handicap site. From April 12th to May 21th and September 4th to November 25th, walk-in sites are $10; from May 22rd to September 3th, sites with full hookups are $16; sites with full hookups and 50 ampere service are $18. Recreational vehicle maximum length 50'. Open from April 12th to November 25th. (208) 476-9029. NRRS (May 23rd to September 4th).

DENT ACRES GROUP CAMPGROUND

From Orofino, go 18 miles northeast on Elk River Road via the Wells Bench Road (2 miles from Dent Acres camp ground). A picnic shelter with electric is available. 3+ acre tent camping zone for up to 200 people and 48 vehicles is $50. Open from early May through early September.

GRANDAD CREEK CAMPGROUND

From project office, go 68 miles north on Silver Creek Road and Musselman Road (gravel roads). 10 primitive sites. All sites are free. Open from spring through fall the months subject to weather conditions.

MINI CAMPS CAMPGROUND

Accessible by boat-in or biking trail, marked by signs. Group camping with maps available. 121 sites primitive tent only sites. All sites are free. Open from spring through the fall months.

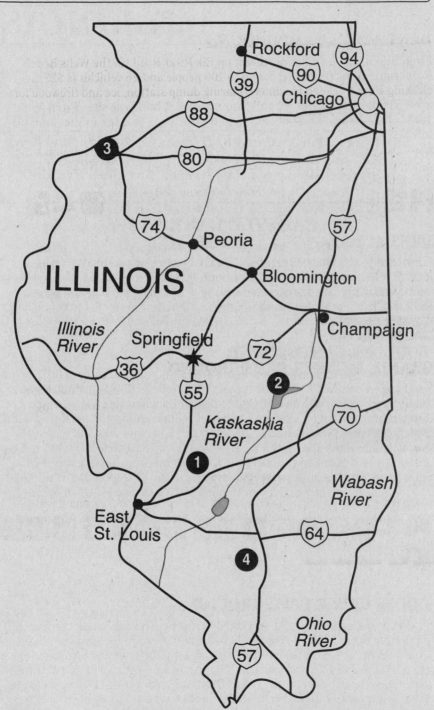

ILLINOIS

STATE CAPITAL:
Springfield
NICKNAME:
Prairie State

21st State - 1818

Site reservation, National Recreation Reservation Service
(NRRS), toll free, 1-877-444-6777; TDD 877-833-6777,
www.recreation.gov, (Master, Visa, American Express
& Discover cards).

CARLYLE LAKE (SL) 1

A 26,000 acre surface area lake located 50 miles east of St. Louis, north of
Carlyle on United States Route 50. Dam East Lakeview parking lot has a
handicap fishing pier. All comfort stations, buildings and camping areas provide
for handicap persons. Dam tours, seaplane usage, visitor center and checkout
time is 4. p.m. For daily lake information, call (618) 594-4637. Project Manager,
Carlyle Lake, 801 Lake Road, Carlyle, IL 62231-9703. (618) 594-2484/5253.

BOULDER CAMPGROUND

From Carlyle, go 6 miles east on United States Route 50, 3.5 miles north (sign)
on County Road 2500E, 0.5 mile east on County Road 1700N, 2.4 miles north
on County Road 2550E, go west(signs). A picnic shelter, amphitheater and a
fish cleaning station are available, and boat rentals are located nearby. 85 sites,
73 with electric, 11 walk-in tent only sites, 21 - 50 ampere, 1 double site, 1
handicap site with . Tent only sites are $10; sites with electric hookups are $14;
a double site is $28. Recreational vehicle maximum length is in excess of 65'.
This campground requires a 2 night minimum stay on weekends and a 3 night
stay on holiday weekends. Open from April 15th to October 15th. (618) 226-
3586. NRRS.

COLES CREEK CAMPGROUND

From Carlyle, go 6 miles east on United States Route 50, 3.5 miles north (sign)
on County Road 2500E, 1 mile west on County Road 1700N, 1 mile south on
County Road 2400E. A fish cleaning station, amphitheater and picnic shelter
are available. 148 sites with electric, 2 handicap sites with water and electric,
27 full hookups, 2 buddy sites, 1 pull through site. Sites with electric hookups
are $14; sites with full hookup are $24; buddy sites are $28. Recreational

vehicle maximum length is in excess of 65'. This campground requires a 2 night minimum stay on weekends and a 3 night stay on holiday weekends. Open from May 1st to September 30th. (618) 226-3211. NRRS.

DAM WEST CAMPGROUND

From Carlyle, go 1 mile north on County Road 1800E. A picnic shelter, fish cleaning station and an amphitheater are available, and boat rentals and a convenience store are located nearby. 109 sites with 50 ampere service, 23 full hookups, 2 double sites, 1 handicap site with full hookups. Sites with single 50 ampere service, 2nd price, are $12; sites with 50 ampere service are $14; premium sites with 50 ampere service are $16; sites with full hookups are $24; double sites are $32; double sites with full hookups are $48. Recreational vehicle maximum length is in excess of 65'. This campground requires a 2 night minimum stay on weekends and a 3 night stay on holiday weekends. Open from April 1st to November 1st. (618) 594-4410. NRRS.

EAST SPILLWAY CAMPGROUND

Below dam. 15 sites, 10 with electric. Sites without electric hookups are $10; sites with electric hookups are $12. Open all year.

LOTUS GROUP CAMPGROUND

Located in Coles Creek recreation area. A group camping area for up to 80 people and 25 vehicles with 10 mini shelters, 4 bunk beds in each, and a sheltered dining area that seats 30 people is $120. A fish cleaning station is available. This campground requires a 2 night minimum stay on weekends and a 3 night stay on holiday weekends. Open from May 1st to September 30th. NRRS.

MCNAIR GROUP CAMPGROUND

A group camping areas with picnic shelter and fish cleaning station. Area A for up to 80 people and 30 vehicles is $120; area B for up to 80 people and 30 vehicles is $150; area C for up to 80 people and 30 vehicle is $90; and area D for up to 96 people and 20 vehicles is $175. Restaurants are located nearby. 50 sites. Call office for directions. When not reserved, sites are rented for $12. This campground requires a 2 night minimum stay on weekends and a 3 night stay on holiday weekends. Open from May 1st to September 30th. NRRS.

LAKE SHELBYVILLE (SL) 2

An 11,100 acre surface area lake located northeast of Shelbyville, 31 miles south of Decatur, southwest of I-57 from Matoon. The visitor center has interpretive audio--visual programs and exhibits. There are dam tours on weekends from Memorial Day weekend through Labor Day, meet at visitor center at 3 p.m. on Saturday and 11 a.m. on Sunday. Seaplane usage, equestrian trail in the area and checkout time is 4 p.m. Unreserved picnic shelters are free. Daily lake information, recording (217) 774-2020. Operations Manager, Lake Shelbyville, RR #4, Box 128B, Shelbyville, IL 62565-9804. (217) 774-3951/3313.

COON CREEK CAMPGROUND

From Findlay, go 2.8 miles south, 0.2 mile west, 1.7 miles south. A fish cleaning station, an amphitheater and horseshoe pits are available. 209 sites with water and electric, 7 full hookups, 5 - 50 ampere, 1 double site with water and 50 ampere, 15 double sites with water and electric, 30 pull through sites, 1 handicap site with water and electric. Sites with electric hookups are $18; sites with full hookups are $22; double sites are $36. Recreational vehicle maximum length is in excess of 65'. This campground requires a 2 day minimum stay on weekends and a 3 night stay on holiday weekends. Open from April 5th to October 7th. (217) 774-2233. NRRS.

FORREST W. "BO" WOOD CAMPGROUND

From Sullivan, go 2.6 miles south on State Road 32, 0.5 mile west. A picnic shelter, amphitheater and fish cleaning station are available. 79 sites with electric hookups, 7 pull through sites, 2 double sites with full hookups, 1 double sites with water and 50 ampere, 16 full hookups, 2 handicap sites with full hookups. Sites with electric hookups are $18; sites with full hookups are $22; double sites are $36. Recreational vehicle maximum length is in excess of 65'.

This campground requires a 2 day minimum stay on weekends and a 3 night stay on holiday weekends. Open from May 24th to October 28th. NRRS (Due to constriction no reservations will be taken during 2007).

LITHIA SPRINGS CAMPGROUND

From Shelbyville, go 3.2 miles east on State Road 16, 2.1 miles north on County Road 2200E, 1.4 miles west. A pcnic shelter, an amphitheater, horseshoe pits and fish cleaning station are available. 115 sites with electric, 93 - 50 amps, 6 double sites, 11 full hookups with 50 ampere, 4 pull through sites, 1 handicap site with water and 50 ampere. Sites with electric hookups are $18; sites with full hookups are $22; double sites with electric are $36. Recreational vehicle maximum length is in excess of 65'. This campground requires a 2 day minimum stay on weekends and a 3 night stay on holiday weekends. Open from April 5th to October 27th. NRRS.

LONE POINT CAMPGROUND

From Findlay, go 2.8 miles south, 0.5 mile east, 0.8 mile south, 0.5 mile east, 0.5 mile south (east of Coon Creek Road). An amphitheater, fish cleaning station and picnic shelter are available, and four group camping areas, Walleye for up to 80 people and 20 vehicles is $160, May Apple for up to 64 people and 15 vehicles is $128, Woodchuck for up to 40 people and 10 vehicles is $80 and Chipmonk for up to 56 people and 10 vehicles is $112. 92 sites, 87 with electric, 2 tent only sites, 2 double sites, 5 pull through sites, 2 full hookup sites, 1 handicap site. All sites are $16; double sites with electric hookups are $32. Recreational vehicle maximum length is in excess of 65'. This campground requires a 2 day minimum stay on weekends and a 3 night stay on holiday weekends. Open from May 3rd to September 3rd. NRRS.

OKAW BLUFF GROUP CAMPGROUND

From Sullivan, go 4.7 miles south on State Road 32. A group camping with horseshoe pits. 2 houses with a maximum 34 persons featuring bunk beds, no linen. Open from March 3rd to November 26. Rates vary. For information and reservation, call (217) 774-3951.

OPOSSUM CREEK CAMPGROUND

From Shelbyville, go 3.4 miles north on State Road 128, 0.9 mile east, 0.5 mile south, 1.2 miles east. A fish cleaning station is available. 79 sites, 54 with electric, 21 tent only sites, 4 full hookups, 1 pull through site, 2 double sites with electric, 1 handicap site with full hookups. Sites with electric hookups are $16; double sites with electric hookups are $32. Recreational vehicle maximum length is in excess of 65'. This campground requires a 2 day minimum stay on weekends and a 3 night stay on holiday weekends. Open from May 3rd to September 3rd. NRRS.

WILBORN CREEK GROUP CAMPGROUND

From Bethany, go 2.5 miles southeast on State Road 121, 4 miles south & 0.5 mile west. A group camping area for up to 80 people and 25 vehicles with 15 sites is $120 and a fish cleaning station is available. This campground requires a 2 day minimum stay on weekends and a 3 night stay on holiday weekends. Open from May 3rd to September 3rd. (217) 774-3951. NRRS.

MISSISSIPPI RIVER PUA (RI) 3

Mississippi River Visitor Center, P. O. Box 2004, Rock Island, IL 61204-2004, (309) 794-5338, is located north of State Road 92 between I-74 and United States Route 67 on Arsenal Island, just north of Rodman Avenue near Government Bridge. Observation area for locking operations, exhibits, theater with seasonal hours of operation and all are handicap accessible. Free sites during winter may have reduced amenities. For information, contact Park Rangers. No's 1-3, L&D #11, Dubuque, IA 52001, (563) 582-0881. No's 4-10, P. O. Box 398, Thomson, IL 61285, (815) 259-3628. No's 12-17, L&D #16, 1611-2nd Ave., Muscatine, IA 52761, (563) 263-7913. No's 18-23, L&D #21, Quincy, IL 62301, (217) 228-0890. See IA, MO & WI listings.

NO. 12. ANDALUSIA SLOUGH CAMPGROUND

From Andalusia across river south of Davenport, IA, go 2 miles west on State Road 92. A picnic shelter is available. 16 sites, some pull through sites. From May 14th to October 27th, sites are $4; from October 28th to May 13th, some sites are available and are free. Open all year.

NO. 19. BEAR CREEK CAMPGROUND

From Quincy, go 12 miles north on State Road 96 to Marcelline, 1.5 miles on Bolton Road, 3 miles west across levee. A picnic shelter is available. 40 sites. All sites are free. Open all year.

NO. 15. BLANCHARD ISLAND CAMPGROUND

From Muscatine, IA bridge, go 1.5 miles east on State Road 92, 4 miles south, second right past Copperas Creek Bridge. 34 sites. From May 14th to October 22nd, sites are $4. From October 23rd to May 13th, some sites are available and are free. Open all year.

NO. 2. BLANDING LANDING CAMPGROUND

From Galena/Junction United States Route 20, south on County Road to Blanding, go west. A picnic shelter is $25, and an amphitheater is available. 37 sites, 7 tent only sites, 30 - 50 ampere. Tent only sites are $10; sites with 50 ampere service are $14. Recreational vehicle maximum length is 50'. This campground requires a 2 day minimum stay on weekends and a 3 day stay on holiday weekends. Open from May 11th to October 28th. (815) 591-2326. NRRS.

NO. 9. FISHERMAN'S CORNER CAMPGROUND

From Hampton, go 1 mile north on State Road 84 or from I 80, 1 mile south on State Road 84, located near L&D #14. An amphitheater and horseshoe pits are available. 56 sites, 5 tent only sites, 51 - 50 ampere handicap sites. Tent only sites are $10; sites with 50 ampere service are $16; premium sites with 50 ampere service are $18. Recreational vehicle maximum length is in excess of 65'. This campground requires a 2 day minimum stay on weekends and a 3 day stay on holiday weekends. Open from April 13th to October 28th. (309) 496-2720. NRRS.

NO. 21. JOHN HAY CAMPGROUND

On highway 106 near East Hannibal. A picnic shelter is available. 8 primitive sites. All sites are free. Open all year.

NO. 7. LOCK & DAM #13 CAMPGROUND

From Fulton, go 2 miles north on State Road 84, west on Lock Road (signs). A picnic shelter is available and a boat launch fee applies. 6 primitive sites. All sites are free. Open all year.

NO. 22. PARK & FISH CAMPGROUND

From Hull, go 0.7 mile west on United States Route 36, 6.1 miles south, IL side of L&D #22. A picnic shelter is available. 6 sites. All sites are free. Open all year.

NO. 5. THOMSON CAUSEWAY CAMPGROUND

From Thomson, go west 4-5 blocks on Main Street, south on Lewis Avenue (signs). Two picnic shelters are $25, a group shelter and an amphitheater are available. Shopping is located nearby. 131 sites, 5 tent only sites, 106 - 50 ampere, 4 pull through sites. Tent only sites are $10; sites with 50 ampere service are $16; premium sites with 50 ampere service are $18. Recreational vehicle maximum length is in excess of 65'. This campground requires a 2 day minimum stay on weekends and a 3 day stay on holiday weekends. Open from April 13th to October 28th. (815) 259-2353. NRRS.

REND LAKE (SL) 4

A 18,900 acre surface area lake located north of Benton, on State Road 14 west of I-57, in south-central Illinois. Checkout time is 4 p.m, visitor center, exhibits, interpretive programs, live snake display and seaplane usage. Boat rentals and trap shooting are located nearby. For daily lake information, recording (618) 629-1828. Project Manager, Rend Lake, 12220 Rend City Road, Benton, IL 62812-9803. (618) 724-2493.

DALE MILLER YOUTH GROUP AREA

From I-57, exit 71, go 2.5 miles west on State Road 14, 2.5 miles north on Rend City Road, east (right) on Rend Lake Dam Road, north (left) on Trail Head Lane. An amphitheater and picnic shelters are available. Boat rentals are located nearby. Off the road vehicles are prohibited without prior approval. Group camping for up to 200 people and 50 vehicles is $150. 5 cabins with bunk beds (sleep 8), trailer and tent sites available. This campground requires a 2 day minimum stay on weekends and a 3 day stay on holiday weekends. Open from April 1st to October 30th. NRRS.

GUN CREEK CAMPGROUND

From Benton, go 6 miles north on I-57, exit 77, 0.2 mile west on State Road 154, go south on Gun Creek Trail & 0.5 mile west on Golf Course Drive. A picnic shelter is $25 and an amphitheater is available. 100 sites with water and electric, 2 pull through sites, 1 handicap site. Sites with water and electric hookups are $14. Recreational vehicle maximum length is in excess of 65'. This campground requires a 2 day minimum stay on weekends and a 3 day stay on holiday weekends. Open from March 30th to November 25th. (618) 629-2338. NRRS.

NORTH SANDUSKY CAMPGROUND

From Benton, go 6 miles north on I-57, exit 77, 6 miles west on State Road 154, south on Rend City Road to stop sign, on the south side of the intersection. A picnic shelter is available and a campground store is located nearby. 118 sites with water and electric, 16 full hookups, 78 - 50 ampere, 4 handicap sites with water and 50 ampere. Sites with water and electric hookups and 50 ampere service are $16; sites with full hookups are $22. Recreational vehicle maximum length is 65'. This campground requires a 2 day minimum stay on weekends and a 3 day stay on holiday weekends. Open from April 1st to October 30th. (618) 625-6115. NRRS.

SHAGBARK GROUP CAMPGROUND

From Benton, go 6 miles north on I-57, exit 77, 6 miles west on State Road 154, south on Rend City Road to stop sign, inside the North Sandusky Campground. A group camping area and picnic shelter are available and a campground store and restaurants are located nearby. 21 sites for up to 200 people and 50 vehicles is $100. Off the road vehicles are prohibited without prior approval. This campground requires a 2 day minimum stay on weekends and a 3 day stay on holiday weekends. Open from April 1st to October 30th. (618) 625-6115. By reservation only. NRRS.

SOUTH MARCUM CAMPGROUND

From Benton, I-57, exit 71, go 2.5 miles west on State Road 14, 2.5 miles north on Rend City Road, east on Rend Lake Dam Road, north on Trail Head Lane. A picnic shelter and an amphitheater are available. A convenient store, boat rentals and horseback riding are nearby. 161 sites, 147 with electric, 14 walk-in tent only sites, 3 handicap sites, 48 - 50 ampere, 2 double sites, 2 full hookups. Tent only sites are $12; sites with electric hookups are $16; sites with full hookups are $22; double sites are $32. Recreational vehicle maximum length is in excess of 65'. This campground requires a 2 day minimum stay on weekends and a 3 day stay on holiday weekends. Open from March 30th to October 30th. (618) 435-3549. NRRS.

SOUTH SANDUSKY CAMPGROUND

From Benton, I-57, exit 71, go 2.5 miles west on State Road 14, 6 miles north on Rend City Road. A picnic shelter and an amphitheater are available. Boat rentals and horseback riding are located nearby. 129 sites, 121 with water and electric, 100 - 50 ampere, 8 walk in tent only sites, 10 full hookups, 3 handicap sites with 50 ampere, 1 premium handicap site with full hookups, 2 handicap sites with 50 ampere, 6 pull through sites. Tent only sites are $12; sites with water and electric hookups are $16; sites with full hookups are $22. Recreational vehicle maximum length is 65'. This campground requires a 2 day minimum stay on weekends and a 3 day stay on holiday weekends. Open from March 30th to October 30th. (618) 625-3011. NRRS.

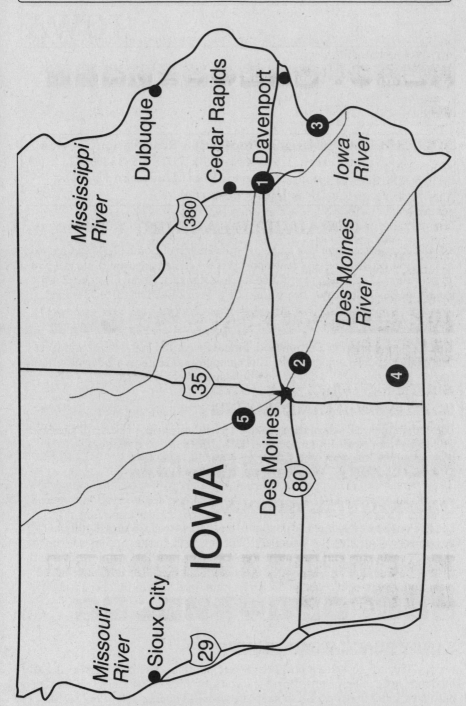

IOWA

STATE CAPITAL:
Des Moines
NICKNAME:
Hawkeye State
29th State - 1846

Site reservation, National Recreation Reservation Service (NRRS), toll free, 1-877-444-6777; TDD 877-833-6777, www.recreation.gov, (Master, Visa, American Express & Discover cards).

CORALVILLE LAKE (RI) 1

A 5,430 acre surface area lake located 3 miles north of Coralville/Iowa City, exit 244 on I-80, 55 miles west of Davenport. Visitor center, checkout time is 5 p.m., and off the road vehicles are prohibited. Park Manager, Coralville Lake, 2850 Prairie du Chien Road, northeast, Iowa City, IA 52240-7820. (319) 338-3543.

DAM COMPLEX

This complex comprises Cottonwood, Linder Point, Tail Waters East and West, and West Overlook campgrounds. This campground requires a 2 day minimum stay on weekends and a 3 day stay on holiday weekends. NRRS.

COTTONWOOD CAMPGROUND

Located on the west side of the spillway. 15 tent only walk-in sites. All sites are $10. Open from April 15th to October 14th. NRRS.

LINDER POINT CAMPGROUND

Located on the west side of the dam, north of access road. 26 sites, 9 full hookups, some walk-in sites, 9 - 50 ampere. Tent only walk-in sites and sites without electric hookups are $10; sites with electric hookups are $14; premium sites with electric hookups are $16; sites with full hookups are $22. Recreations vehicle maximum length is in excess of 65'. Open from April 15th to October 14th.

SANDY BEACH CAMPGROUND

From I-380, exit 10, go east on 120th Street, south on Curtis Bridge Road, east on Sandy Road, follow signs. Horse shoe pits. 60 sites, 50 with electric, 10 tent only sites, 2 full hookups, 1 handicap site with full hookups. Tent only walk-in sites are $10; premium sites with electric hookups are $16; sites with full hookups are $20. Recreational vehicle maximum length is in excess of 65'. This campground requires a 2 day minimum stay on weekends and a 3 day stay on holiday weekends. Open from May 1st to September 29th. NRRS.

SUGAR BOTTOM CAMPGROUND

From I-80, north on I-380, exit 4, go east on Penn Street to north Front Street (Mehaffey Bridge Road), cross Mehaffey bridge, 1.3 miles south (right). Amphitheater, horseshoe pits and four group camping areas, A & C for up to 60 people and 20 vehicles is $160, B1 for up to 24 people and 8 vehicles is $64 and B2 for up to 30 people and 10 vehicles is $80. A shopping mall is located nearby. 249 sites, 17 tent only sites, 13 full hookups, 35 - 50 ampere, 1 handicap site with electric, 1 premium handicap site with electric, 1 handicap site with full hookups, 33 pull through sites. Tent only walk-in sites are $10; sites with electric hookups are $14; premium sites with electric hookups are $16; sites with 50 ampere service are $18; sites with full hookups are $22. Recreation maximum vehicle length is in excess of 65'. This campground requires a 2 day minimum stay on weekends and a 3 day stay on holiday weekends. Open from May 1st to September 29th. NRRS.

TAIL WATER EAST CAMPGROUND

Located below the dam, on the east side of the outlet. Fish cleaning station. 28 sites, 22 with electric, 5 tent only walk-in sites, 5 - 50 ampere, 1 handicap site with water and 50 ampere, 1 pull through site. Tent only walk-in sites and sites without electric hookups are $10; sites with electric hookups are $14; premium sites with electric hookups are $16; sites with 50 ampere service are $18. Recreational vehicle maximum length is in excess of 65'. Open from April 15th to October 14th.

TAIL WATER WEST CAMPGROUND

Located below the dam on the west side of the outlet. A picnic shelter and fish cleaning station are available. 30 sites, 9 tent only walk-in sites. Tent only walk-in sites are $10; sites without electric hookups are $12. Open from April 15th to October 14th.

WEST OVERLOOK CAMPGROUND

Located on the west side of dam, north of the dam access road. A picnic shelter and fish cleaning station are available. 89 sites with electric, 1 handicap site, 1 pull through site. Sites with electric hookups are $14; premium sites with electric hookups are $16. Open from April 15th to October 14th.

LAKE RED ROCK (RI) 2

A 15,000 acre surface area lake located 4 miles southwest of Pella off State Road 163, southeast of Des Moines in southwest Iowa. Visitor center, checkout time is 4 p.m., and camp fire programs are available. For camping/lake information, recording, call (641) 828-7522. Operations Manager, Lake Red Rock, 1105 Highway T-15, Knoxville, IA 50138-9522. (641) 828-7522/628-8690.

HOWELL STATION CAMPGROUND

From Pella/Junction State Road 163, go 1 mile west on State Road 28, 5 miles southwest on County Road T-15, east on Idaho, south on 198th Place, go south (signs). Amphitheater with weekend programs from Memorial Day to Labor Day, and a fish cleaning station is available. 143 sites with electric, 66 - 50 ampere, 2 handicap sites, 1 full hookup. All sites with electric hookups are $20. Recreational vehicle maximum length is in excess of 65'. This campground requires a 2 day minimum stay on weekends and a 3 day stay on holiday weekends. Open from March 29th to October 29th. NRRS.

IVAN'S CAMPGROUND

Located below the dam on the south side of the outlet. Fish cleaning station. 22 sites. All sites are $16. Open from April 12th to October 1st.

NORTH OVERLOOK CAMPGROUND

From the Junction of County Road G-28, go 3 miles south on County Road T-15. A picnic shelter is available and there is an amphitheater with weekend programs from Memorial Day to Labor Day. 55 sites, 46 with 50 ampere, 9 tent only sites, 1 full hookup. Tent only sites are $10; sites with 50 ampere service are $16. Recreational vehicle maximum length is in excess of 65'. This campground requires a 2 day minimum stay on weekends and a 3 day stay on holiday weekends. Open from April 26th to October 1st. NRRS.

WALLASHUCK CAMPGROUND

From Pella, go 4 miles west on County Road G-28, 2 miles south on 190th Avenue. There is an amphitheater with campfire programs from Memorial Day to Labor Day and a fish cleaning station is available. 83 sites, 23 - 50 ampere, 1 handicap site, 1 full hookup. All sites with electric hookups are $16. Recreational vehicle maximum length is in excess of 65'. This campground requires a 2 day minimum stay on weekends and a 3 day stay on holiday weekends. Open from April 26th to October 15th. NRRS.

WHITEBREAST CAMPGROUND

From Knoxville, go 8 miles northeast on County Road T-15, 2 miles north on County Road S-71. Two group camping areas, HE1 for up to 96 people and 24 vehicles is $192 and HE2 for up to 56 people and 14 vehicles is $112, and a picnic shelter, an amphitheater and fish cleaning station are available. 111 sites with electric, 31 - 50 ampere. All sites with electric hookups are $16. Recreational vehicle maximum length is 60'. This campground requires a 2 day minimum stay on weekends and a 3 day stay on holiday weekends. Open from April 26th to October 1st. NRRS.

MISSISSIPPI RIVER PUA (RI) 3

Free sites during winter may have reduced amenities. For information, contact Park Rangers: No's 1-3, L&D #11, 2530 Kerper Blvd., Suite #3,Dubuque, IA 52001, (563) 582-0881. No's 4-10, P. O. Box 398, Thomson, IL 61285, (815) 259-3628. No's 12-17, L&D #16, 1611-2nd Avenue, Muscatine, IA 52761, (563) 263-7913. See IL, MO & WI listings.

NO. 6. BULGER'S HOLLOW CAMPGROUND

From Clinton, go 3 miles north on Unites States Route 67, 1 mile east on 170th Street. A picnic shelter is $25, and horseshoe pits are available. 26 sites, 9 tent only sites. From May 10th to September 15th, sites are $4. From September 16th to May 9th, sites are free with some exceptions - call first. Open all year.

NO. 13. CLARKS FERRY CAMPGROUND

From Muscatine, go 15 miles east on State Road 22 (signs). A picnic shelter is $25, an amphitheater, horseshoe pits and firewood are available. 45 sites with 50 ampere service. Sites with 50 ampere service are $16; premium sites with 50 ampere service are $18. This campground requires a 2 day minimum stay on weekends and a 3 day stay on holiday weekends. Open from April 13th to October 8th. (563) 381-4043. NRRS.

NO. 17. FERRY LANDING CAMPGROUND

From Muscatine, go 25 miles south on Unites States Route 61, east on State Road 99 (signs), L&D #17. 20 sites. All sites are free. Open all year.

NO. 3. PLEASANT CREEK CAMPGROUND

From Dubuque, go 24 miles south on Unites States Route 52 (signs), L&D #12. Self registration. 55 sites. From May 15th to October 15th, sites are $4. From October 16th to May 14th, sites are free. Open all year.

NO. 14. SHADY CREEK CAMPGROUND

From Muscatine, go 10 miles east on State Road 22 (signs). A picnic shelter is $25, and horseshoe pits and an amphitheater are available. 53 sites with 50 ampere service. Sites with 50 ampere service are $16; premium sites with 50 ampere service are $18. Recreational vehicle maximum length is in excess of 65'. This campground requires a 2 day minimum stay on weekends and a 3 day stay on holiday weekends. Open all year. (563) 262-8090. NRRS.

RATHBUN LAKE (KC) 4

An 11,000 acre surface area lake located 7 miles north of Centerville off State Road 5, 85 miles southeast of Des Moines, in southeast Iowa near the Missouri state line. A fish hatchery is located below the dam. For information call (641) 647-2464. Resource Manager, Rathbun Lake, 20112 Highway J-5-T, Centerville, IA 52544-8308.

BRIDGEVIEW CAMPGROUND

From Moravia, go 10 miles west on Highway 142, follow signs. A picnic shelter for up to 24 people and 12 vehicles, a fish cleaning station is available and an all terrain vehicle park is nearby. 114 sites, 103 with electric hookups, 39 - 50 ampere, 6 pull through sites, 7 double sites with electric. Sites without electric hookups are $12; sites with electric hookups are $16; premium sites with 50 ampere service are $18; double sites with electric are $32. Recreational vehicle maximum length is in excess of 65'. This campground requires a 2 day stay minimum on weekends and a 3 day stay on holiday weekends. Open from May 1st to September 29th. NRRS.

BUCK CREEK CAMPGROUND

From Centerville, go 5 miles north on Highway 5, 4 miles northwest on County Road J-29, 2 miles north on County Road J-5-T, follow signs. A picnic shelter and a fish cleaning station are available. 42 sites with electric hookups, 5 - 50 ampere,10 pull through sites. Sites with electric hookups are $16; premium sites with 50 ampere service are $18. Recreational vehicle maximum length is in excess of 65'. This campground requires a 2 day stay minimum on weekends and a 3 day stay on holiday weekends. Open from May 12th to September 29th. NRRS.

ISLAND VIEW CAMPGROUND

From Centerville, go 2.5 miles north on State Road 5, 3.8 miles northwest on County Road J-29, 0.2 mile north on County Road J-5-T. A group camping area, GCA 1 for up to 100 people and 24 vehicles is $125 from Sunday through Thursday and $250 for Friday and Saturday. Four picnic shelters, IV 5 & DS each for up to 200 people and 50 vehicles, BD for up to 75 people and 20 vehicles and PENN for up to 50 people and 20 vehicles are from $25 to $50, and a fish cleaning station is available. 194 sites with electric, 101 - 50 ampere, 3 double sites, 7 pull through sites. A site without electric hookups is $12; sites with electric hookups are $16; sites with 50 ampere service are $18; double sites are $32. Recreational vehicle maximum length is in excess of 65'. This campground requires a 2 day stay minimum on weekends and a 3 day stay on holiday weekends. Open from May 1st to September 29th. NRRS.

PRAIRIE RIDGE CAMPGROUND

From Moravia, go 4 miles west on Highway J-18, 2.5 miles south on 200th Avenue, follow signs. A group camping area for up to 72 people and 18 vehicles is $50 Sunday through Thursday and $100 on Friday and Saturday, a picnic shelter for up to 40 people and 12 vehicles is $20, a fish cleaning station is available, and firewood is available for a fee. 54 sites with 50 ampere, 2 pull through sites. Sites with 50 ampere service are $18. Recreational vehicle maximum length is in excess of 65'. This campground requires a 2 day stay minimum on weekends and a 3 day stay on holiday weekends. Open from May 1st to September 29th. NRRS.

ROLLING COVE CAMPGROUND

From Centerville, go west on Highway 2, 6 miles north on County Road T-14, 2.5 miles west, 2.5 miles north on 150th Avenue, 1 mile east on 435th Street, follow signs. A fish cleaning station is available. 32 sites, 1 pull through site. All sites are $12. Recreational vehicle maximum length is in excess of 65'. This campground requires a 2 day stay minimum on weekends and a 3 day stay on holiday weekends. Open from May 1st to September 29th.

SAYLORVILLE LAKE (RI) 5

A 5,950 acre surface area lake located north of Des Moines Area, north of Johnston, exit 131 off I-35/80, on Merle Hay Road, north on northwest Beaver Drive. Visitor center, (515) 964-0672. The Neal Smith Trail runs for 23.7 miles from Big Creek Beach to Des Moines. For lake information/recording, call (515) 276-0433. Park Manager, Saylorville Lake, 5600 northwest 78th Avenue, Johnston, IA 50131. (515) 276-4656/270-6173.

ACORN VALLEY CAMPGROUND

From I-35/80 north of Des Moines, exit 131 on the Johnson/Saylorville Road, go 2.8 miles north on Merle Hay Road through Johnston, at 4 way stop sign go 3.7 miles northwest (left) on Beaver Drive, just past the National Weather Service Building turn right onto Northwest Corydon Drive and right into the campground. Firewood is available nearby and a picnic shelter is availaable. 99 sites, 33 with electric, 66 tent only walk-in sites, 1 handicap site with water and electric. Tent only walk-in sites are $12; sites with electric hookups are $16; premium sites with electric hookups are $18, sites with water and electric hookups are $22. Recreational vehicle maximum length is 65'. Open from May 1st to September 29th. (515) 276-0429. NRRS.

BOB SHETLER CAMPGROUND

From I-35/80 north of Des Moines, exit 131 (Johnson/Saylorville Road), go 2.8 miles north on Merle Hay Road through Johnston, at the 4 way stop sign go 1 mile northwest (left) on Beaver Drive, at large concrete water storage tank on right, go 0.8 mile northwest (right) on 78th Avenue, turn right at T-intersection, 0.4 mile. A picnic shelter and a fish cleaning station are available, and firewood is available for a fee. 67 sites with electric, 1 full hookup, 1 handicap site, 8 pull through sites. Sites with electric hookups are $16. Recreational vehicle maximum length is in excess of 65'. Open from May 1st to September 27th. (515) 276-0873. NRRS.

CHERRY GLEN CAMPGROUND

From I-35/80 north of Des Moines, exit 90, go 2.4 miles on Highway 160 to its end, continue 4.1 miles on Highway 415 north, at campground sign, left turn lane, 0.6 mile on northwest 94th Avenue. Picnic shelters and fish cleaning station are available. Bike rentals and firewood are available nearby. 125 sites with electric, 6 - 50 ampere, 2 full hookups, 3 handicap sites. Sites with electric hookups are $16; premium sites with electric hookups are $18; premium sites with water and electric hookups are $22; sites with full hookups are $24. Recreational vehilcle maximum length is in excess of 65'. Open from March 30th to October 30th. (515) 964-8792. NRRS.

PRAIRIE FLOWER NORTH & SOUTH CAMPGROUND

From I-35 north of Des Moines, exit 90, go 2.4 miles on Highway 160 to its end, continue 5.6 miles on Highway 415, at campground sign, left turn lane, 0.2 mile on northwest Lake Drive. Ten group camping areas, Elderbery and Knapweed for up to 24 people and 8 vehicles are $56; Fleabane for up to 36 people and 12 vehicles is $84; May Weed and June Berry for up to 48 people and 16 vehicles are $112; Ox-eye for up to 60 people and 20 vehicles is $140;

Nipplewart for up to 72 people and 24 vehicles is $168; Goldenrod and Ironwood for up to 84 people and 28 vehicles are $196; and Leadplant with 50 ampere service for up to 84 people and 58 vehicles is $224. Bike rentals and firewood are available nearby. 154 sites with electric, 110 - 50 ampere, 1 handicap site, 2 pull through sites. Sites with electric hookups are $16; premium sites with electric hookups are $18; sites with water and 50 ampere service are $20; sites with full hookups and 50 ampere service are $22. Recreational vehilcle maximum length is in excess of 65'. Open from May 1st to October 30th. (515) 984-6925. NRRS.

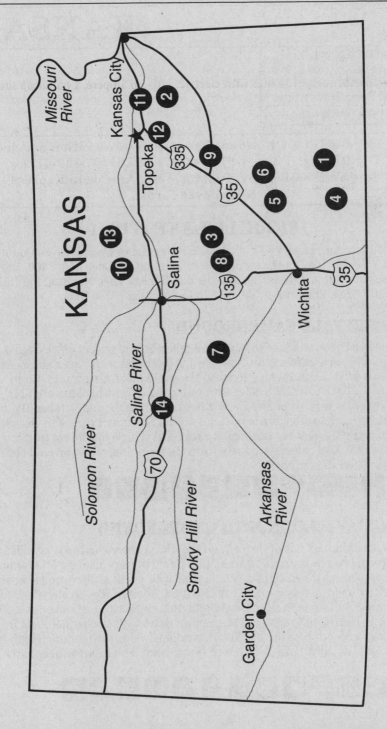

KANSAS

STATE CAPITAL:
Topeka
NICKNAME:
Sunflower State

34th State - 1861

Site reservation, National Recreation Reservation Service
(NRRS), toll free, 1-877-444-6777; TDD 877-833-6777,
www.recreation.gov, (Master, Visa, American Express
& Discover cards).

BIG HILL LAKE (TU) 1

A 1,240 acre surface area lake located 4.5 miles east of Cherryvale on County
Road 5000, 11 miles southwest of Parsons and United States Route 400, 160
miles southwest of Kansas City in southeast Kansas. Lake Manager, Big Hill
Lake, P. O. Box 426, Cherryvale, KS 67335-0426. (620) 336-2741.

CHERRYVALE CAMPGROUND

Located on the west side of the dam, 0.3 mile north of project office (signs). A
group camping area for up to 75 people and 9 vehicles with 7 sites and a picnic
shelter is $100. 23 sites with water and electric, 2 pull through sites. From
March 31st to October 30th, sites with water and electric hookups are $14;
premium sites with water and electric hookups are $16; from October 31st to
March 30th, sites with electric hookups are $12; premium sites with electric
hookups are $14, reduced services. Recreational vehicle maximum length is in
excess of 65'. This campground requires a 3 day minimum stay on weekends for
groups. Open all year. NRRS.

MOUND VALLEY NORTH CAMPGROUND

Located on the east side of the dam on the lake. A change house is provided at
the beach, two group camping areas, 0G2 for up to 64 people and 0G3 for up
to 32 people and 16 vehicles are $32 (add $8 with picnic shelter), and a picnic
shelter for up to 32 people and 5 vehicles is $8. 82 sites, 76 with electric, 2 full
hookups, 8 pull through sites, 2 handicap sites. Sites without hookups are $10;
sites with electric hookups are $14; premium sites with electric hookups are
$16; sites with full hookups are $17. Recreational vehicle maximum length is
in excess of 65'. (620) 328-2050. Open from March 30th to September 30th.
NRRS.

TIMBER HILL CAMPGROUND

From the dam on the east side, go 3 miles north, west on gravel road. 20 sites, some pull through sites. All sites are $8. Open from March 31st to October 30th.

CLINTON LAKE (KC) 2

A 7,000 acre surface area lake with 85 miles of shoreline is located 1 mile southwest of Lawrence, west of United States Route 59, 45 miles west of Kansas City. Resource Manager, Clinton Lake, 872 north. 1402 Road, Lawrence, KS 66049-9176. (785) 843-7665.

ASH GROUP CAMPGROUND

Located near Walnut/Hickory parks. Group camping areas for 10 to 75 persons and 26 vehicles are $50. A picnic shelter, fish cleaning station and horseshoe pits are available. Shopping is located nearby. Open from May 1st to September 30th. NRRS (Through Walnut campground).

BLOOMINGTON EAST PARK

From Lawrence, go 4 miles west on Highway 40 (6th Street), 5 miles west (left) on County Road 442 to Stull, 6 miles south (left) on County Road 1023, 4 miles northeast (left) on County Road 6 through Clinton, follow signs. Contains Cedar Ridge, Hickory and Walnut campgrounds.

BLOOMINGTON WEST GROUP CAMPGROUND

From Lawrence, go 4 miles west on Highway 40 (6th Street), 5 miles west (left) on County Road 442 to Stull, 6 miles south (left) on County Road 1023, 4 miles northeast (left) on County Road 4, 0.5 mile east (right) on County Road 1200N, first gravel road on left (Located near north corner of Clinton). Group camping area with 25 sites (approximately 60' each in length) for 25 to 150 people is $100. A picnic shelter and horseshoe pits are available. Open from April 15th to October 14th. NRRS.

CEDAR RIDGE CAMPGROUND

Horseshoe pits and a fish cleaning station. 97 sites with water and electric, 13 - 50 ampere, 61 pull through sites. Sites with water and electric hookups are $18.

Recreational vehicle maximum length is in excess of 65'. Open from April 1st to October 13th. NRRS.

ELM GROUP CAMPGROUND

Located near Walnut/Hickory campgrounds. Group camping areas for 10 to 75 persons and 26 vehicles is $50 and a picnic shelter is available. Pick up the gate keys at the Walnut Creek Campground. Open from May 1st to September 30th. NRRS.

HICKORY/WALNUT CAMPGROUND

An amphitheater and fish cleaning station are available. 221 sites, 94 with electric, 10 handicap sites, 15 pull through sites. Sites without hookups are $12; sites with electric hookups are $16; sites in the Oak Loop with hookups are $10. Recreational vehicle maximum length is in excess of 65'. Open from May 1st to September 30th. NRRS.

ROCKHAVEN CAMPGROUND

From Stull, go 6 miles south on State Road 1023, 3 miles east on State Road 458, 0.8 mile north on County Road 700E, gravel road. Horse/mule camping. 50 sites. Sites are $6 for self pay and $8 if collected by a ranger. Open from April 1st to October 31st.

WOODRIDGE CAMPGROUND

From Stull, go 3.4 miles south on County Road 1023, 1 mile east on County Road 2, 0.4 mile north on County Road 350E, gravel road. Trail primitive tent only camping and 450 acre primitive area. All camping is free. Open all year.

COUNCIL GROVE LAKE (TU) 3

A 3,310 acre surface area lake located 1.5 miles northwest of Council Grove off United States Route 56 and State Road 177, 101 miles southwest of Kansas City. An all terrain vehicle area is located below the dam and checkout time is 4 p.m.

Swimming is permitted unless otherwise posted. Free sites during winter with reduced amenities. Lake Manager, Council Grove Lake, 945 Lake Road, Council Grove, KS 66846-9322. (620) 767-5195.

CANNING CREEK COVE CAMPGROUND

From Council Grove, go 1.5 miles north on State Road 177, west across Dam Road, 2 miles right on City Lake Road. Two group camping areas from $75 to $120, 2 night minimum stay and two picnic shelters (requires a $10 reservation fee), S1, with full hookups, for up to 50 people and 40 vehicles is $150 and S2, premium with water and electric hookups for up to 50 people and 25 vehicles is $75. 42 sites, 35 with electric, 7 - 50 ampere, 6 pull through sites. Sites without hookups are $10; sites with electric hookups are $15; sites with water and electric hookups are $16; premium sites with water and electric hookups are $17; sites with water and 50 ampere service are $18. Recreational vehicle maximum length is in excess of 65'. This campground requires a 2 day minimum stay on weekends and a 3 day stay on holiday weekends from April 1st to October 30th. Open from April 1st to October 31st. (620) 767-6745. NRRS (April 15th to September 30th).

CUSTER PARK

From Council Grove/Junction United States Route 56, go 3.5 miles north on State Road 55/177, go west. 10 sites. All sites are $7. Open from March 1st to December 31st.

KANSAS VIEW CAMPGROUND

From Council Grove/Junction United States Route 56, go 1.5 miles north on State Road 57/177, go west. A group camping area is $30 and a picnic shelter is available. 5 sites. From April 1st to October 31st, sites without hookups are $7; from November 1st to March 31st, some sites are available and are free with frost free water hydrants available at Neosho campground and the office area. Open all year.

KIT CARSON COVE CAMPGROUND

From Council Grove/Junction United States Route 56, go 2 miles north on State Road 177/57, go west. 25 sites, 14 with water and electric hookups, 1 primitive site. From March 1st to October 31st, a primitive site is $8; sites with electric hookups are $14; from November 1st to December 31st, water is available from frost free hydrants at the Neosho campground and near the office. Open from March 1st to December 31st.

MARINA COVE CAMPGROUND

From Council Grove, go 1.5 miles north on State Road 177, 1 mile west on Dam Road, 1.5 miles west, on right. A fish cleaning station is available. 4 sites. From April 1st to October 31st, a site without hookups is $8; sites with electric hookups are $12; from November 1st to March 31st, some sites without hookups are available and are free with frost free water hydrants located at Neosho campground and the office area. Open all year.

NEOSHO CAMPGROUND

From Council Grove, go 1.5 miles north on State Road 177, 1 mile west on Dam Road, 1 mile right to City Lake Road, 0.3 mile west, on right. 8 sites. From April 1st to October 31st, sites without water and electric hookups are $12; a site with water and electric hookups is $14; from November 1st to March 31st, some sites without hookups are available and are free with frost free water hydrants located in the park. Open all year.

RICHEY COVE CAMPGROUND

From Council Grove/Junction United States Route 56, go 2.8 miles on State Road 57/177, west side. A group camping area for up to 50 people and 16 vehicles is $75 with a 2 night minimum stay and a picnic shelter is available. 42 sites, 40 sites with electric, 2 tent only sites, 1 full hookups. From April 1st to October 31st, a tent only site is $11; a premium tent only site is $12; sites with electric hookups are $15; sites with water and electric hookups are $17; a site with full hookups are $20; from November 1st to March 31st, some sites without hookups are available and are free with frost free water hydrants located in the park. Recreational vehicle maximum length is in excess of 65'. This campground requires a 2 day minimum stay on weekends and a 3 day stay on holiday weekends. Open all year. (620) 767-5800. NRRS (April 15th to September 30th).

SANTA FE TRAIL CAMPGROUND

From Council Grove, go 1.5 miles north on State Road 177, 1 mile west on Dam Road, 1 mile west on City Lake Road, 1 mile west, on right. Group camping area for up to 50 people and 32 vehicles is $120 with a 2 night minimum stay, and a picnic shelter is available. 35 sites, 3 full hookups, 1 pull through site. Sites without hookups are $11; sites with electric hookups are $15; sites with water and electric hookups are $16; a site with full hookups is $18. This campground requires a 2 day minimum stay on weekends and a 3 day stay on holiday weekends. Open from April 1st to October 30th. Walk-in season during October. (620) 767-7125. NRRS (April 15th to September 30th).

ELK CITY LAKE (TU) 4

A 4,122 acre surface area lake located 5 miles northwest of Independence and United States Route 160, 127 miles east of Wichita in southern Kansas. Lake Manager, P. O. Box 426, Cherryvale, KS 67335-0426. (620) 336-2741.

CARD CREEK CAMPGROUND

From Elk City/Junction State Road 39, go 7 miles southeast on United States Route 160, 1.3 miles north, 1.7 miles northwest. A picnic shelter is $25. 20 sites, 4 primitive tent only sites, some pull through sites. From April 1st to October 31st, primitive sites are $8; sites with electric hookups are $12; from November 1st to March 31st, tent only sites are free; sites with electric hookups are $11. Reduced services during the winter. Open all year.

OUTLET CHANNEL CAMPGROUND

From Elk City, go 7 miles northwest of Independence on County Road below dam, west side of spillway. A picnic shelter is $25. 15 sites. From April 1st to October 31st, sites are $8; from November 1st to March 31st, sites are free. Open all year.

FALL RIVER LAKE (TU) 5

A 2,450 acre surface area lake located 4 miles northwest of Fall River off United States Route 400, 70 miles east of Wichita. All terrain vehicles, golf carts, etc., must be street legal with tags and lights. Lake Manager, Fall River Lake, Route. 1, Box 243E, Fall River, KS 67047-9738. (620) 658-4445.

DAMSITE CAMPGROUND

From United States Route 400/Junction Highway 99, go 7.8 miles east, 0.9 mile north, 2.4 miles east, on right. A group camping area for up to 150 people and 30 vehicles is $84 and the picnic shelter is free. there is a campground store is nearby. 33 sites, 28 with electric, 10 - 50 ampere, 18 full hookups. From April 1st to October 31st, sites without hookups are $13; sites with water and electric hookups are $17; sites with full hookups and 30 ampere service are $20; sites with full hookups and 50 ampere service are $21; from November 1st to March 31st, sites with electric hookups are $5 to $10. Recreational vehicle maximum length is in excess of 65'. Open all year. NRRS.

ROCK RIDGE COVE NORTH CAMPGROUND

From United States Route 400/Junction Highway 99, go 7.8 miles east, 1.7 miles north, 1.5 miles west (low water crossing), 0.9 mile east. 44 sites, 25 with electric. From April 1st to October 31st, sites without hookups are $9; sites with electric hookups are $13; from November 1st to March 31st, sites with electric hookups are $5. Open all year.

WHITE HALL BAY CAMPGROUND

From United States Route 400, at mile marker 344 (Z 50 Road), go 0.09 mile north (left), 2.8 miles east (right) across the dam, 0.8 mile north (left), 0.7 mile west (left), 1.7 miles north (right) to a low water crossing, continue north for 0.1 mile, 0.4 miles west, 1.1 miles south to park. A group camping area for up to 60 people and 18 vehicles is $84, and three picnic shelters, GS 24 & GS 25 for up to 40 people and 12 vehicles, and GS 36 for up to 150 people and 30 vehicles are from $36 to $50. there is a campground store is nearby. 33 sites, 27 sites with electric, 8 - 50 ampere, 9 full hookups. From April 1st to October 31st, sites without hookups are $13; sites with electric hookups are $17; sites with full hookups and 50 ampere service are $21; from November 1st to March 31st, sites with electric hookups are $5. Recreational vehicle maximum length is in excess of 65'. Open all year. NRRS.

JOHN REDMOND DAM & RESERVIOR (TU) 6

A 9,400 acre surface area lake located 6 miles north and west of Burlington off United States Route 75, 110 miles southwest of Kansas City. There is off the road vehicle area at Otter Creek that provides 140 acres for dirt bikes and all terrain vehicles. Lake Manager, John Redmond Dam, 1565 Embankment Road southwest, Burlington, KS 66839-8911. (620) 364-8613.

DAMSITE AREA CAMPGROUND

From New Strawn, go 1 mile southwest. Three picnic shelters for up to 50 people and 26 vehicles with a required reservation fee of $10, horseshoe pits, and three group camping areas, GCA 1 for up to 100 people and 21 vehicles, GCA 2 for up to 70 people and 11 vehicles and GCA 3 for up to 40 people and 9 vehicles with some pull through sites from $30 to $80 (NRRS). 32 sites with water and electric, some pull through sites. From April 1st to October 31st, sites without electric hookups are $10; sites with water and electric hookups are $15. From November 1st to March 31st some sites are available and are free, no services. This campground requires a 2 day minimum stay on weekends. Open all year.

HARTFORD RAMP PARK

From Hartford, go 0.5 mile east on gravel road. Primitive camping is free.

RIVERSIDE EAST CAMPGROUND

From Burlington, go 3.5 miles north on Highway 75, 1.5 miles west on Embankment Road (signs). Two picnic shelters, GPS 4 for up to 50 people and 15 vehicles and GPS 5 for up to 50 people and 10 vehicles which require a reservation fee of $10. 53 sites with water and electric, 6 pull through sites. Sites with water and electric hookups are $12. Recreational vehicle maximum length is in excess of 65'. This campground requires a 2 day minimum stay on weekends. Open from April 1st to October 31st. NRRS (May 1st to September 30th).

RIVERSIDE WEST CAMPGROUND

From Burlington, go 3.5 miles north on Highway 75, 1.5 miles west on Embankment Road (signs). A picnic shelter for up to 100 people and 30 vehicles which requires a reservation fee of $10. There is a universal access ramp to the fishing dock. 37 sites, 19 with water and electric, 12 - 50 ampere, 3 pull through sites. Sites with water and electric hookups are $15. Recreational vehicle maximum length is in excess of 65'. This campground requires a 2 day minimum stay on weekends. Open from April 1st to October 31st. NRRS (May 1st to September 15th).

WEST WINGWALL

Located below the dam. 6 sites. All sites are $10. Open from April 1st to October 31st.

KANOPOLIS LAKE (KC) 7

A 3,400 acre surface area lake with 41 miles of shoreline is located 31 miles southwest of Salina off Highway 141, 85 miles northwest of Wichita. Operations Manager, Kanopolis Lake, 105 Riverside Drive, Marquette, KS 67464-7464. (785) 546-2294.

BOLDT BLUFF CAMPGROUND

From the dam, go 2 miles south on K-141, 5 miles west on Avenue T (gravel), 3 miles north on 25th Road (gravel), 2 miles east on Avenue Q. Primitive camping area with no designated sites. Camping is free. Open all year.

RIVERSIDE CAMPGROUND

From Salina, go 10 miles west on Highway 140, 14 miles south on Highway 141, 0.5 mile east. 40 sites, 9 with water and electric, 31 primitive sites. From May 1st to September 30th, primitive sites are $12; sites with electric hookups are $18. From October 1st to April 30th some sites are available and are free, $4 with electric. Recreational vehicle maximum length is in excess of 65'. This campground requires a 2 day minimum stay on weekends and a 3 day stay on holiday weekends. Open all year. NRRS.

VENANGO CAMPGROUND

From the dam go north on Highway 141, on left. A primitive group camping area for up to 50 people and 21 vehicles with a shelter house. Four picnic shelters, GA 1 for up to 30 people and 13 vehicles, GK 2 for up to 30 people and

9 vehicles, GL 3 for up to people and 16 vehicles and GB 4 for up to 50 people
and 21 vehicles are $20. 205 sites, 87 with electric, 24 - 50 ampere, 17 pull
through sites, 4 tent only sites. From May 1st to September 30th, tent only sites
and sites without hookups are $12; sites with electric hookups and premium
sites with electric hookups are $16; sites with water and electric hookups, a
premium site with water and electric hookups, sites with water and 50 ampere
service and premium sites with water and 50 ampere service are $18. From
October 1st to April 30th, during the walk-in season, some sites are available
and are free, $4 with electric hookups. Recreational vehicle maximum length is
in excess of 65'. This campground requires a 2 day minimum stay on weekends
and a 3 day stay on holiday weekends. Open all year. NRRS.

YANKEE RUN

From the dam, go 2 miles south on K-141, 5 miles west on Avenue T (gravel), 3
miles north on 25th Road (gravel), 1 miles east on Avenue Q, 1 mile north on
26th Road (gravel). Primitive camping area with no designated sites. Camping
is free. Open all year.

MARION RESERVOIR (TU) 8

A 6,200 acre surface area lake located 3 miles northwest of Marion off United
States Route 56, 46 miles northeast of Wichita. Unregistered vehicles, all
terrain vehicles, golf carts, etc., are prohibited. Lake Manager, Marion
Reservoir, 2105 Pawnee Road, Marion, KS 66861-9740. (620) 382-2101.

COTTONWOOD POINT CAMPGROUND

From Marion, go 3 miles west on United States Route 56, 2 miles north on Old
Mill Road (signs). Two group camping areas, GS 1 & GS 2 for up to 80 epople
and 15 vehicles are $80, and two picnic shelter, PSA & PSB for up to 60 people
and 20 vehicles are $20. 94 sites with water and electric, 41 - 50 ampere, 7 pull
through sites, 1 handicap site. Sites with water and electric hookups are $15;
sites with water and 50 ampere service are $18. Recreational vehicle maximum
length is 50'. This campground requires a 2 day minimum stay on weekends
and a 3 day stay on holiday weekends. Open from March 15th to November
15th. NRRS (April 10th to October 15th).

FRENCH CREEK COVE CAMPGROUND

From Marion, go 7 miles west on United States Route 56, 1 mile north on Kansas, 1 mile east on 210th Street. 20 sites with electric. From March 15th to November 15th, sites with electric hookups are $10. From November 16th to March 14th, some sites are available and are free with reduced services. Open all year.

HILLSBORO COVE CAMPGROUND

From Marion, go 4 miles west on United States Route 56, north on Nighthawk, go east. A group camping area for up to 80 people and 15 vehicles is $80. 51 sites with electric, 8 pull through sites. Sites with electic hookups are $15; sites with water and electric hookups are $17. Recreational vehicle maximum length is 50'. This campground requires a 2 day minimum stay on weekends and a 3 day stay on holiday weekends. Open from March 15th to November 15th. NRRS (April 10th to October 15th).

MARION COVE CAMPGROUND

From Marion, go 3 miles west on United States Route 56, 1 mile north on Pawnee, past project office, on left. 6 sites. From March 15th to November 15th, sites are $7. From November 16th to March 14th, some sites are available and are free with reduced services. Open all year.

MELVERN LAKE (KC) 9

A 6,900 acre surface area lake with 101 miles of shoreline is located 3.5 miles west of Melvern on State Road 31, west of United States Route 75, north of I-35, 39 miles south of Topeka. Interpretive programs, project office has displays, exhibits, etc. Group tours provided upon request. Free sites during winter may have reduced amenities. Project Office, Melvern Lake, 31051 Melvern Parkway, Melvern, KS 66510-9759. (785) 549-3318.

ARROW ROCK CAMPGROUND

From Olivet/Junction United States Route 75, go 1 mile west on County Road K-276, 1 mile north on south Fairlawn Road, 1 mile west on Arrow Rock Parkway. The picnic shelter is free. Horseshoe pits and a fish cleaning station are available. 45 sites, 19 with electric, 5 pull through sites, 1 handicap site with water and electric. From May 1st to September 30th, sites without electric hookups are $12; sites with electric hookups are $16; sites with water and electric hookups are $17. From October 1st to April 30th some sites are available and are free. Recreational vehicle maximum length is in excess of 65'. This campground requires a 2 day minimum stay on weekends and a 3 day stay on holiday weekends. Open all year. NRRS (May 1st to September 30th).

COEUR D'ALENE PARK

From Melvern/Junction United States Route 75, go 1 mile south on Melvern Lake Parkway, 1 mile northwest on Coeur D'Alene Parkway. Picnic shelter, horseshoe pits and a fish cleaning station are available. 60 sites, 35 with electric, 1 handicap pull through full hookup site with 50 ampere. From May 1st to September 30th, sites without hookups are $12; sites with electric hookups are $16; a site with full hookups is $19. From October 1st to April 30th, some sites are available and are free. Recreational vehicle maximum length is 50'. This campground requires a 2 day minimum stay on weekends and a 3 day stay on holiday weekends. Open all year. NRRS (May 1st to Sept. 30th).

OUTLET PARK

From Melvern/Junction United States Route 75, go 0.3 mile west on Merlvern Lake Parkway, 0.3 mile west on Cutoff Road, 0.5 mile north on River Pond Parkway, below dam. Gasoline engines are prohibited. Youth group camping area for up to 50 people and 20 vehicles, a picnic shelter for up to 100 people and 25 vehicles, an amphitheater, horseshoe pits and fish cleaning station are available and a change house is located at the beach. 150 sites with water and electric, 90 pull through sites, 89 full hookups, 51 - 50 ampere, 5 triple sites, 1 handicap site. From April 1st to October 31st, sites with water and electric hookups are $17; sites with full hookups are $19; premium sites with full hookups are $20; triple sites with water and electric hookups are $51. From November 1st to March 31st, some sites are available and are free. Recreational vehicle maximum length is in excess of 65'. This campground requires a 2 day minimum stay on weekends and a 3 day stay on Memorial Day and Labor Day weekends. Open all year. NRRS (April 1st to October 31st).

SUNDANCE

From Lebo/Junction I-35/United States Route 50, go 4.5 miles north. The picnic shelter is free. 30 sites. All sites are free. Open all year.

TURKEY POINT CAMPGROUND

From Osage City, go south on County Road K-170, 2 miles east on 301st Street, 1 mile south on Indian Hills, 0.5 mile south on Turkey Point Parkway. Group camping area for up to 100 people and 30 vehicles with shelter is $40, fish cleaning station and horseshoe pits are available. 50 sites, 36 with electric, 20 - 50 ampere, 3 pull through sites. From May 1st to September 30th, sites without hookups are $12; sites with water and electric hookups are $17; sites with water and 50 ampere service are $18. From October 1st to April 30th some sites are available and are free. Recreactional vehicle maximum length is 65'. This campground requires a 2 day minimum stay on weekends and a 3 day stay on Memorial Day and Labor Day weekends. Open all year. NRRS (May 1st to September 30th).

![icons]

MILFORD LAKE (KC) 10

A 15,700 acre surface area lake located 5 miles northwest of Junction City/I-70, on Highway K-57, west of United States Route 77, 65 miles west of Topeka. Project Office/Information Center has displays and exhibits along with a 24 hour accessible brochure information area. Off the road vehicle area for vehicles less than 50" wide only. Free sites during winter may have reduced amenities. Project Manager, Milford Lake, 4020 West Highway K/57, Junction City, KS 66441-8997. (785) 238-4643.

CURTIS CREEK

From Junction City/I-70, exit 290, go 5 miles north on Milford Lake Road, 6 miles west on County Road 837. 84 sites, 61 with electric, 8 tent only sites. Sites without electric hookups and tent only sites are $12; sites with electric hookups are $16; sites with water and electric hookups are $18. Recreational vehicle maximum length is in excess of 65'. This campground requires a 2 day minimum stay on weekends and a 3 day stay on holiday weekends. Open from April 15th to September 30th. NRRS.

FARNUM CREEK GROUP CAMPGROUND

From Milford/Junction I-70, exit 295, go 11 miles north on United States Route 77. A fish cleaning station is available. 80 sites, 46 with water and electric, 5 - 50 ampere, 5 pull through sites, 4 tent only sites. Tent only sites and sites without electric hookups are $10; sites with electric hookups are $16; sites with

50 ampere service are $17.. Recreational vehicle maximum length is 60'. This campground requires a 2 day minimum stay on weekends and a 3 day stay on holiday weekends. Open from April 15th to September 30th.

SCHOOL CREEK CAMPGROUND

From Wakefield, go 1 mile west on State Road 82. 56 sites, 12 primitve sites. From April 15th to September 30th, sites are $8; from October 1st to April 14th, some sites are available and are free. Recreational vehicle maximum length 30'. Open all year.

TIMBER CREEK CAMPGROUND

From Wakefield, go 1 mile east on State Road 82. 36 sites. From April 15th to September 30th, sites are $8; from October 1st to April 14th, some sites are available and are free. Open all year.

WEST ROLLING HILLS CAMPGROUND

From Junction City/Junction I-70, exit 290, go 5 miles north on Highway 244 (Milford Lake Road). A fish cleaning station is available. 60 sites, 30 with electric, 11 sites with 50 ampere, 12 tent only sites, 6 sites with hookups (RVs) - $15. Tent only sites are $12; sites with electric hookups are $18; sites with 50 ampere service are $19. There is also a free primitive area open all year. Recreational vehicle maximum length is in excess of 65'. This campground requires a 2 day minimum stay on weekends and a 3 day stay on holiday weekends. Open from April 15th to September 30th. NRRS.

PERRY LAKE (KC) 11

An 11,150 acre surface area lake located 3 miles northwest of Perry off United States Route 24, 15 miles northeast of Topeka. Unregistered vehicles, off the road vehicles, motorcycles, golf carts, etc., are prohibited. Project Manager, Perry Lake, 10419 Perry Park Drive, Perry, KS 66073-9717. (785) 597-5144.

LONGVIEW PARK

From Oskaloosa, go 5.5 miles west on State Road 92, 2.1 miles south on Ferguson Road, 1.5 miles west on 86th Street. A group tent camping area for up to 100 people and 15 vehicles is $30 and a picnic shelter is available. 45 sites, 26 with electric, 6 tent only sites, 1 pull through site. Tent only sites and sites without hookups are $12; sites with electric hookups are $16. There is a $5 visitor fee in effect on weekends and holidays. Recreational vehicle maximum length is in excess of 65'. This campground requires a 2 day minimum stay on weekends and a 3 day stay on holiday weekends. Open from May 1st to September 30th. NRRS.

OLD TOWN CAMPGROUND

From Oskaloosa, go 6 miles west on State Road 92, on the south side before the bridge (signs). A picnic shelter for up to 100 people and 20 vehicles is $20, and a group camping area is $30. 76 sites, 33 with electric, 2 pull through sites. Sites without hookups are $12; sites with electric hookups are $16. Recreational vehicle maximum length is in excess of 65'. This campground requires a 2 day minimum stay on weekends and a 3 day stay on Memorial Day and Labor Day weekends. Open from May 1st to September 30th. NRRS.

ROCK CREEK CAMPGROUND

From Perry/Junction Highway 24, go 3 miles north on State Road 237, east to Rock Creek Park Road. A picnic shelter for up to 100 people and 6 vehicles is $30 and a fish cleaning station is available. 141 sites, 65 with electric, 20 tent only sites, 28 - 50 ampere, 2 pull through sites. Sites without hookups and tent only sites are $12; sites with electric hookups are $16; sites with water and electric hookups are $17; sites with water and 50 ampere service are $18. There is some primitive camping in a designated area. Recreational vehicle maximum length is in excess of 65'. This campground requires a 2 day minimum stay on weekends and a 3 day stay on Memorial Day and Labor Day weekends. Open from April 16th to October 15th. NRRS.

SLOUGH CREEK CAMPGROUND

From Perry/Junction Highway 24, go 7 miles north on Ferguson Road, 1 mile southwest on Slough Creek Road. A picnic shelter is $20, two group camping areas, G East for up to 125 people and 15 vehicles and G West for up to 100 people and 10 vehicles are $30, and a fish cleaning station is available. No dogs are permitted in the Locust Loop. 273 sites, 118 with electric hookups, 18 tent only sites, 2 handicap sites, 14 - 50 ampere, 15 pull through sites. Tent only sites and sites without hookups are $12; sites with electric hookups are $16; sites with water and electric hookups and premium sites with water and electric hookups are $17; premium sites with water and 50 ampere service are $18. There is a $5 visitor fee in effect for weekends and holidays. Recreational vehicle maximum length is in excess of 65'. This campground requires a 2 day minimum stay on weekends and a 3 day stay on holiday weekends. Open from April 16th to October 15th. NRRS.

POMONA LAKE (KC) 12

A 4000 acre surface area lake located 17 miles west of Ottawa, on State Road 268/68, 1 mile north on Pomona Dam Road, 35 miles south of Topeka. Project Manager, Pomona Lake, 5260 Pomona Dam Road, Vassar, KS 66543-9743. (785) 453-2201.

CARBOLYN CAMPGROUND

From Lyndon, go 4.5 miles north on United States Route 75, east before the Dragoon Creek bridge (signs). A picnic shelter is available. 32 sites, 29 with electric, 15 - 50 ampere. Sites without hookups are $12; sites with electric hookups and sites with water and electric hookups are $16. Recreational vehicle maximum length is 55'. This campground requires a 2 day minimum stay on weekends and a 3 day stay on holiday weekends. Open from May 1st to September 30th.

CEDAR CAMPGROUND

From Michigan Valley, go 2 miles west on East 213th Street, 1 mile north on South Shawnee Heights Road, 3 miles west on East 205th Street, follow the signs. 8 primitive sites. All sites are free. Open all year.

MICHIGAN VALLEY CAMPGROUND

From Michigan Valley, go 1 mile south, 1 mile west on the northwest side of the dam. Wigeler group camping area for up to 100 people and 2 vehicles is $30 and may be reserved only through NRRS from May 1st to October 31st, two picnic shelters, #5 for up to 200 people and 41 vehicles and #3 for up to 50 people and 11 vehicles are $25 to $30, and an amphitheater is available. 87 sites, 51 with electric, 9 full hookups, 3 pull through sites, 1 handicap site with water and electric. Sites without hookups are $12; sites with electric hookups are $16; premium sites with electric hookups are $18; sites with full hookups are $20. Recreational vehicle maximum length is in excess of 65'. This campground requires a 2 day minimum stay on weekends and a 3 day stay on holiday weekends. Open from May 1st to September 30th. NRRS.

OUTLET AREA CAMPGROUND

From Michigan Valley, go 2 miles south, 1.5 miles west, gravel road, below dam. Picnic shelters and an amphitheater are available. 36 sites with water and electric. From April 1st to October 31st, sites with water and electric hookups are $16. From November 1st to March 31st, sites with electric hookups are $10. Open all year. NRRS (April 1st to October 31st).

WOLF CREEK CAMPGROUND

From Michigan Valley, go 1 mile south, 1 mile west to dam, 1 mile northwest. A group camping area for up to 125 people and 48 vehicles with 23 sites is $12 and a picnic shelter is available. There is an 18 hole Disc Golf Coarse available. 78 sites, 45 with water and electric, 3 handicap site with water and electric. From May 1st to September 30th, sites without hookups are $12; sites with water and electric hookups are $16. During April and October, group camping only. Recreational vehicle maximum length is 65'. This campground requires a 2 day minimum stay on weekends and a 3 day stay on holiday weekends. Open from April 1st to October 31st. NRRS.

110 MILE CAMPGROUND

From Michigan Valley, go 2 miles west on east 213th Street, 1 mile north on South Shawnee Heights Road, 1.5 miles west on East 205th Street (signs). No drinking water from October 1st to April 30th. A group camping area and a horse camp may be reserved from May 1st to September 30th. 25 primitive sites. All sites are free. Open all year.

TUTTLE CREEK LAKE (KC) 13

A 12,570 acre surface area lake located 5 miles north of Manhattan on United States Route 24 and State Road 13, 55 miles west of Topeka. there is an off the road vehicle and cycle area. Free sites during winter may have reduced amenities. Project Manager, Tuttle Creek Lake, 5020 Tuttle Creek Boulevard, Manhattan, KS 66502-8812. (785) 539-8511.

STOCKDALE CAMPGROUND

From the dam, go 6 miles west on United States Route 24/77, 1.5 miles on County Road 895, 2.5 miles east (right) on County Road 396. A picnic shelter is available. 14 sites, 2 tent only walk-in sites, 3 pull through sites, plus some random camping. From April 15th to September 30th, sites are $12; random camping is $8; from October 1st to April 14th, some sites are available and are free. Recreational vehicle maximum length is in excess of 65'. This campground requires a 2 day minimum stay on weekends and a 3 day stay on holiday weekends. Open all year. NRRS.

TUTTLE CREEK COVE CAMPGROUND

From the dam at the project office, go 0.1 mile east on State Road 13, 2.5 miles north on County Road 897. A picnic shelter is available. 56 sites, 39 handicap sites with water and 50 ampere, 4 tent only walk in sites, 5 pull through sites. Sites without electric hookups are $12; sites with water and electric hookups are $18. Open all year. NRRS (April 15th to October 31).

WILSON LAKE (KC) 14

A 9000 acre surface area lake located 7 miles south of Lucas on State Road 232, 135 miles northwest of Wichita. Off the road vehicles are prohibited. Free sites during winter may have reduced amenities. Resource Manager, Wilson Lake, 4860 Outlet Boulevard, Sylvan Grove, KS 67481. (785) 658-2551.

LUCAS CAMPGROUND

From Wilson/Junction I-70, exit 206, go 9 miles north on State Road 232, park on left. A group camping area for up to 100 people and 50 vehicles with water and electric hookups and 15 sites is $150, and a picnic shelter is available. 104 sites, 73 with electric, 3 double sites, 32 pull through sites. From April 15th to September 30th, tent only sites and sites without hookups are $12; sites with electric hookups are $16; sites with water and electric hookups, premium sites with water and electric hookups and sites with water and 50 ampere service are $18; double sites without electric hookups are $24; double sites with water and electric hookups are $36. From October 1st to April 14th, walk in tent only sites at Whitetail Ridge are $12. Recreational vehicle maximum length is in excess of 65'. This campground requires a 2 day minimum stay on weekends and a 3 day stay on holiday weekends. Open all year. NRRS (April 15th to September 30th).

MINOOKA CAMPGROUND

From Dorrance/Junction I-70, exit 199, go 7 miles north on Dorrance Road
(signs). A group camping area for up to 100 people and 20 vehicles is $150,
a picnic shelter is $20, and a fish cleaning station and an amphitheater
are available. 165 sites, 106 with electric, 16 - 50 ampere, 5 primitive tent
only walk-in sites, 4 double sites, 17 pull through sites. From April 15th to
September 30th, tent only sites and sites without hookups are $12; sites with
electric hookups are $16; sites with water and electric hookups are $18; double
sites without hookups are $24; a premium double site with electric hookups is
$36; from October 1st to April 14th, during the walk-in season, all sites, other
than tent only walk-in sites, are available and are free, no showers, with utilities
$8. Recreational vehicle maximum length is in excess of 65'. This campground
requires a 2 day minimum stay on weekends and a 3 day stay on holiday
weekends. Open all year. NRRS (April 15th to September 30th).

SYLVAN CAMPGROUND

From Lucas, go 7 miles south on State Road 232, below the dam on the north
side of the spillway. A picnic shelter for up to 50 people and 20 vehicles is $20,
group camping area for up to 50 people and 20 vehicles is $100, reservation
at the office, and horseshoe pits are available. 28 sites, 25 with water and
electric, 17 pull through sites, 12 handicap sites with water and electric. From
April 15th to October 15th, sites without hookups are $12; premium sites with
electric hookups are $18; from October 16th to April 14th, during the walk-
in season, all sites are free, with utilities $8. Recreational vehicle maximum
length is in excess of 65'. This campground requires a 2 day minimum stay on
weekends and a 3 day stay on holiday weekends. Open all year. NRRS (April 15
to September 30).

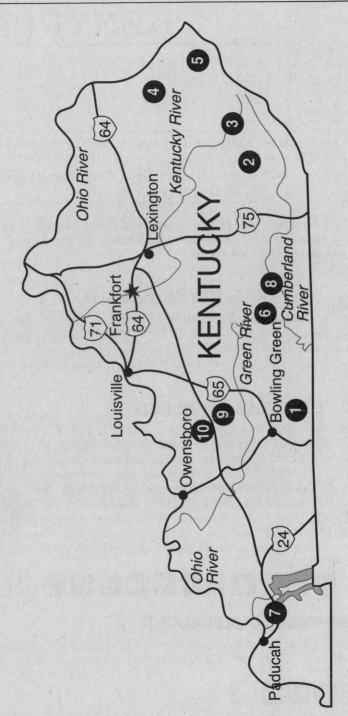

KENTUCKY

STATE CAPITAL:
Frankfort
NICKNAME:
Bluegrass State
15th State - 1792

Site reservation, National Recreation Reservation Service
(NRRS), toll free, 1-877-444-6777; TDD 877-833-6777,
www.recreation.gov, (Master, Visa, American Express
& Discover cards).

Louisville District - All fee campgrounds may charge a visitor
fee. Nashville District - Fees may be higher on weekends.
A visitors fee may be charged.

BARREN RIVER LAKE (LO) 1

A 10,000 acre surface area lake located 20 miles east of Bowling Green, 1.5
miles southwest of Finney on State Road 252 or State Road 1533. Alcohol and
off the road vehicles are prohibited, checkout time is 5 p.m., and visitors to 9:30
p.m. Park Manager, Barren River Lake, 11088 Finney Road, Glasgow, KY 42141-
9642. (270) 646-2055.

BAILEY'S POINT CAMPGROUND

From Cedar Springs/Junction United States Route 231/31E, go 2 miles north
on State Road 252, 1.5 miles east on County Road 517 (signs). An amphitheater,
horseshoe pits, ice and firewood are available and a picnic shelter for up to 100
people and 25 vehicles. 215 sites, 158 with water and 50 ampere service, 20
pull through sites, 5 handicap sites with water and 50 ampere. Sites without
hookups, 2nd price, are $14; sites without hookups and sites with water
hookups are $17; sites with water and 50 ampere service are $21. Recreational
vehicle maximum length is in excess of 65'. This campground requires a 3 night
minimum stay on holiday weekends. Open from April 20th to October 21st.
(270) 622-6959. NRRS.

BEAVER CREEK CAMPGROUND

From Rocky Hill, go 2.5 miles east on State Road 252, across lake bridge, 1.4
miles southwest. 12 primitive sites. All sites are $10. Open from April 20th to
September 16th.

TAILWATER CAMPGROUND

Located below the dam, Junction State Road 252/1533, go north. A group primitive tent camping area for up to 100 people and 1 vehicle is $50, a picnic shelter for up to 100 people and 25 vehicles, and an amphitheater and horseshoe pits are available. 48 sites with water and 50 ampere service, 2 handicap sites. From April 20th to September 16th, sites with water and 50 ampere service are $17; from September 17th to April 19th, some sites are available and are free, reduced services. Recreational vehicle maximum length is in excess of 65'. This campground requires a 3 night minimum stay on holiday weekends. Open all year. (270) 622-7732. NRRS (April 20th to September 16th).

THE NARROWS CAMPGROUND

From Lucas, go 1.7 miles west, (signs). Boat rentals are nearby, horseshoe pits, ice, firewood and a picnic shelter are available. 90 sites with water and 50 ampere service, 2 pull through sites, 2 handicap sites. Sites with water and 50 ampere service are $21. Recreational vehicle maximum length is in excess of 65'. This campground requires a 3 night minimum stay on holiday weekends. Open from April 20th to September 16th. (270) 646-3094. NRRS.

BUCKHORN LAKE (LO) 2

A 1,230 acre surface area lake located 28 miles west of Hazard, north of Daniel Boone National Forest on State Road 28, 0.5 mile from Buckhorn in southeast Kentucky. Alcohol is prohibited by local law. Resource Manager, Buckhorn Lake, Buckhorn, KY 41721. (606) 398-7251.

BUCKHORN BOAT-IN CAMPS

Accessible by boat only, near the emergency spillway, dock provided. 15 primitive sites. All sites are $8. This campground requires a 3 night minimum stay on holiday weekends. Open from May 1st to September 7th (Varies with summer pool elevation).

BUCKHORN CAMPGROUND

Located on the west side of Stilling Basin below the dam. A picnic shelter is $25 to $50, two group camping areas, cable TV hookups, horseshoe pits, firewood and ice are available, and a convenience store and restaurants are located nearby. 45 sites, 31 with water and electric, 29 - 50 ampere, 10 double sites without electric, 2 double sites with 50 ampere, 4 tent only sites, 4 walk-in tent only sites, plus 14 overflow sites, 1 full hookup with 50 ampere, 1 handicap site with water and 50 ampere. Tent only sites are $10; sites with water and 50 ampere service are $18; double sites without hookups are $25; double sites with water and 50 ampere service are $27. Recreational vehicle maximum length is 50'. This campground requires a 3 night minimum stay on holiday weekends. Oen from April 13th to October 15th. (606) 398-7220. NRRS.

TRACE BRANCH CAMPGROUND

From Krypton, go 1.3 miles south on State Road 451, 2.1 miles southwest on Campbell Creek Road. Horseshoe pits are available and a picnic shelter with water and electric is $50. 28 sites, 15 - 50 ampere, 13 double sites, 1 pull through site, 1 handicap site with water and 50 ampere, overflow area. Sites without electric hookups are $10; sites with water and 50 ampere service are $18. Recreational vehicle maximum length is 50'. This campground requires a 3 night minimum stay on holiday weekends. Open from May 1st to September 30th (Varies with pool elevation). NRRS.

CARR CREEK LAKE (LO) 3

A 710 acre surface area lake located 16 miles east of Hazard on State Road 15, northwest of Jefferson National Forest, east of Daniel Boone National Forest in southeast Kentucky. Resource Manager, Carr Fork Lake, 843 Sassafras Creek Road, Sassafras, KY 41759-8806. (606) 642-3308/3307.

LITTCARR CAMPGROUND

From the dam/Junction State Road 1089, 5.2 miles east on State Road 15, 2.4 miles northeast on State Road 160, go north. Ice and firewood for a fee, 24 hour gate attendants, picnic shelter and horseshoe pits are available, and a grocery store is located nearby. 45 sites with water and electric, 3 handicap sites with water and electric. Sites with water and electric hookups are $18. Recreational vehicle maximum length is 50'. This campground requires a 3 night minimum stay on holiday weekends. Open from April 1st to October 14th. (606) 642-3052. NRRS.

LITTCARR #1 CAMPGROUND

From the dam/Junction State Road 15, go 2.4 miles northeast on State Road 160. Horseshoe pits are available. 6 primitive sites. All sites are $10. Open from April 1st to late October.

DEWEY LAKE (HU) 4

A 1,100 acre surface area lake located 10 miles south of Van Lear on State Road 302/3 in east Kentucky, southwest of Huntington, West Virginia. For lake information call (606) 886-6398. Off the road vehicles are prohibited. Resource Manager, Dewey Lake, HC 70, Box 540, Van Lear, KY 41265. (606) 886-6709/789-4521.

SHORELINE CAMPGROUNDS I & II

Boat-in only access. There are boat rentals nearby. 30 primitive sites, 15 on each campground. All sites are $5. Open from May 1st to October 31st.

FISHTRAP LAKE (HU) 5

A 1,130 acre surface area lake located 10 miles south of Pikeville on United States Route 460, in southeast Kentucky, near the Virginia/West Virginia state lines. Checkout time is 4 p.m. For lake information call (606) 437-9426. Resource Manager, Fishtrap Lake, 2204 Fishtrap Road, Shelbiana, KY 41562. (606) 437-7496.

GRAPEVINE CAMPGROUND

From Phyllis, go 0.5 mile west on State Road 194. Three picnic shelters for up to 100 people and 50 vehicles are $50. 28 sites, 10 with water and electric. Sites without electric hookups are $8; sites with water and electric hookups are $12. Open from Friday before Memorial Day through Labor Day. (606) 835-4564.

GREEN RIVER LAKE (LO) 6

An 8,210 acre surface area lake located 9 miles south of Campbellsville on State Road 55, 95 miles south of Louisville. Alcohol is prohibited by local law and off the road vehicles are prohibited. Park Manager, Green River Lake, 544 Lake Road, Campbellsville, KY 42718-9705. (270) 465-4463.

HOLMES BEND CAMPGROUND

From Columbia/Junction State Road 206, exit 49, go 1.2 miles north on State Road 55, 1 mile northeast on State Road 551, 3.8 miles north on Holmes Bend Road. Boat rentals and a convenience store are nearby. A picnic shelter, firewood, ice, and an amphitheater are available. 125 sites, 102 with 50 ampere service, 6 handicap sites. Sites without hookups are $17; sites with 50 ampere service are $20. Recreational vehicle maximum length is in excess of 65'. This campground requires a 3 night minimum stay on holiday weekends. Open from April 20th to October 20th. (270) 384-4623. NRRS.

PIKES RIDGE CAMPGROUND

From Knifley, 4.8 miles northwest on State Road 76, southwest on Pikes Ridge Road (signs). A picnic shelter for up to 100 people is available and a convenience store is nearby. 60 sites, 21 with water and electric, 3 handicap sites. Sites without hookups are $15; sites with water and electric hookups are $17. Recreational vehicle maximum length is in excess of 65'. This campground requires a 3 night minimum stay on holiday weekends. Open from April 20th to September 22nd. (270) 465-6488. NRRS.

SMITH RIDGE CAMPGROUND

From Campbellsville, go 1 mile east on Highway 70, 3 miles south on State Road 372, west (right) on County Park Road (signs). Group camping area for up to 100 people, boat sgtorage and rentals, and a convenience store are located nearby, and an amphitheater and cabins are available. 80 sites, 62 with 50 ampere service, 5 handicap sites. Sites without hookups are $17; sites with water and 50 ampere service are $20. Recreational vehicle maximum length is in excess of 65'. This campground requires a 3 night minimum stay on holiday weekends. Open from April 20th September 22nd. (270) 789-2743. NRRS.

WILSON CREEK CAMPGROUND

From Campbellsville, go 4 miles east on State Road 70, 7 miles east on State Road 76, on right. 5 primitive sites. All sites are free. Open all year.

LAKE BARKLEY (NV) 7

A 57,920 acre surface area lake southeast of Junction I-24/United States Route 62 near Gilbertsville, east of Paducah, continuing south into Tennessee. Checkout time is 3 p.m. There is a display on early life styles and river usage at the visitor center. Resource Manager, Lake Barkley, Box 218, Highway 62, Grand Rivers, KY 42045-0218. (270) 362-4236. See TN listing.

CANAL CAMPGROUND

From Paducah, east on I-24 to Junction with "The Trace" (Land Between the Lakes), go 3 miles south on The Trace, go east. An amphitheater is available and a group loop camping area for up to 64 people and 30 vehicles with shelter is $160. 115 sites with water and electric, 9 full hookups, 29 - 50 ampere, 9 handicap sites with water and 50 ampere, 9 handicap sites with water and electric, 6 handicap pull through sites with water and 50 ampere, 15 pull through sites. Restaurants are located nearby. Sites with water and electric hookups are $14; sites with water and electric hookups, 2nd price, and sites with water and 50 ampere service are $17; premium sites with water and electric hookups and premium sites with water and 50 ampere service are $21; full hookups are $25. Recreational vehicle maximum length is in excess of 65'. This campground requires a 3 night minimum stay on holiday weekends. Open from April 1st to October 27th. (270) 362-4840. NRRS.

EUREKA CAMPGROUND

Across the spillway on east side of the dam. A picnic shelter for up to 100 people and 50 vehicles is $35. A convenience store is located nearby. 26 sites with water and electric, 3 pull through sites. Sites with water and electric hookups are $15; sites with water and electric hookups, 3rd price, are $16; premium sites with water and electric hookups are $20. Recreational vehicle maximum length is in excess of 65'. This campground requires a 2 night minimum stay on weekends and a 3 night stay on holiday weekends. Open from April 27th to September 3rd. (270) 388-9459. NRRS.

HURRICANE CREEK CAMPGROUND

From Cadiz, go 7.5 miles north on State Road 139, 6.5 miles west on State Road 276, 0.3 mile north on State Road 724, go west. A convenience store is located nearby. 51 sites, 45 with water and electric, 9 with 50 ampere service, 1 handicap tent only site, 1 handicap site with electric, 7 tent only sites, 11 pull through sites. Tent only walk-in sites are $10; a tent only site with water and 50 ampere service, a tent only site with water and electric hookups, sites with electric hookups, sites with water and electric hookups and sites with water and 50 ampere service are $16; premium sites with water and electric hookups and a site with water and 50 ampere service is $19. Recreational vehicle maximum length is in excess of 65'. This campground requires a 2 night minimum stay on weekends and a 3 night stay on holiday weekends. Open from April 27th to September 3rd. (270) 522-8821. NRRS.

LAKE CUMBERLAND (NV) 8

A 50,000 acre surface area lake located south of Lexington near the Tennessee state line, south of the Cumberland Parkway. Wolf Creek Dam is located on United States Route 127, 4.2 miles south of Junction of State Road 55/United States Route 127. Various exhibits at the visitor center in the office. The water level on the lake has been drawn down as a precaution due to seepage while repairs are under construction. Resource Manager, Lake Cumberland, 855 Boat Dock Road, Somerset, KY 42501-0450. (606) 679-6337/6338.

CUMBERLAND POINT CAMPGROUND

From Nancy, go 0.2 mile east on State Road 80, 1 mile south on State Road 235, 8 miles southeast on State Road 761. A picnic shelter for up to 300 people and 100 vehicles is $50 and an amphitheater is available. 30 sites with water and electric. Sites with water and electric hookups are $18; a premium site with water and electric hookups is $22. Recreational vehicle maximum length is in excess of 65'. This campground requires a 2 night minimum stay on weekends and a 3 night stay on holiday weekends. Open from April 19th to September 24th. (606) 871-7886. NRRS.

FALL CREEK CAMPGROUND

From Monticello, go 0.4 mile northwest on State Road 92, 1.5 miles northeast on State Road 90, 6 miles north on State Road 1275, go northwest. A picnic shelter is available. 10 sites with electric. Sites with electric hookups are $20. Open from April 1st to October 30th. (606) 348-6042.

FISHING CREEK CAMPGROUND

From Somerset/Junction United States Route 27, go 5.5 miles west on State Road 80, exit prior to lake bridge 2 miles north on Highway 1248 (signs). A convenience store is located nearby. 47 sites with electric, 20 tent only sites, 2 pull through sites, 1 handicap site with electric. Tent only sites with electric are $15; tent only sites with water and electric are $19; premium tent only sites with water and electric and premium standard sites with water and electric hookups are $20; premium sites with water and electric hookups are $24. Recreational vehicle maximum length is in excess of 65'. This campground requires a 2 night minimum stay on weekends and a 3 night stay on holiday weekends. Open from April 20th to September 26th. (606) 679-5174. NRRS.

KENDALL CAMPGROUND

From Jamestown, go 10 miles south on United States Route 127, right on Kendall Road before crossing the dam, signs. A picnic shelter for up to 600 people and 100 vehicles is $50, firewood, horseshoe pits and a fish cleaning station are available, and a convenience store is located nearby. 96 sites with water and electric, 55 - 50 ampere service, 5 pull through sites, 1 full hookup, 6 handicap sites with water and 50 ampere. Sites with water and 50 ampere service are $15; premium sites with water and electric hookups are $20. Recreational vehicle maximum length is in excess of 65'. This campground requires a 2 night minimum stay on weekends and a 3 night stay on holiday weekends. Open all year. (270) 343-4660. NRRS.

WAITSBORO CAMPGROUND

From Somerset, go 5 miles south on United States Route 27, west (right) on Waitsboro Road (signs). Two picnic shelters for up to 15 people and 1 vehicle are $35. Restaurants are located nearby. 25 sites, 20 with electric, 5 tent only sites, 1 full hookup, 2 pull through sites. Tent only sites are $14; a premium tent only site is $15; a tent only site with water and electric is $17; sites with water and electric hookups are $19; a site with full hookups is $20; premium sites with water and electric hookups are $24. Recreational vehicle maximum length is in excess of 65'. This campground requires a 2 night minimum stay on weekends and a 3 night stay on holiday weekends. Open from April 6th to October 15th. (606) 561-5513. NRRS.

NOLIN LAKE (LO) 9

A 5,795 acre surface area lake located 2 miles north of Mammoth Cave National Park on State Road 13/52, 15 miles north of Brownsville on State Road 259, 22 miles south on Leitchfield on State Road 259. Alcohol is prohibited by local law. Mammoth Cave Nationa Park is located nearby. Park Manager, Nolin Lake, 2150 Nolin Dam Road, P. O. Box 339, Bee Springs, KY 42207-0289. (270) 286-4511.

DOG CREEK CAMPGROUND

From Munfordville, go 18 miles west on State Road 88, 1 mile south on State Road 1015 (signs). A picnic shelter is available. 70 sites, 24 sites with water and electric, 12 pull through sites, some 50 ampere, 2 handicap sites. Sites without hookups are $12; premium sites without hookups are $16; sites with water and electric hookups are $18. Recreational vehicle maximum length is in excess of 65'. This campground requires a 3 night minimum stay on holiday weekends. Open from April 20th to September 23rd. (270) 524-5454. NRRS.

MOUTARDIER CAMPGROUND

From Leitchfield, go 16 miles south on State Road 259 (signs), 2 miles southeast on State Road 2067. Boat rentals are nearby, a picnic shelter, horseshoe pits and a fish cleaning station are available. Moutardier Marina, (270) 286-4069. 167 sites, 81 with water and electric, 28 pull through sites, 2 handicap sites. Sites without hookups are $14; premium sites without hookups are $18; sites with water and electric hookups are $21. Recreational vehicle maximum length is in excess of 65'. This campground requires a 3 night minimum stay on holiday weekends. Open from April 20th to October 28th. (270) 286-4230. NRRS.

WAX CAMPGROUND

From Munfordville, go 20 miles west on State Road 88. Boat rentals are nearby, a picnic shelter, horse shoe pits and a fish cleaning station are available. Wax Marina, (270) 242-7205. 110 sites, 56 sites with water and electric, 7 pull through sites, 2 handicap sites. Sites without hookups are $14; premium sites without hookups are $18; sites with water and electric hookups are $21. Recreational vehicle maximum length is in excess of 65'. This campground requires a 3 night minimum stay on holiday weekends. Open from April 20th to September 23rd. (270) 242-7578. NRRS.

ROUGH RIVER LAKE (LO) 10

A 5,100 acre surface area lake located 1.4 miles north of Falls of Rough Post Office on State Road 79, 51 miles north of Bowling Green. Alcohol is prohibited by local law, off the road vehicles are prohibited, checkout time is 4:30 p.m., horse trails are nearby and a golf course is in the area. Sites during winter may have reduced amenities. A large number are lakeside sites. Park Manager, Rough River Lake, 14500 Falls of Rough Road, Falls of Rough, KY 40119-9801. (270) 257-2061.

AXTEL CAMPGROUND

From Harned, go 9 miles south on State Road 259, 0.5 mile west on State Road 79, on left. Boat rentals are nearby and a picnic shelter is available. 158 sites, 40 - 50 ampere, 2 handicap sites with water and 50 ampere. Sites without electric hookups (2nd price) are $14; sites without electric hookups are $16; sites with water and 50 ampere service are $21. Recreational vehicle maximum length is 45'. This campground requires a 3 night minimum stay on holiday weekends. Open all year. (270) 257-2584. NRRS (April 13th to September 21st).

CAVE CREEK CAMPGROUND

From the dam, go 2.9 miles south on State Road 79, 0.8 mile east on State Road 736. 86 sites, 16 - 50 ampere, 8 handicap sites without electric, 2 handicap sites with water and 50 ampere. Sites without hookups are $9; sites without hookups (2nd price) are $11; sites with 50 ampere service are $13. Recreational vehicle maximum length is 40'. This campground requires a 3 night minimum stay on holiday weekends. Open from May 1st to September 15th. (270) 879-4304. NRRS (May 1st to September 30th).

LAUREL BRANCH CAMPGROUND

From Mc Daniels, go 1 mile northwest on State Road 259, 0.4 mile southwest on State Road 110 (signs). 77 sites, 35 with water and electric, 2 handicap sites with water and 50 ampere. From May 1st to September 30th, sites without electric hookups are $13; sites with water and 50 ampere service are $18; from October 1st to April 30th, sites are $10 to $13. Recreational vehicle maximum length is 40'. This campground requires a 2 night minimum stay on weekends and a 3 night stay on holiday weekends. Open all year. (270) 257-8839. NRRS (April 13th to September 21st).

NORTH FORK CAMPGROUND

From Mc Daniels, go 2 miles north on State Road 259. A picnic shelter is
available. 106 sites, 1 handicap site with water and 50 ampere, 49 - 50 ampere,
2 pull through sites. Sites without hookups are $16; sites with water and 50
ampere service are $19. Recreational vehicle maximum length is 60'. This
campground requires a 3 night minimum stay on holiday weekends. Open from
May 1st to September 15th. (270) 257-8139. NRRS.

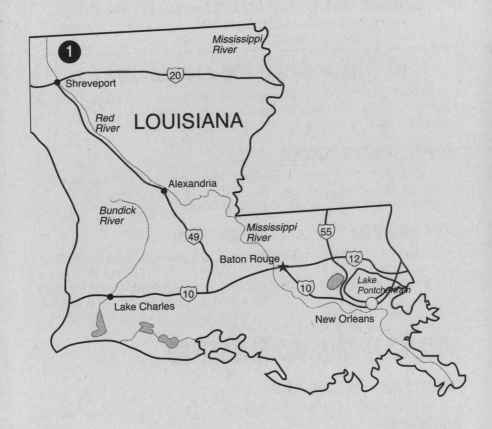

LOUISIANA

STATE CAPITAL:
Baton Rouge
NICKNAME:
Pelican State
18th State - 1812

Site reservation, National Recreation Reservation Service (NRRS), toll free, 1-877-444-6777; TDD 877-833-6777, www.recreation.gov, (Master, Visa, American Express & Discover cards).

BAYOU BODCAU RESERVOIR (VK) 1

Dry Reservoir - 34,000 acres, located 20 miles northeast of Shreveport and I-20, 18 miles north on State Road 157. Park Manager, Louisiana Field Office, 3505 South Grand Street, Monroe, LA 7120. (318) 322-6391, ext. 104.

HORSE CAMPGROUND

Located on the north end of the dam near the spillway. Large groups should call for a permit and information. There are over 50 miles of horse trails available. Primitive camping. Camping is free. Open all year.

TOM MERRILL AREA CAMPGROUND

From Haughton/Fillmore exit on I-20, go 15 miles north on State Road 157, 3 miles east at Bellevue (Bodcau Dam Road, sign). Durdiln Hill Trail starts at this campground and extends for 6 miles for hikers and mountain bikers. A picnic shelter is $35. 20 sites, 10 with electric, some pull through sites. Sites without electric hookups are $6; sites with electric hookups are $12. Recreational vehicle maximum length 20'. Open all year.

SOUTH ABUTMENT AREA

Located on the upstream side of the dam. 12 sites. All sites are $6. Open all year.

WENK'S LANDING

From Minden on I-20, go 17 miles north on United States Route 371 through Cotton Valley, on the left before Sarepta (signs). Primitive camping in designated areas only. Camping is free. Open all year.

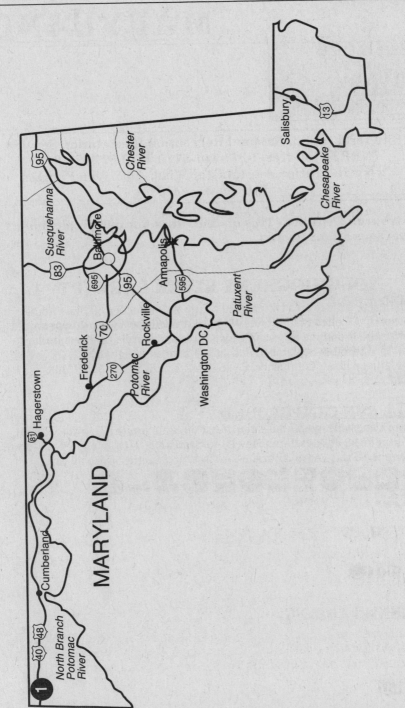

MARYLAND

STATE CAPITAL:
Annapolis
NICKNAME:
Free State

7th State - 1788

Site reservation, National Recreation Reservation Service (NRRS), toll free, 1-877-444-6777; TDD 877-833-6777, www.recreation.gov, (Master, Visa, American Express & Discover cards).

Pittsburgh Disttrict - This district does not permit alcoholic beverages at any project.

YOUGHIOGHENY RIVER LAKE (PT) 1

A 2,840 acre surface area lake located south of Confluence off State Route 281, north of United States Route 40, in southwest Pennsylvania spanning the Mason-Dixon Line between Pennsylvania and Maryland. Trout stockings from April through September. Resource Manager, Youghiogheny River Lake, 497 Flanigan Road, Confluence, PA 15424-1932. (814) 395-3242/3166. See PA listing.

MILL RUN CAMPGROUND
From Friendsville, go 3.7 miles northeast on State Route 53, 1 mile west on Mill Run Road. 30 sites. From May 1st to September 11th, sites are $12. From September 12th to April 30th, sites are free, no facilities. Open all year.

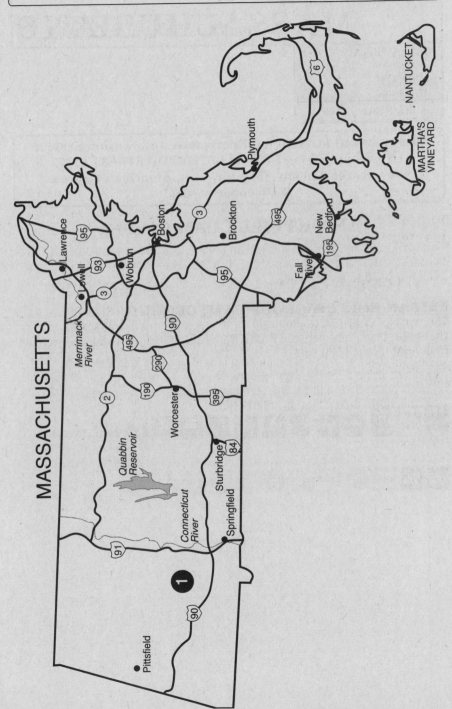

MASSACHUSETTS

MASSACHUSETTS

STATE CAPITAL:
Boston
NICKNAME:
Bay State

6th State - 1788

Site reservation, National Recreation Reservation Service (NRRS), toll free, 1-877-444-6777; TDD 877-833-6777, www.recreation.gov, (Master, Visa, American Express & Discover cards).

KNIGHTVILLE DAM (NAE) 1

Located 4 miles south of Chesterfield and State Road 143 in west-central Massachusetts. Knightville Dam, RR 1, Box 285, Huntington, MA 01050-9942. (413) 667-3430/(508) 249-2547.

INDIAN HOLLOW GROUP CAMPGROUND

From Chesterfield, go 4 miles southeast on State Road 143, access on South Street. Two group camping areas, GN1 for up to 100 people and 31 vehicles is $90 and GS1 for up to 100 people and 41 vehicles is $85. Amphitheater and a picnic shelter is $75. This campground requires a 2 night minimum stay on weekends and a 3 night stay on holiday weekends. Open from May 18th September 9th. By reservation only. NRRS.

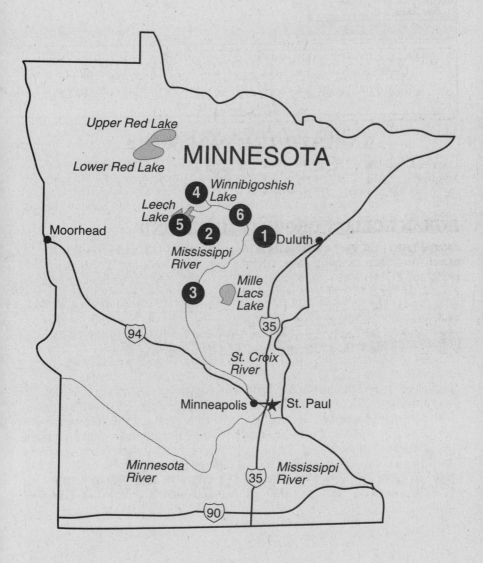

MINNESOTA

STATE CAPITAL:
St. Paul

NICKNAME:
North Star State

32nd State - 1858

Site reservation, National Recreation Reservation Service (NRRS), toll free, 1-877-444-6777; TDD 877-833-6777, www.recreation.gov, (Master, Visa, American Express & Discover cards).

BIG SANDY LAKE (SP) 1

A 9,400 acre surface area lake located off State Road 65, north of Mc Gregor, 60 miles west of Duluth. Interpretive facility and interpretive programs. An old lock house has been turned into an interpretive display. Checkout time is noon and off the road vehicles are prohibited. Resource Manager, Big Sandy Lake, 22205 531st Lane, Mc Gregor, MN 55760-0192. (218) 426-3482.

SANDY LAKE CAMPGROUND

From McGregor, go 13 miles north on State Road 65, go south, located at the outlet of Big Sandy Lake. Two group camping areas for up to 25 people and 3 vehicles are $25, fish cleaning station musem, and horseshoe pits are available, a picnic shelter for up to 40 people and 20 vehicles is $25, and firewood is availabale for a fee. 58 sites, 54 with electric, 8 tent only walk-in sites, 8 pull through sites, 5 double sites with electric, 1 handicap site with electric. From May 1st to September 20th, tent only sites without electric are $12; tent only sites with electric are $14; sites with electric hookups are $22; double sites with electric are $44; during April and from September 21st to October 31st, tent only sites without electric are $6; tent only sites with electric are $10; sites with electric hookups are $16; double sites with electric are $32. Recreational vehicle maximum length is in excess of 65'. This campground requires a 2 night minimum stay on weekends and a 3 night stay on holiday weekends. Open from April 1st to October 31st. NRRS (May 1st to September 20th).

CROSS LAKE (SP) 2

A 13,660 acre surface area lake with 119 miles of shoreline located at Cross Lake off State Road 210, on County Road 3/66, 100 miles southwest of Duluth. Interpretive programs, checkout time is noon and off the road vehicles are prohibited. Resource Manager, Cross Lake, 35507 County Road 66, Box 36, Cross Lake, MN 56422-0036. (218) 692-2025.

CROSS LAKE CAMPGROUND

From Crosby/Junction State Road 210, go 12 miles north on State Road 6, 6 miles west on County Road 11, northeast on County Road 3. A fish cleaning station and picnic shelter are available, and firewood is available for a fee. A handicap accessible fishing and swimming area are available. 119 sites, 69 with electric, 1 pull through, 6 tent only sites, 1 handicap site with electric. From April 1st to April 30th and September 17th to October 31st, tent only sites and sites without electric hookups are $9; sites with electric hookups are $12; from May 1st to September 16th, tents only sites and sites without electric hookups are $18; sites with electric hookups are $24. This campground requires a 2 night minimum stay on weekends and a 3 night stay on holiday weekends. Open from April 1st to October 31st. NRRS (May 1st to September 18th).

GULL LAKE (SP) 3

Located north of Brainerd off State Road 371, 115 miles southwest of Duluth, 130 miles north of Minneapolis. Burial Mound display, checkout time is noon and off the road vehicles are prohibited. Resource Manager, Gull Lake, 10867 East Gull Lake Drive, Brainerd, MN 56401-9413. (218) 829-3334.

GULL LAKE CAMPGROUND

From Brainerd, go 10 miles northwest on State Road 371, west on County Road 125 to dam. A fish cleaning station is available, a picnic shelter for up to 40 people and 10 vehicles is $35 and firewood is available for a fee. Shopping is located nearby. Showers are open from May 1st to October 1st, and water is available from April 15th to November 1st. 39 sites with electric, 1 handicap site. From October 1st to April 30th, sites are $12; from May 1st to September 30th, sites with electric hookups are $24. This campground requires a 2 night minimum stay on weekends and a 3 night stay on holiday weekends. Open all year. NRRS (May 1st to September 30th).

LAKE WINNIBIGOSHISH (SP) 4

A 67,000 acre surface area lake located northwest of Deer River and north of United States Route 2, off State Road 46, 102 miles northwest of Duluth. Off the road vehicles prohibited and checkout time is noon. Resource Manager, Lake Winnibigoshish, 34385 Highway 2, Grand Rapids, MN 55744-9663. (218) 326-6128.

WINNIE DAM CAMPGROUND

From Deer River, go 1 mile northwest on United States Route 2, 12 miles north (right) on State Road 46, 2 miles west (left) on County Road 9 (signs). A picnic shelter and a fish cleaning station are available, and firewood is available for a fee. 22 sites with electric, 1 handicap site. Sites with electric hookups are $18. Recreational vehicle maximum length is in excess of 65'. This campground requires a 2 night minimum stay on weekends and a 3 night stay on holiday weekends. Open from May 1st to October 31st. NRRS (May 1st to Sept. 15th).

LEECH LAKE (SP) 5

A 126,000 acre surface area lake located east of Walker on State Road 371, 35 miles west of Grand Rapids, 120 miles west of Duluth, 30 miles southwest of Deer River. Interpretive programs and a snowmobile trail are available, checkout time is noon and off the road vehicles are prohibited. Resource Manager, Leech Lake, P. O. Box 111, Federal Dam, MN 56641-0111. (218) 654-3145.

LEECH LAKE CAMPGROUND

From Cass Lake/Junction United States Road 2, 8 miles south on Highway 8, southwest side of dam. A fish cleaning station, firewood is available for a fee, horseshoe pits and a group camping area are available, and a cafe and boat rentals are nearby. A picnic shelter for up to 50 people and 15 vehicles is $25. 77 sites, 74 with electric, 23 - 50 ampere, 3 pull through sites, 5 full hookups, 4 tent only sites, 2 handicap sites with water and electric. Tent only walk-in sites are $10; sites with electric hookups and sites with 50 ampere service are $20; sites with full hookup are $30; double sites are $36. Recreational vehicle maximum length is in excess of 65'. This campground requires a 2 night minimum stay on weekends and a 3 night stay on holiday weekends. Open from May 1st to October 31st. (218) 654-3145, Ext. 2. NRRS (May 1st to September 30th).

POKEGAMA LAKE (SP) 6

A 16,000 acre surface area lake located west of Grand Rapids off United States Route 2 and 169, 82 miles northwest of Duluth. Checkout time is noon and off the road vehicles are prohibited. Resource Manager, Pokegama Lake, 34385 Highway 2, Grand Rapids, MN 55744-9663. (218) 326-6128.

POKEGAMA DAM CAMPGROUND

From Grand Rapids, go 2 miles west on United States Route 2, south (left, signs) of road. A picnic shelter for up to 50 people and 50 vehicles is $35, a fish cleaning station is available, and firewood is available for a fee. 21 sites, 19 sites - 50 ampere, 2 tent only sites, 1 handicap site. Tent only sites are $12; sites with 50 ampere service are $24. Recreational vehicle maximum length is in excess of 65'. This campground requires a 2 night minimum stay on weekends and a 3 night stay on holiday weekends. Open from April 1st to October 31st. NRRS (May 1st to September 15th).

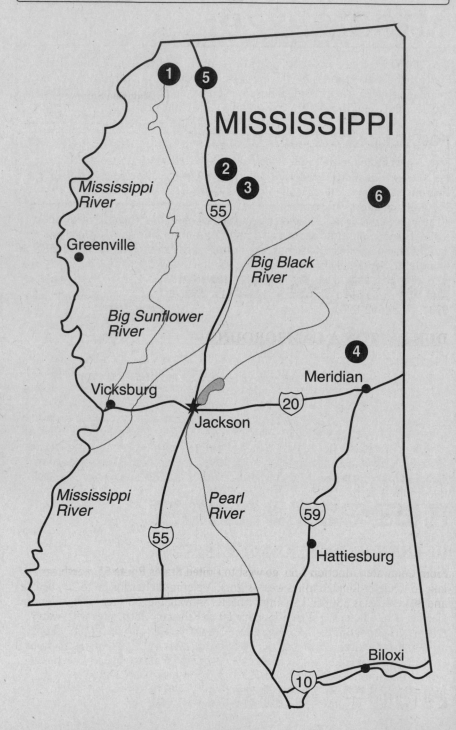

MISSISSIPPI

STATE CAPITAL:
Jackson
NICKNAME:
Magnolia State

20th State - 1817

Site reservation, National Recreation Reservation Service (NRRS), toll free, 1-877-444-6777; TDD 877-833-6777, www.recreation.gov, (Master, Visa, American Express & Discover cards).

ARKABUTLA LAKE (VK) 1

A 12,730 acre surface area lake located north of Arkabutla on State Road 301, 30 miles south of Memphis, Tennessee. Visitors to 10 p.m., and checkout time is 4 p.m. Free sites during winter may have reduced amenities. Resource Manager, Arkabutla Lake Field Office, 3905 Arkabutla Dam Road, Coldwater, MS 38618-9737. (662) 562-6261.

DUB PATTON A CAMPGROUND

From Arkabutla, go north on Scenic Loop 304 across the dam, north side (signs). An amphitheater is available and two picnic shelters for up to 100 people and 30 vehicles are $30. 66 sites with water and electric, 2 full hookups, 10 tent only sites, 1 handicap site. From January 1st to February 28th, tent only sites with water and electric and sites with water and electric hookups are $10; premium sites with water and electric hookups and sites with full hookups are $16; from March 1st to October 31st, tent only sites with water and electric and sites with water and electric hookups are $12; premium sites with water and electric hookups and sites with full hookups are $18. Recreational vehicle maximum length is 50'. Open all year. NRRS.

HERNANDO POINT CAMPGROUND

From Coldwater/Junction I-55, go west to United States Route 51, north across lake to Wheeler Road, 6 miles west (signs). A picnic shelter for up to 100 people and 30 vehicles is $30, and an amphitheater is available. 83 sites with water and electric, 1 handicap site. From January 1st to February 28th, sites with water and electric hookups are $10; premium sites with water and electric hookups are $16; from March 1st to October 31st, sites with water and electric hookups are $12; premium sites with water and electric hookups are $18. Recreational vehicle maximum length is in excess of 65'. Open all year. NRRS.

KELLY'S CROSSING CAMPGROUND

From Arkabutla, go 0.3 mile east, 3 miles north. 24 primitive sites. Sites are $5. Recreational vehicle maximum length is 20' Open all year.

OUTLET CHANNEL CAMPGROUND

From Arkabutla, go 4.5 miles north on Scenic Loop Road, below dam (signs). A picnic shelter is $30. 65 sites, plus primitive area. Sites are $6. Recreational vehicle maximum length is 20'. Open all year.

PLEASANT HILL CAMPGROUND

From Hernando, go 5 miles west on State Road 304, 5 miles south on Fogg Road. 10 sites. Sites are $5. Recreational vehicle maximum length is 20'. Open all year.

SOUTH ABUTMENT CAMPGROUND

From Arkabutla, go north to the dam on Scenic Loop 304 (signs). A group camping area with 2 sites is $50 and a picnic shelter for up to 100 people and 30 vehicles is $30. 80 sites with electric, 1 handicap site. From November 1st to February 28th, sites with electric hookups are $8; from March 1st to October 31st, sites with electric hookups are $10. Recreational vehicle maximum length is 60'. Open all year. NRRS.

ENID LAKE (VK) 2

A 15,560 acre surface area lake located 26 miles north of Grenada, 1.7 miles east of Enid, off I-55, exit 233 on State Road 233, 65 miles south of Memphis, Tennessee. Visitors to 10 p.m. Resource Manager, Enid Lake, 931 County Road 36, Enid, MS 38927. (662) 563-4571.

BYNUM CREEK LANDING

From Water Valley/Junction State Road 7, go 8.3 miles northwest on State Road 315, 2.8 miles southwest, 2.4 miles southeast on an all weather road. 5 primitive sites. All sites are free. Recreational vehicle maximum length is 20'. Open all year.

CHICKASAW HILL CAMPGROUND

From Pope, go 8.8 miles southeast, 1.6 miles southwest. A picnic shelter is $30 and an amphitheater is available. 51 sites with water and electric, 15 tent only sites, 12 pull through sites. From November 1st to February 28th, sites with water and electric hookups are $10; from March 1st to October 31st, sites with water and electric hookups are $14. Recreational vehicle maximum length is 65'. This campground requires a 2 night minimum stay on weekends and a 3 night stay on holiday weekends. Open all year. NRRS.

LONG BRANCH CAMPGROUND

From I-55 south of Enid, exit 227, go 3.8 miles Northeast on State Road 32, 1.9 miles north. 14 primitive sites. From November 1st to February 28, sites are $5; from March 1st to October 31st, sites are $6. Recreational vehicle maximum length is 20'. Open all year.

PERSIMMON HILL CAMPGROUND

From I-55, exit 233, go 1 mile east on County Road 36 to dam, south end of dam (signs). Picnic shelters are $30. 72 sites with water and electric, 2 pull through sites. From November 1st to February 28th, sites with water and electric hookups are $10; premium sites with water and electric hookups are $12; from March 1st to October 31st, sites with water and electric hookups are $16; premium sites with water and electric hookups are $18. Recreational vehicle maximum length is 65'. This campground requires a 2 night minimum stay on weekends and a 3 night stay on holiday weekends. Open all year. NRRS.

PLUM POINT CAMPGROUND

From Pope, go 5.3 miles southeast, 3.7 miles southeast on an all weather road. 10 primitive sites. From November 1st to February 28th, sites are $5; from March 1st to October 31st, sites are $6. Recreational vehicle maximum length is 20'. Open all year.

POINT PLEASANT CAMPGROUND

From I-55 south of Enid, exit 227, go 6.3 miles Northeast on State Road 32, go northwest. 3 primitive sites. All sites are free. Recreational vehicle maximum length is 20'. Open all year.

WALLACE CREEK CAMPGROUND

From I-55, exit 233, go 2.5 miles east on County Road 36 to the dam, across the spillway on west side of the dam (signs). Picnic shelters, an amphitheater and fish cleaning station are available. 99 sites with water and electric, 7 pull through sites, 3 handicap sites. From November 1st to February 28, sites with water and electric hookups, 2nd price, are $10; sites with water and electric hookus and premium sites with water and electric hookups, 2nd price, are $12; from March 1st to October 31st, sites with water and electric hookups and premium sites with water and electric hookups, 2nd price, are $16; premium sites with water and electric hookups are $18. Recreational vehicle maximum length is 65'. This campground requires a 2 night minimum stay on weekends and a 3 night stay on holiday weekends. Open all year. NRRS.

WATER VALLEY LANDING CAMPGROUND

From Water Valley/Junction State Road 315, go 2 miles south on State Road 7, 5.3 miles west on State Road 32, 3.2 miles northwest. A picnic shelter is $30. 29 sites with water and electric. Sites with water and electric hookups are $14. Recreational vehicle maximum length is 60'. This campground requires a 2 night minimum stay on weekends and a 3 night stay on holiday weekends. Open March 1st to October 31st. NRRS.

GRENADA LAKE (VK) 3

A 35,820 acre surface area lake with 148 miles of shoreline located 2 miles northeast of Grenada, I-55, exit 206, east on State Road 8, 99 miles south of Memphis, Tennessee. There are displays and exhibits at the visitor center and a sports complex area is located below dam. Free sites during winter may have reduced amenities. Resource Manager, Grenada Lake Field Office, P. O. Box 903, Grenada, MS 38902-0903. (662) 226-1679/5911.

GRENADA LANDING A (OLD FORT) CAMPGROUND

From the Dam, on the south side. A picnic shelter is $30. 21 primitive sites. From April 1st to September 30th, sites are $6; from October 1st to March 31st, some sites are available and are free. Recreational vehicle maximum length is 20'. Open all year.

NORTH ABUTMENT CAMPGROUND

From I-55 north of Grenada, exit 55, go 5 miles Northeast on State Road 7, go south. A picnic shelter is $30, an amphitheater and fish cleaning station are available, and a convenience store and restaurants are located nearby. 36 sites with water and electric, 4 pull through sites, 2 handicap sites. Sites with water and electric hookups are $18. Recreational vehicle maximum length is 40'. This campground requires a 2 night minimum stay on weekends and a 3 night stay on holiday weekends. Open all year. NRRS.

NORTH GRAYSPORT CAMPGROUND

From Gore Springs/Junction State Road 8, go 5.8 miles north across the bridge on the east side. An amphitheater is available. 29 sites, 25 with water and electric, 3 handicap sites with water and electric. Sites with water and electric hookups are $10. Recreational vehicle maximum length is 55'. This campground requires a 2 night minimum stay on weekends and a 3 night stay on holiday weekends. Open all year. (662) 226-1679. NRRS (March 1st to October 31st).

SKUNA-TURKEY CREEK CAMPGROUND

From Coffeeville, go 4.5 miles southeast on State Road 330, 2.1 miles south, 3.8 miles west. 6 sites. All sites are free. Recreational vehicle maximum length is 20'. Open all year.

OKATIBBEE LAKE (MB) 4

A 4,000 acre surface area lake with 28 miles of shoreline located 10 miles north of junction I-20/I-59, northwest of Meridian off State Road 19, 20 miles west of the Alabama state line. Project Manager, Okatibbee Lake, P. O. Box 98, Collinsville, MS 39325-0098. (601) 626-8431.

GIN CREEK CAMPGROUND

From Collinsville/Junction State Road 19, go 2.8 miles north on County Road 17 (West Lauderdale School Road) past "T", 1 mile east, on right. 7 primitive sites. All sites are $6. Open all year.

TWILTLEY BRANCH CAMPGROUND

From Collinsville/Junction State Road 19, go 1 mile east on County Road 17, exit 1.7 miles east and south. Visitors to 9:30 p.m., for a fee and checkout time is 3 p.m. Three group camping areas, sites 63 and 64 are for up to 24 people and 9 vehicles, and site 65 is for up to 48 people and 24 vehicles, priced from $30 to $60, and a picnic shelter is available. 62 handicap sites, 50 with water and electric, 4 pull through sites. Sites without electric hookups are $10; sites with water and electric hookups are $16; premium sites with water and electric hookups are $18. Recreational vehicle maximum length is in excess of is 65'. This campground requires a 2 night minimum stay on weekends and a 3 night stay on holiday weekends. Open all year. (601) 626-8068. NRRS.

SARDIS LAKE (VK) 5

A 32,100 acre surface area lake located northeast of Batesville and I-55, exit 246, on State Road 35, 9 miles southeast of Sardis, 50 miles south of Memphis, Tennessee. Checkout time is 2 p.m., and a golf coarse is located at a nearby state park. Free sites during winter may have reduced amenities. Project Manager, Sardis Lake Field Office, 29949 Highway 315, Sardis, MS 38666-3066. (662) 563-4531.

BEACH POINT CAMPGROUND

From Sardis/Junction I-55, exit 8 miles east on State Road 315. 14 primitive sites. From April 1st to September 30th, sites are $6; from October 1st to March 31st, some sites are available and are free. Recreational vehicle maximum length is 20'. Open all year.

CLEAR CREEK CAMPGROUND

From Oxford/Junction State Road 7, go 10.5 miles northwest on State Road 314, 2 miles southwest. A picnic shelter is $30. 32 sites with water and electric, 2 handicap sites. From November 1st to February 28th, sites with water and electric hookups are $7; from March 1st to October 31st, sites with water and electric hookups are $10. Recreational vehicle maximum length is 65'. This campground requires a 2 night minimum stay on weekends and a 3 night stay on holiday weekends. Open all year. NRRS (April 1st to September 30th).

HURRICANE LANDING CAMPGROUND

From Abbeville, go 3.6 miles west (left) at sign. 16 primitive sites. From April 1st to September 30th, sites are $6; from October 1st to March 31st, some sites are available and are free. Recreational vehicle maximum length is 20'. Open all year.

OAK GROVE AREA CAMPGROUND

From Batesville, I-55, exit 246, go east on State Road 35, below the dam. An amphitheater and a picnic shelter are available. 82 sites, 1 pull through site. Will probably be closed all of 2007 for upgrading to a Class A campground (Call for information).

PATS BLUFF CAMPGROUND

From Batesville/I-55, exit 243A, go 9 miles on Highway 6, go north on County Road, watch for signs. A picnic shelter is $30. 18 sites. From April 1st to September 30th, sites are $6; from October 1st to March 31st, some sites are available and are free. Recreational vehicle maximum length is 20'. Open all year.

SLEEPY BEND CAMPGROUND

On the northwest side of Lower Lake, below John Kyle State Park. 50 sites. From April 1st to September 30th, sites are $5; from October 1st to March 31st, some sites are available and are free. Recreational vehicle maximum length is 20'. Open all year.

TENNESSEE-TOMBIGBEE WATERWAY (MB) 6

The Tennessee-Tombigbee Waterway is a navigable link between the lower Tennessee Valley and the Gulf of Mexico. Stretching 234 miles from Demopolis, AL to Pickwick Lake in the northeast corner of MS., this man-make channel has a series of ten locks and dams forming ten pools. Fishing piers are available. Off the road vehicles are prohibited. Jamie L. Whitten Historical Center, Fulton, MS (662) 862-5414 and the Bay Springs Resource & Visitor Center, Bay Springs Lake, near Dennis, MS (662) 423-1287, open daily except during winter months and on some federal holidays. Interpretive exhibits, artifacts, 120 seat auditorium with audio/visual equipment, group tours, (662) 862-5414. Checkout time is 3 p.m., visitor vehicle to 9 p.m., a fee applies. Contact Resource Manager, Waterway Management Center, 3606 West Plymouth Road, Columbus, MS 39701. (662) 327-2142.

BLUE BLUFF CAMPGROUND

From Aberdeen/Junction Commerce Street (Highway 145), go north on Meridian (center of downtown), cross railroad tracks and bridge, 1st right (signs). A picnic shelter, fish cleaning station and handicap accessible fishing are available. 92 sites with water and electric, 3 pull through sites, 4 full hookups, 4 - 50 ampere, 2 handicap sites with water and electric, 1 handicap site with water and 50 ampere. Sites with water and electric hookups are $16; sites with waterfront and sites with full hookups are $18. Recreational vehicle maximum length is in excess of 65'. This campground requires a 2 night minimum stay on weekends and a 3 night stay on holidays. Open all year. (662) 369-2832. NRRS (March 1st to September 15th).

DEWAYNE HAYES CAMPGROUND

From Columbus, go 4 miles north on United States Route 45, 1.5 miles west on State Road 373, 2 miles southwest on Stenson Creek Road, 0.5 mile left on Barton's Ferry Road. A fish cleaning station and picnic shelter are available, and an interactive water sprayground (New - replaces swimming beach). 110 sites, 100 with water and electric, 10 primitive tent only walk-in sites, 25 full hookups, 3 handicap sites. Tent only walk-in sites are $10; sites with water and electric hookups are $16; premium sites with water and electric hookups are $18; sites with full hookups are $20. Recreational vehicle maximum length is in excess of 65'. This campground requires a 2 night minimum stay on weekends and a 3 night stay on holidays. Open all year. (662) 434-6939. NRRS (March 1st to September 15th).

PINEY GROVE CAMPGROUND

(Bay Springs Lake, Dennis, MS) From Tishomingo, go west on State Road 25, south on State Road 30, go southeast. Picnic shelters, a fish cleaning station and an amphitheater are available. 141 sites with water and electric, 6 pull through sites, 2 handicap sites. Sites with water and electric are $18; premium sites with water and electric are $20. There are also 10 primitive sites, access by water, free. Recreational vehicle maximum length is in excess of 65'. This campground requires a 2 night minimum stay on weekends and a 3 night stay on holidays. Open from March 23rd to November 11th. (662) 862-7070. NRRS.

TOWN CREEK CAMPGROUND

From Columbus/Junction United States Route 45 north, go west on State Road 50, 1 mile west of Tenn-Tom Bridge on State Road 50, 1.5 miles north, turn right on J. Witherspoon Road. A fish cleaning station is available. 110 sites, 100 with water and electric, 10 primitive tent only walk-in sites, 3 pull through sites, 16 full hookups, 4 handicap sites. Tent only walk-in sites are $10; sites with water and electric hookups are $16; premium sites with water and electric hookups and sites with full hookups are $18. There is a $3 fee for 3rd and 4th vehicles and for visitors. Recreational vehicle maximum length is in excess of 65'. This campground requires a 2 night minimum stay on weekends and a 3 night stay on holidays. Open all year. (662)494-4885. NRRS (March 1st to September 15th).

WHITTEN CAMPGROUND

Adjacent to the city of Fulton. From Junction United States Route 78, go north on Highway 25, west on Main Street to Waterway, 2 miles north (signs). Picnic shelters and an amphitheater are available, and alcohol is prohibited. 61 sites with water and electric, 3 pull through sites, 4 handicap sites. Sites with water and electric hookups are $18; premium sites with water and electric hookups are $20. A fee is charged for the 3rd and 4th vehicles. Recreational vehicle maximum length is in excess of 65'. This campground requires a 2 night minimum stay on weekends and a 3 night stay on holidays. Open all year. (662) 862-7070. NRRS.

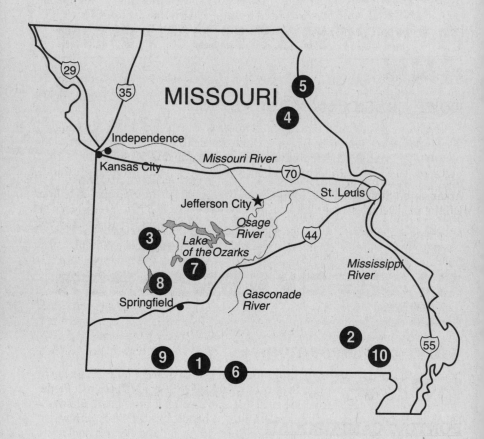

MISSOURI

MISSOURI

STATE CAPITAL:
Jefferson City
NICKNAME:
Show-Me State

24th State - 1821

Site reservation, National Recreation Reservation Service
(NRRS), toll free, 1-877-444-6777; TDD 877-833-6777,
www.recreation.gov, (Master, Visa, American Express
& Discover cards).

**Little Rock District - Where posted, a fee is charged for use of
dump station by non-campers. An extra fee may be charged for
sites with water hookups.**

BULL SHOALS LAKE (LR) 1

A 45,440 surface area acre lake located 15 miles west of Mountain Home,
Arkansas on State Road 178, southeast of Branson near the Missouri state line.
Off the road vehicles are prohibited and checkout time is 3 p.m. Free sites in off
season may have reduced amenities. Resource Manager, Bull Shoals Lake, P. O.
Box 367, Mountain Home, AR 72653. (870) 425-2700. See AR listing.

BEAVER CREEK CAMPGROUND

From Kissee Mills (sign), go 2.5 miles south on Route O. A picnic shelter for up
to 50 people and 1 vehicle is $40. 36 sites, 13 - 50 ampere, 1 pull through site.
Sites with electric hookups are $16. Recreational vehicle maximum length is
40'. This campground requires a 2 night minimum stay on weekends and a 3
night stay on holiday weekends. Open from March 1st to October 31st. (870)
546-3708. NRRS.

PONTIAC CAMPGROUND

From Junction United States Route 160, go 4.7 miles south on State Road 5, 7.3
miles southwest to Pontiac on Route W, 0.2 mile south. A picnic shelter for up
to 50 people and 10 vehicles is $40. 39 sites, 31 with electric, 1 double site. Sites
without electric hookups are $12; sites with electric hookups are $16; a double
site is $32. Recreational vehicle maximum length is 40'. This campground

requires a 2 night minimum stay on weekends and a 3 night stay on holiday weekends. Open from April 1st to September 30th. (870) 679-2222. NRRS (May 19th to September 15th).

RIVER RUN CAMPGROUND

From Forsyth, go east on State Road 60 across bridge, south across bridge (sign), go west. 32 sites with electric. Sites with electric hookups are $16; double sites are $32. Recreational vehicle maximum length is 40'. This campground requires a 2 night minimum stay on weekends and a 3 night stay on holiday weekends. Open from March 1st to October 31st. (870) 546-3646).

THEODOSIA CAMPGROUND

From Isabella (sign), go 3 miles west on United States Route 160, across bridge, go south (left). A picnic shelter is $40 and a convenience store is located nearby. 31 sites with electric, 6 - 50 ampere, 1 double site. Sites with electric hookups are $16; a double site is $32. Recreational vehicle maximum length is 45'. This campground requires a 2 night minimum stay on weekends and a 3 night stay on holiday weekends. Open from April 1st to October 31st. (870) 273-4626. NRRS.

CLEARWATER LAKE (LR) 2

A 1,600 acre surface area lake located 5 miles southwest of Piedmont on County Road HH, off State Road 34, east of Springfield, northwest of Mark Twain National Forest, in southeast Missouri. Primitive camping is permitted project wide with a permit. A fee is charged for non camper use of the dump station. Free sites in off season may have reduced amenities. Operations Manager, Clearwater Lake, RR 3, Box 3559D, Piedmont, MO 63957-9559. (573) 223-7777.

BLUFF VIEW CAMPGROUND

From Piedmont/Junction State Road 34, go 0.9 mile north on State Road 49, 6.9 miles west on County Road AA. A picnic shelter for up to 40 people and 9 vehicles is $40. 60 sites, 44 with electric, 20 - 50 ampere. Sites without electric hookups are $12; sites with electric hookups are $16; sites with water and 50 ampere service are $20. Recreational vehicle maximum length is in excess of 65'. This campground requires a 2 night minimum stay on weekends and a 3 night stay on holidays. Open from May 13th to September 13th. NRRS.

NEW HIGHWAY K CAMPGROUND

From Annapolis, go 5 miles southwest on County Road K, after bridge, west side (signs). A picnic shelter for up to 40 people and 16 vehicles is $50. 84 sites, 55 with electric, 20 - 59 ampere, 2 pull through sites. Sites without electric hookups are $12; sites with electric hookups are $16; sites with water and 50 ampere service are $20. Recreational vehicle maximum length is 60'. This campground requires a 2 night minimum stay on weekends and a 3 night stay on holidays. Open from April 1st to October 31st. NRRS (May 19th to September 15th).

PIEDMONT CAMPGROUND

From Piedmont, go 7 miles southwest on State Road 34, 5.6 miles southwest on County Road HH, 1.5 miles northeast on Lake Road (signs). Group camping area for up to 40 people and 10 vehicles is $40 and two picnic shelters for up to 50 people and 11 vehicles are $50. 94 sites, 83 with electric, 9 - 50 ampere, 7 pull through sites, 1 handicap site with electric. Sites without electric hookups are $12; sites with electric hookups are $16; sites with water and 50 ampere service are $20. Recreational vehicle maximum length is in excess of 65'. This campground requires a 2 night minimum stay on weekends and a 3 night stay on holidays. Open from April 1st to September 30th. NRRS (May 15th to September 15th).

RIVER ROAD LEFT BANK CAMPGROUND

From Piedmont, go 6 miles southwest on State Road 34, 5.6 miles southwest on County Road HH, below dam. Three picnic shelters, S1 & S2 for up to 50 people and 16 vehicles, and Zebo for up to 50 people and 9 vehicles are $50. A convenience store is located nearby. 112 sites, 99 with electric, 6 - 50 ampere, 11 pull through sites, 1 handicap site with water and 50 ampere, 1 handicap site with electric. Sites without electric hookups are $12; sites with electric hookups are $16; sites with water and 50 ampere service are $20. Recreational vehicle maximum length is in excess of 65'. This campground requires a 2 night minimum stay on weekends and a 3 night stay on holidays. Open January 1st to October 31st. NRRS (May 14th to September 14th).

WEBB CREEK CAMPGROUND

From Ellington, to 2.6 miles southeast on State Road 21, 10.3 miles southeast on County Road H. A picnic shelter is available. 35 sites, 25 with electric, some pull through sites, overflow camping nearby. Sites without electric hookups are $12; sites with electric hookups are $16. Open from May 15th to September 15th.

HARRY S TRUMAN LAKE (KC) 3

A 55,600 acre surface area lake located near Warsaw on United States Route 65, 94 miles southeast of Kansas City. Exhibit area, interpretive programs and checkout time is 6 p.m. Golf courses are located at Warsaw and Clinton. Resource Manager, Harry S. Truman Lake, Route. 2, Box 29A, Warsaw, MO 65355-9603. (660) 438-7317.

BERRY BEND CAMPGROUND

From Warsaw, go 4.4 miles west on State Road 7, 3 miles west on State Road Z, 1.8 miles south on Berry Bend Road. A picnic shelter, amphitheater, horseshoe pits and change house are available. 189 sites, 115 with electric, 4 pull through sites, 11 handicap sites. From October 16th to April 13th, walk-in sites without electric are $8; from April 14th to October 15th, sites without electric hookups are $12; premium sites without electric hookups are $14; sites with electric hookups are $16; premium sites with electric hookups are $18. Recreational vehicle maximum length is in excess of 65'. This campground requires a 2 night minimum stay on weekends and a 3 night stay on holiday weekends. Open all year. (660) 438-3872. NRRS (April 15th to October 15th).

BERRY BEND EQUESTRIAN CAMPGROUND

From Warsaw, go 4.4 miles west on State Road 7, 3 miles west on State Road Z, 1.8 miles south on Berry Bend Road. Campers must have a horse. Two picnic shelters for up to 64 people and 30 vehicles are $25, group camping area is available, and call for special rules on horses (660) 438-3812). 89 sites, 24 with electric. From April 15th to October 15th, sites without electric hookups are $12; premium sites without electric hookps are $14; sites with electric hookups are $16; premium sites with electric hookups are $18. From October 16th to April 14th, walk-in sites are $6. Recreational vehicle maximum length is in excess of 65'. This campground requires a 2 night minimum stay on weekends and a 3 night stay on holiday weekends. Open all year. NRRS (April 15th to October 14th).

BUCKSAW CAMPGROUND

From Clinton, go 7.8 miles east on State Road 7, 2.5 miles south on County Road U (signs). An amphitheater, fish cleaning station, and a change house are available, boat rentals are nearby, and there is a handicap accessible swimming area. 306 sites, 123 with electric, 38 pull through sites, 12 - 50 ampere, 8 handicap sites. From October 16th to April 14th, walk-in sites are $6; from April 15th to October 15th, sites without electric hookups are $12; premium sites without electric hookups are $14; sites with electric hookups are $16; premium sites with electric hookups are $18; premium sites with 50 ampere service are $20. Recreational vehicle maximum length is in excess of 65'. This campground requires a 2 night minimum stay on weekends and a 3 night stay on holiday weekends. Open all year. (660) 447-3402. NRRS (April 15th to October 15th).

LONG SHOAL CAMPGROUND

From Warsaw, go 4.4 miles west on State Road 7 (signs). A picnic shelter for up to 48 people and 25 vehicles is $20, boat rentals are nearby and a change house is available, and there is a handicap accessible swimming area. 130 sites, 3 pull through sites, 2 full hookups, 6 handicap sites. From October 16th to April 14th, walk-in sites without electric hookups are $6; from April 15th to October 15th, sites without electric hookups are $12; premium sites without electric hookups are $14; sites with electric hookups are $16; premium sites with electric hookups are $18. Recreational vehicle maximum length is in excess of 65'. This campground requires a 2 night minimum stay on weekends and a 3 night stay on holiday weekends. Open all year. (660) 438-2342. NRRS (April 15th to October 13th).

OSAGE BLUFF CAMPGROUND

From Warsaw/Junction State Road 7, go 3 miles south on United States Route 65, 3 miles southwest on State Road 83, go 1 mile west on State Road 295(signs). Boat rentals are located nearby. 68 sites, 4 handicap sites. From October 16th to April 14th, sites without electric hookups are $8; from April 14th to October 14th, sites without electric hookups are $12; premium sites without electric hookups are $14; sites with electric hookups are $16; premium sites with electric hookups are $18. Recreational vehicle maximum length is in excess of 65'. This campground requires a 2 night minimum stay on weekends and a 3 night stay on holiday weekends. Open all year. NRRS (April 14th to October 14th).

SPARROWFOOT CAMPGROUND

From Clinton, go 6 miles south on State Road 13, 1.5 miles east (signs). Three picnic shelters for up to 48 people and 30 vehicles are $20, horseshoe pits and a change house are available. 108 sites, 3 pull through sites, 3 handicap sites. From October 16th to April 14th, sites without electric hookups are $6; from April 15th to October 15th, sites without electric hookups are $12; sites with electric hookups are $16; premium sites with electric hookups are $18. Recreational vehicle maximum length is in excess of 65'. This campground requires a 2 night minimum stay on weekends and a 3 night stay on holiday weekends. Open all year. NRRS (April 15th to October 15th).

TALLEY BEND CAMPGROUND

From Lowry City/Junction State Road 13, go 7 miles east on County Road C, on the south side across bridge (signs). 84 sites, 78 with electric, 8 pull through sites, 3 handicap sites. From October 1st to April 14th, sites without electric hookups are $12; from April 15th to September 30th, sites without electric hookups are $12; sites with electric hookups are $16; premium sites with electric hookups are $18. Recreational vehicle maximum length is in excess of 65'. This campground requires a 2 night minimum stay on weekends and a 3 night stay on holiday weekends. Open all year. NRRS (April 15th to October 15th).

THIBAUT POINT CAMPGROUND

From Warsaw, go 4.3 miles north on United States Route 65, 2.8 miles west on County Road T, 1 mile south on County Road 218 on a gravel road. Three group camping areas (Handicap accessible), PRC for tent groups up to 150 people and 20 vehicles is $50, GSB for up to 150 people and 40 vehicles is $80, and GRP with electric for up to 150 people and 40 vehicles is $100, and two picnic shelters for up to 64 people and 1 vehicle are $25. Horseshoe pits and a change house are available. 50 sites, 1 full hookup, 5 handicap sites. From October 1st to April 14th, sites without electric are $8; from April 15th to September 30th, sites without electric hookups are $12; sites with electric hookups are $16; premium sites with electric hookups are $18. Recreational vehicle maximum length is in excess of 65'. This campground requires a 2 night minimum stay on weekends and a 3 night stay on holiday weekends. Open all year. (660) 438-2767. NRRS (April 15th to September 30th).

WINDSOR CROSSING CAMPGROUND

From Lincoln, go 11.7 miles west on County Road C, 2.3 miles south on County Road PP, on the east side (signs). A change house is available. 47 sites, 6 pull through sites, 3 handicap sites. From October 16th to April 14th, sites without electric hookups are $6; from April 15th to October 15th, sites without electric hookups are $8. Recreational vehicle maximum length is in excess of 65'. This campground requires a 2 night minimum stay on weekends and a 3 night stay on holiday weekends. Open all year. (660) 477-9275. NRRS (April 15th to September 30th).

MARK TWAIN LAKE (SL) 4

An 18,600 acre surface area lake located 14 miles southeast of Monroe City on State Road J, 120 miles northwest of St. Louis. Checkout time is 4 p.m., visitor center, self guided tours of Hydroelectric Power Plant on weekends from May through August, and special events throughout summer. The David C. Berti shooting range is available and located under three covered shelters which are handicap accessible. For lake information, 24 hours, recorded, call (573) 735-2619. Mark Twain Birth Place State Historical Site at lake (State Park, managed by the Department of Natural Resources). Operations Manager, Mark Twain Lake, 20642 Highway J, Monroe City, MO 63456-9359. (573) 735-4097.

FRANK RUSSELL CAMPGROUND

From Monroe City/Junction United States Route 36, go 4 miles east on United States Route 24/36, 9 miles south on Route J, 1 mile north of dam. An amphitheater is available, and there is a horse corral with stalls on a first come first served basis. 65 sites with electric. Sites with electric hookups are $15. Recreational vehicle maximum length is in excess of 65'. This campground requires a 2 night minimum stay on weekends and a 3 night stay on holidays. Open from April 20th to October 8th. NRRS (April 20th to October 9th).

INDIAN CREEK CAMPGROUND

From Monroe City, go 6 miles south on United States Route 24, 1.7 miles south on Route HH. A group camping area is by reservation only at $30, two picnic shelters for up to 100 people and 1 vehicle are $30 and a fish cleaning station and an amphitheater are available. 247 sites, 203 with electric, 20 primitive tent only hike-in sites, 55 full hookups, 1 handicap site. Tent sites are $8; sites without electic hookups are $7.50; sites with electric hookups are $16; sites with full hookups are $22. Recreational vehicle maximum length is in excess of 65'. This campground requires a 2 night minimum stay on weekends and a 3 night stay on holiday weekends. Open from March 30th to November 19th. NRRS.

JOHN C. "JACK" BRISCOE GROUP CAMPGROUND

At the dam, south side, go 0.5 mile on Route J. Six group camping areas, GRP1 & GRP4 for up to 32 people and 4 vehicles are $60 and GRP2, GRP5 & GRP6 for up to 24 people and 3 vehicles are $45, a picnic shelter for up to 125 people and 10 vehicles is $30. A visitor center and horseshoe pits are available. 20 sites. Sites are $15 per site, a minimum of 3 sites are required. Check in at the Frank Russell Recreation Area. Recreational vehicle maximum length is 60'. This campground requires a 2 night minimum stay on weekends and a 3 night stay on holidays. Open from April 20th to September 10th. NRRS.

RAY BEHRENS CAMPGROUND

From Perry/Junction State Road 154, go 6.6 miles north on Route J, north side. A picnic shelter for up to 125 people and 1 vehicle is $30, an amphitheater and a fish cleaning station are available. 165 sites with water and electric, 133 - 50 ampere, 1 handicap site. Sites with water and electric hookups are $15; sites with full hookups are $20. Recreational vehicle maximum length is in excess of 65'. This campground requires a 2 night minimum stay on weekends and a 3 night stay on holiday weekends. Open from March 30th to November 19th. NRRS (April 1st to October 22nd).

MISSISSIPPI RIVER (PUA) (RI) 5

Information, contact Park Ranger, RR #4, L&D # 21, Quincy, IL 62301, (217) 228-0890. See IL, IA & WI listings.

FENWAY LANDING CAMPGROUND

From Canton, go 4.5 miles north on United States Route 61, go east on County Road 454, the camping area is located just across the levee. 15 sites. All sites are free. Open all year.

NORFOLK LAKE (LR) 6

Located 4 miles northeast of Norfolk, Arkansas, on Arkansas State Road 177, near the Missouri state line. Resource Manager, Norfolk Lake, P. O. Box 2070, Mountain Home, AR 72654. (501) 425-2700. See AR listing.

TECUMSEH CAMPGROUND

At Tecumseh on both sides of the lake. 7 sites. All sites are $9. Open from April 1st to September 30th.

UDALL CAMPGROUND

From Udall, go 1.5 miles west on State Road O, 0.7 miles on access road. 7 sites. All sites are $9. Open from April 1st to September 30th.

POMME DE TERRE LAKE (KC) 7

A 7,790 acre surface area lake with 113 miles of shoreline located 3 miles south of Hermitage on State Road 254, 140 miles southeast of Kansas City. Free sites in off season may have reduced amenities. There is a reservation fee of $20 for picnic shelters. Resource Manager, Pomme de Terre Lake, Route 2, Box 2160, Hermitage, MO 65668-9509. (417) 745-6411.

DAMSITE CAMPGROUND

From Hermitage, go 3 miles southeast on State Road 254, go west at Carson's Corner. Two picnic shelters and an amphitheater are available, and there is a handicap accessible fishing area. 129 sites, 64 with electric, 10 tent only sites, 22 pull through sites, some 50 ampere, 2 handicap sites. From April 16th to October 15th, tent only sites and sites without electric hookups are $12; premium sites without electric hookups are $14; sites with electric hookups are $16; premium sites with electric hookups are $18; sites with water and electric hookups are $20; sites with full hookups are $22. From October 15th to April 14th, some sites without hookups are $12. Recreational vehicle maximum length is 45'. This campground requires a 2 night minimum stay on weekends and a 3 night stay on holiday weekends. Open all year. (417) 745-2244. NRRS (April 16th to October 15th).

LIGHTFOOT LANDING CAMPGROUND

From Elkton, go 2.3 miles south on State Road 83, 3.4 miles east on County Road RB. Three group camping areas for up to 50 people and 16 vehicles are $30, a picnic shelter for up to 50 people and 16 vehicles, and a heated fishing pier and horseshoe pits are available. Boat rentals are located nearby. 40 sites, 29 with water and electric, 5 tent only sites, 6 pull through sites, 29 - 50 ampere, 1 handicap site with water and 50 ampere. From April 15th to October 14th, tent only sites are $12; sites without electric hookups are $14; sites with water and 50 ampere service are $20. From October 15th to April 14th, tent only sites are available and are free. Recreational vehicle maximum length is in excess of 65'. This campground requires a 2 night minimum stay on weekends and a 3 night stay on holiday weekends. Open all year. (417) 282-6890. NRRS (April 16th to October 14th).

NEMO LANDING CAMPGROUND

From Nemo/Junction County Road D, go 1 mile southwest on State Road 64 before bridge. A picnic shelter, amphitheater and horseshoe pits are available, and boat rentals are nearby. 119 sites, 55 with electric, 3 tent only sites, 17 pull through sites, 2 - 50 ampere, 1 handicap site with water and 50 ampere. From April 16th to October 15th, tent only sites and sites without electric hookups are $12; premium sites without electric hookups are $14; sites with electric hookups are $16; premium sites with electric hookups and a site with water and 50 ampere service are $18; premium sites with water and electric hookups and a premium site with water and 50 ampere service are $20. From October 16th to April 15th, some sites without electric hookups are available and are free; sites with water and 50 ampere service are $18. Recreational vehicle maximum length is 60'. This campground requires a 2 night minimum stay on weekends and a 3 night stay on holiday weekends. Open all year. (417) 993-5529. NRRS (April 16th to October 15th).

OUTLET CAMPGROUND

From Hermitage, go 3 miles southeast on State Road 254, go west at Carson's Corner, below dam on west side of outlet. A group camping area is $30, a picnic shelter and horseshoe pits are available. 28 sites, 14 with electric, 10 pull through sites. Sites without hookups are $10; sites with electric hookups are $14. From October 16th to April 15th, some sites without electric hookups are available and are free. Recreational vehicle maximum length is 50'. This campground requires a 2 night minimum stay on weekends and a 3 night stay on holidays. Open all year. (417) 745-2290. NRRS (April 16th to October 15th).

PITTSBURG LANDING CAMPGROUND

From Pittsburg/Junction County Road J, go 1 mile south on State Road 64, 3 miles east on County Road RA. A picnic shelter is available. 40 primitive sites. All sites are free. Open all year.

WHEATLAND CAMPGROUND

From Wheatland/Junction United States Route 54, go 4.2 miles south on State Road 83, 2 miles east on State Road 254, 1 mile south on State Road 205. A picnic shelter for up to 75 people is $20. 83 sites, 67 with electric, 9 tent only sites, 8 pull through sites, 14 - 50 ampere, 1 handicap site with water and electric. From April 16th to October 15th, sites without electric hookups are $12; premium sites without electric hookups are $14; sites with electric hookups are $16; sites with water and electric hookups and water and 50 ampere service are $20. From October 16th to April 15th, sites without electric hookups are available and are free. Recreational vehicle maximum length is 35'. This campground requires a 2 night minimum stay on weekends and a 3 night stay on holiday weekends. Open all year. (417) 282-5267. NRRS (April 16th to October 15th).

STOCKTON LAKE (KC) 8

A 24,900 acre surface area lake with 298 miles of shoreline is located on east side of Stockton on State Road 32, 136 miles southeast of Kansas City. Free sites in off season may have reduced amenities. Operations Manager, Stockton Lake, 16435 East Stockton Lake Drive, Stockton, MO 65785-9471. (417) 276-3113.

CEDAR RIDGE CAMPGROUND

From Bona/Junction State Road 215, go 0.5 mile north on State Road 245, 0.7 mile north on County Road RA. A picnic shelter is available and there is a convenience store nearby. 54 sites, 21 with electric hookups, 12 tent only sites, plus 5 overflow. From April 16th to September 30th, tent only sites are $12; sites without electric hookups are $12; premium sites without electric hookups are $14; sites with electric hookups are $16; premium sites with electric hookups are $18; from October 1st to April 15th, sites without electric hookups are available and are free. Recreational vehicle maximum length is 60'. This campground requires a 2 night minimum stay on weekends and a 3 night stay on holiday weekends. Open all year.(417) 995-2045. NRRS (April 16th to September 30th).

CRABTREE COVE CAMPGROUND

From Stockton/Junction State Road 39, go 3.5 miles east on State Road 32, go southwest. A picnic shelter is available and there is a handicap accessible fishing area. 61 sites, 31 with electric, 4 tent only sites, plus 5 overflow, 3 pull through sites, 2 handicap sites without electric, 1 handicap site with electric. From April 16th to September 30th, tent only sites are $10; sites without electric hookups are $12; premium sites without electric hookups are $14; sites with electric hookups are $16; premium sites with electric hookups are $18; from October 1st to October 31st and from March 15th to April 15th, sites without electric hookups are available and are free. Recreational vehicle maximum length is 50'. This campground requires a 2 night minimum stay on weekends and a 3 night stay on holiday weekends. Open all year. NRRS (April 13th to September 30th).

HAWKER POINT NORTH & SOUTH CAMPGROUND

From Stockton/Junction State Road 32, go 6.2 miles south on State Road 39, 5.2 miles east on County Road H. 62 sites, 30 with electric, 6 at the equestrian trail head, 1 pull through site. Equestrian sites are $10; from April 16th to September 30th, sites without electric hookups are $12; premium sites without electric hookups are $14; sites with electric hookups are $16; premium sites with electric hookups are $18; from October 1st to April 15th, some sites without electric hookups are available and are free. Recreational vehicle maximum length is 60'. This campground requires a 2 night minimum stay on weekends and a 3 night stay on holiday weekends. Open all year. (417) 276-7266. NRRS (April 16th to September 30th).

MASTERS EAST & WEST CAMPGROUN

From Fair Play/Junction State Road 123, go 3.7 miles west on State Road 32, 2.6 miles south on County Road RA, go west. A group camping area for up to 34 people and 18 vehicles is from $30 to $35 and a picnic shelter is $30. Scuba diving is permitted. 66 sites, 8 overflow sites, 9 pull through sites. Sites, 3rd price, are $12; sites, 2nd price, are $10; premium sites are $14. Recreational vehicle maximum length is 60'. May 11th to September 9th. (417) 276-6847. NRRS.

ORLEANS TRAIL NORTH & SOUTH CAMPGROUND

rom Stockton, southeast corner, go 0.5 mile east on County Road RB, 0.5 mile right on Blake Street. A group camping area for up to 90 people and 45 vehicles with 12 sites and electric hookups is from $85 to $110 and a picnic shelter is $30. 118 sites, 5 at the equestrian trail head, 4 pull through sites. From May

11th to September 9th, sites are $12; from September 10th to May 10th, some sites are available and are free. Recreational vehicle maximum length is 50'. This campground requires a 2 night minimum stay on weekends and a 3 night stay on holiday weekends. Open all year. (417) 276-6948. NRRS (May 11th to September 9th).

RUARK BLUFF EAST CAMPGROUND

From Greenfield/Junction United States Route 160, go 6.4 miles north on County Road H, before the bridge. A group camping area for up to 80 people and 36 vehicles is $85 Monday through Thursday and $110 Friday through Sunday and on holidays. There is a handicap accessible fishing area. 91 sites, 28 with electric, 6 tent only sites, 4 pull through sites, 1 handicap site. From April 16th to September 30th, sites without electric hookups are $12; premium sites without electric hookups are $14; sites with electric hookups are $16; premium sites with electric hookups are $18; from October 1st to April 15th, sites without electric hookups are available and are free. Recreational vehicle maximum length is in excess of 65'. This campground requires a 2 night minimum stay on weekends and a 3 night stay on holiday weekends. Open all year. (417) 637-5303. NRRS (April 16th to September 30th).

RUARK BLUFF WEST CAMPGROUND

From Greenfield/Junction United States Route 160, go 6.4 miles north on County Road H, before bridge. A group camping area for up to 75 people and 35 vehicles and 11 sites with electric hookups is $85 Monday through Thursday and $110 Friday through Sunday and on holidays. 74 sites, 46 with electric, 1 handicap site. Sites without electric hookups are $12; premium sites without electric hookups are $14; sites with electric hookups are $16; premium sites with electric hookups are $18. Recreational vehicle maximum length 25'. Recreational vehicle maximum length is 50'. This campground requires a 2 night minimum stay on weekends and a 3 night stay on holiday weekends. Open from April 16th to September 30th. (417) 637-5279. NRRS.

TABLE ROCK LAKE (LR) 9

A 43,100 acre surface area lake located 3.4 miles southwest of Branson on State Road 165, west of United States Route 65. Exhibits, auditorium audio-visual presentations, nature trail, off the road vehicles are prohibited, checkout time is 3 p.m., and free sites in off season may have reduced amenities. Resource Manager, Upper White River Project Office, 4600 State Road 165 Ste. A, Branson, MO 65616-8976. (417) 334-4101. See AR listing.

AUNT'S CREEK CAMPGROUND

From Branson West/Junction State Road 76, go 3.9 miles southwest on State Road 13, 2.7 miles west on County Road 00 & County Road 00-9 (signs). A picnic shelter for up to 60 people and 25 vehicles is $50. A convenience store and restaurants are located nearby. 56 sites, 53 with electric, 10 - 50 ampere, 6 pull through sites. Sites without electric hookups are $12; sites with electric hookups are $16; a double site is $28. Recreational vehicle maximum length is in excess of 65'. This campground requires a 3 night minimum stay on holiday weekends. Open from May 1st to October 28th. (417) 739-2792. NRRS.

BAXTER CAMPGROUND

From Lampe/Junction State Road 13, go 4.8 miles west on State Road H (signs). 54 sites, 25 with electric, 1 - 50 ampere, 2 tent only sites, 2 pull through sites. Tent only sites and sites without electric hookups are $12; sites with electric hookups are $16. Recreational vehicle maximum length is in excess of 65'. This campground requires a 3 night minimum stay on holiday weekends. Open from April 1st to September 30th. (417) 779-5370. NRRS.

BIG M CAMPGROUND

From Mano/Junction State Road east, go 1.3 miles southeast on State Road M (signs). A picnic shelter is available and a convenience store is located nearby. 54 sites, 16 with electric, 10 full hookups, 1 double site with electric, 1 pull through site. Sites without electric hookups are $12; sites with electric hookups are $16; sites with water and electric hookups are $18; a double site is $28. Recreational vehicle maximum length is in excess of 65'. This campground requires a 3 night minimum stay on holiday weekends. Open from April 1st to September 14th). (417) 271-3190. NRRS.

CAMPBELL POINT CAMPGROUND

From Shell Knob/Junction County Road 39-5, go 5.1 miles southeast on State Road YY. A picnic shelter for up to 60 people and 20 vehicles is $50, and there is a convenience store nearby. 76 sites, 38 with electric, 3 - 50 ampere, 2 full hookup, 1 double site, 4 pull through sites. Sites without electric are $12; sites with electric hookups are $16; a double site is $20. Recreational vehicle maximum length is in excess of 65'. This campground requires a 3 night minimum stay on holiday weekends. Open from April 1st to September 27th. (417) 858-3903. NRRS.

CAPE FAIR CAMPGROUND

From Reeds Springs/Junction State Road 248, go 1.4 miles south on State Road 13, 8 miles west on State Road 76 to Cape Fair, southwest on County Road 76-82 (signs). A picnic shelter for up to 60 people and 25 vehicles is $50. 82 sites, 69 with electric, 1 double site, 7 pull through sites. Sites without electric hookups are $12; sites with electric hookups are $16; sites with water and electric hookups are $17; a double site is $28. Recreational vehicle maximum length is in excess of 65'. This campground requires a 3 night minimum stay on holiday weekends. Open from April 1st to October 28th. (417) 538-2220. NRRS.

EAGLE ROCK CAMPGROUND

From Eagle Rock, go 3 miles south on State Road 86, right before bridge (signs). There is a convenience store nearby. 63 sites, 29 with electric, 1 full hookup, 6 pull through sites. Sites without electric hookups are $12; sites with electric hookups are $16; premium sites with water and electric hookups are $17; a site with full hookups is $18. Recreational vehicle maximum length is in excess of 65'. This campground requires a 3 night minimum stay on holiday weekends. Open from April 1st to October 30th). (417) 271-3215. NRRS.

INDIAN POINT CAMPGROUND

From Branson West/Junction State Road 13, go 3 miles west on State Road 76, 2.8 miles south on Indian Point Road. A group camping area for up to 64 people and 11 vehicles is $80, a picnic shelter for up to 60 people and 25 vehicles is $50, and a fish hatchery is nearby. 86 sites, 77 with electric, 36 - 50 ampere, 2 tent only sites, 1 full hookup. Sites without electric hookups are $12; sites with electric hookups are $16; sites with water and electric hookups are $17; 1 site with full hookups is $18. Recreational vehicle maximum length is in excess of 65'. This campground requires a 3 night minimum stay on holiday weekends. Open from April 1st to October 28th. (417) 338-2121. NRRS.

LONG CREEK CAMPGROUND

From Ridgedale/Junction United States Route 65, go 3 miles west on State Road 86, south on 86/50 prior to bridge (signs). A picnic shelter for up to 60 people and 25 vehicles is $50, and a convenience store is nearby. 47 sites, 36 with electric, 2 pull through sites. Tent only sites and sites without electric hookups are $12; sites with electric hookups are $16; sites with water and electric hookups and sites with water and 50 ampere service are $17. Recreational vehicle maximum length is 55'. This campground requires a 3 night minimum stay on holiday weekends. Open April 1st to October 31st. (417) 334-8427. NRRS.

MILL CREEK CAMPGROUND

From Lampe, go 4 miles north on State Road 13, 1 mile west on County Road RB. A picnic shelter for up to 60 people and 18 vehicles is $50, and a convenience store is nearby. 68 sites, 60 with electric, 1 double site, 19 pull through sites. Sites without electric hookups are $12; sites with electric hookups are $16; sites with water and electric hookups are $17; a double site is $20. Recreational vehicle maximum length is in excess of 65'. This campground requires a 3 night minimum stay on holiday weekends. Open from April 1st to October 28th. (417) 779-5378. NRRS.

OLD HIGHWAY 86 CAMPGRUND

From Ridgedale/Junction United States Route 65, go 7.6 miles west on State Road 86, north on State Road UU. Two picnic shelters, SR1 for up to 60 people and 22 vehicles and SR2 for up to 60 people and 10 vehicles are $50. 71 sites, 63 with electric, 33 - 50 ampere, 6 tent only sites, 1 pull through site. Tent only sites are $12; tent only sites with electric are $16; premium tent only sites with electric are $17; premium sites with electric hookups and sites with 50 ampere service are $17; premium sites with water and electric hookups and premium sites with water and 50 ampere service are $18. Recreational vehicle maximum length is in excess of 65'. This campground requires a 3 night minimum stay on holiday weekends. Open from April 1st to October 31st. (417) 779-5376. NRRS (May 1st to October 30th.

VINEY CREEK CAMPGROUND

From Golden, go 4 miles north on State Road J. 46 sites, 24 with water and electric, 1 tent only site, 9 pull through sites. A tent only site and sites without electric hookups are $12; sites with electric hookups are $17. Recreational vehicle maximum length is 50'. Open from May 1st to September 12th. (417) 271-3860. NRRS.

VIOLA CAMPGROUND

From Viola, go 5 miles south on State Road 39, west on State Road 39/48. 57 sites, 26 with electric, 2 double sites, 2 pull through sites. Sites without electric hookups are $12; sites with electric hookups are $16; sites with water and electric hookups are $17; double sites are $20. Recreational vehicle maximum length is in excess of 65'. This campground requires a 3 night minimum stay on holiday weekends. Open from April 1st to September 12th. (417) 858-3904. NRRS.

WAPPAPELLO LAKE (SL) 10

An 8,400 acre surface area lake located 16 miles northeast of Poplar Bluff, north of United States Route 60, east of United States Route 67, on State Road T, 150 miles south of St. Louis. Checkout time is 4 p.m., and campers are required to register at the office for free sites. Interpretation programs, special events during summer and seaplane usage. Overflow camping below the dam is open only when all Corps and private campgrounds in the surrounding area are full, and there is a $3 fee for primitive sites. Daily lake information, (573) 222-8139/1-877-LAKEVIEW, Visitor Center, (573) 222-8773. Operations Manager, Wappapello Lake, 10992 Highway T, Wappapello, MO 63966-9603. (573) 222-8562.

BLUE SPRINGS CAMPGROUND

From the dam, go 17 miles north on State Road D, 1.8 miles south on State Road BB, 1.5 miles west on County Road 531. 2 primitive sites. All sites are free.

CHAONIA LANDING CAMPGROUND

From Poplar Bluff/Junction United States Route 67, go 3.5 miles east on State Road 172, 2.8 miles northeast on State Road W. 12 sites. All sites are $9. Recreational vehicle maximum length is 22'. Open all year.

GREENVILLE CAMPGROUND

From Greenville, go 2.5 miles south on United States Route 67, before bridge (signs). A picnic shelter for up to 100 people and 55 vehicles is $50, an amphitheater and horseshoe pits are available. 104 single sites and 8 double sites with water and electric, 5 hike-in sites, 3 handicap sites, 1 pull through sites. Sites with water and electric hookups are $16; double sites with water and electric hookups are $32. Recreational vehicle maximum length is in excess of 65'. Open from March 30th to November 20th. (573) 224-3884. NRRS.

ISLANDS CAMPING AREA

Accessible by boat only. Located near dam, southwest side, off shore from Wappapello State Park. Check in at the Redman Creek gatehouse. 6 primitive sites. All sites are $9. Open all year. NRRS.

JOHNSON TRACT NATURAL AREA

From Greenville, go 1.3 miles south on United States Route 67, 2 miles south on State Road D, parking lot on west side across from intersection with County Road 534. 2 primitive hike-in sites. All sites are free.

LOST CREEK LANDING

From dam, go 11 miles north on State Road D, west on Corps Road 9. 3 primitive sites. All sites are free.

NOTHERN PRIMITIVE CAMPING ZONE

Primitive camping is available on all Corps public lands south of Highway 34 to PA 34 on the east side of the St. Francis River and all Corps public lands on the west side, north of where Highway FF intersects with Highway 67. All camping in these areas is free. Open all year.

PEOPLES CREEK CAMPGROUND

From the dam, go 1.7 miles north on State Road D (signs). Group camping area and four picnic shelters, SO6 for up to 30 people and 12 vehicles, SO7 for up to 75 people and 25 vehicles, SO8 & SO9 for up to 15 people and 5 vehicles are $50, and there is a handicap accessible fishing area. 57 single sites with electric, 1 double site with electric, 2 pull through sites, 19 full hookups with 50 ampere service, 1 handicap site. Sites with electric hookups are $16; sites with full hookups and 50 ampere servce are $18; double sites with electric hookups are $32. Recreational vehicle maximum length is in excess of 65'. Open all year. (573) 222-8234. NRRS.

POSSUM CREEK CAMPGROUND

From the dam, go 3 miles north on State Road D, 1.5 miles west on County Road 521 and Road 7. 2 primitive sites. All sites are free.

REDMAN CREEK CAMPGROUND

From the dam, go 1 mile south on State Road T (signs). Three picnic shelters, SO1 for up to 85 people and 30 vehicles, SO2 for up to 600 people and 200 vehicles and SO3 for up to 150 people and 48 vehicles are $50, horseshoe pits are available and boat rentals are located nearby. 116 single sites, 100 with electric, 6 double sites, 4 pull through sites, 70 full hookups with 50 ampere service, 6 handicap sites, 6 boat-in sites. Boat-in sites are $9; sites with electric hookups are $16; sites with full hookups and 50 ampere service are $18; double sites without electric hookups are $32; double sites with full hookups are $36. Open all year. (573) 222-8233. NRRS.

SULPHUR SPRINGS CAMPGROUND

From Greenville, go 1.3 miles south on United States Route 67, 3.2 miles south on State Road D, west on Road 17. 4 primitive sites. All sites are free.

OZARK TRAIL

The Ozark Trail transverses approximately 30 miles through the Wappapello Lake Project and passes within 100' of 19 designated parking areas south of U. S. Highway 67. Free primitive camping is permitted on Corps of Engineer land within 100' of this trail. There are no facilities.

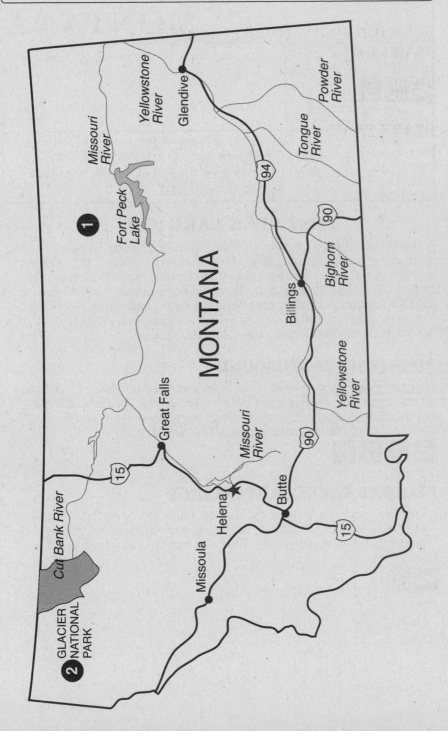

MONTANA

STATE CAPITAL:
Helena
NICKNAME:
Treasure State

41st State - 1889

Site reservation, National Recreation Reservation Service
(NRRS), toll free, 1-877-444-6777; TDD 877-833-6777,
www.recreation.gov, (Master, Visa, American Express
& Discover cards).

FORT PECK LAKE (OM) 1

A 240,000 acre surface area lake with 1520 miles of shoreline is located 10 miles
southwest of Nashua on State Road 117, in northeast Montana, 112 miles west
of North Dakota state line, 76 miles south of Canada. Power Plant Museum
tours by appointment Labor Day to Memorial Day and tours for Memorial Day
to Labor Day are hourly every day starting at 9 a.m., and ending at 4:45 p.m.
For sea plane usage, contact the office. Lake Manager, Fort Peck Lake, P. O. Box
208, Ft. Peck, MT 59223-0208. (406) 526-3411/3224.

BONETRAIL CAMPGROUND

West of the dam on State Road 24, 60 miles southwest on Willow Creek Road
(gravel, impassable when wet, dirt last 30 miles). Picnic shelter is available
and the nearest dump station is 60 miles. 6 primitive sites. All sites are free.
Recreational vehicle maximum length is 16'. Open all year.

CROOKED CREEK CAMPGROUND

From Winnett, southern end of the lake, on Route 200, go north on Drag Ridge
Trail (gravel, weather permitting). Boat ramp is open depending on lake level.
Undesignated sites, primitive, free. Maximum recreational vehicle length is 25'.
Open all year.

DEVILS CREEK CAMPGROUND

From the dam, go south on State Road 24, west on State Road 200 to Jordan, 50 miles northwest on gravel road. A picnic shelter is available and the nearest dump station is 50 miles. 6 primitive sites. All sites are free. Recreational vehicle maximum length 16'. Open all year.

DUCK CREEK CAMPGROUND

From the west end of the dam on State Road 24, go south (signs) on paved road to park. 9 primitive sites, free. Maximum recreational vehicle length is 40'. Open all year.

DOWNSTREAM CAMPGROUND

Located west of spillway below the dam. Picnic shelters are available and group camping area for up to 200 people and 40 vehicles(includes 10 handicap sites) is $120. There is a convenience store located nearby. 74 sites, 71 with electric, 3 tent only sites, 7 handicap sites, 18 - 50 ampere, 1 pull through site. From April 27th to October 31, sites without electric and tent only sites are $10; from May 2nd to September 6th, sites with electric hookups and sites with 50 ampere service are $12. Recreational vehicle maximum length is in excess of 65'. Open from April 27th to October 31st. (406) 526-3224. NRRS (Mid May to early September).

FLAT LAKE CAMPGROUND

From Fort Peck, go 5.7 miles south on State Road 24. A picnic shelter is available and the nearest dump station is 6 miles. 3 primitive sites. All sites are free.

FLOOD PLAIN CAMPGROUND

From the east end of the dam on State Road 24, go north on State Road 117, just before the C.M. Russell Wildlife Refuge Office, on the right. 5 primitive sites, free. Maximum recreational vehicle length is 50'. Open all year.

FOURCHETTE BAY CAMPGROUND

From Malta/JCT I-2, go 60 miles south on gravel road, impassable when wet. A picnic shelter is available and the nearest dump station is 60 miles. 44 primitive sites. All sites are free. Recreational vehicle maximum length is 20'. Open all year.

MCGUIRE CREEK CAMPGROUND

From the dam, go 37 miles southeast on State Road 24 (dirt, impassable when wet), west side. The nearest dump station is 45 miles. 10 primitive sites. All sites are free. Recreational vehicle maximum length is 16. Open all year.

NELSON CREEK CAMPGROUND

From Ft. Peck, go 44 miles southeast on State Road 24, 7 miles west on a gravel road. A picnic shelter is available and the nearest dump station is 45 miles. 16 primitive sites. All sites are free. Recreational vehicle maximum length is 40'. Open all year.

THE PINES CAMPGROUND

From Junction State Road 117, go 4 miles west on State Road 24, 12 miles southwest on Willow Creek Road (gravel) and 15 miles south on Pines Road (gravel). A picnic shelter and fish cleaning station are available, and the nearest dump station is 33 miles. 25 primitive sites. All sites are free. Recreational vehicle maximum length is 30'. All year.

WEST END CAMPGROUND

Located on the lake side, west side of dam. A picnic shelter is available and the nearest dump station is 3 miles. 13 sites with electric. Sites with electric hookups are from $10; overflow sites are $5. Recreational vehicle maximum length is 35'. Open from Memorial Day to Labor Day.

LAKE KOOCANUSA (SEA) 2

A 46,500 acre surface area lake located 17 miles northeast of Libby in northwest Montana on State Road 37. Campsites are available on project lands with some amenities. Visitor center provides powerhouse tours. Blue ribbon fishing area and Murray Springs Fish Hatchery. Libby Dam Project, 17115 Highway 37, Libby, MT 59923-9703. (406) 293-5577.

ALEXANDER CREEK CAMPGROUND

Located 1 mile below the dam on the west shore of Kootenai River off Powerhouse Road, gravel. 2 primitive sites. All sites are free.

BLACKWELL FLATS CAMPGROUND

Located 3 miles below the dam on the west shore of Kootenai River on Forrest Service Road 228, gravel. 7 primitive sites, some pull through sites. All sites are free.

DUNN CREEK FLATS CAMPGROUND

Located 2.5 miles below the dam on the east shore of Kootenai River on Route 37, gravel. 13 primitive sites, some pull through sites. All sites are free.

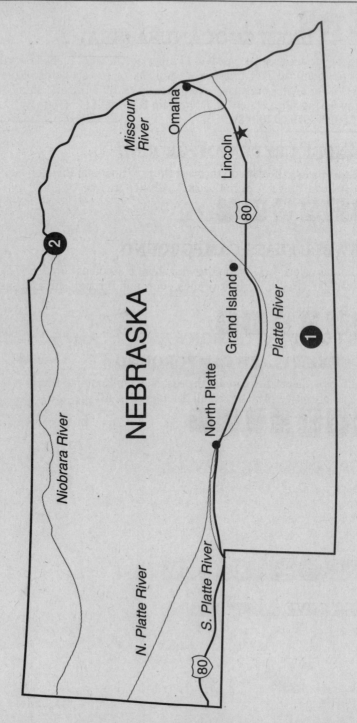

NEBRASKA

STATE CAPITAL:
Lincoln
NICKNAME:
Cornhusker State

37th State - 1867

Site reservation, National Recreation Reservation Service (NRRS), toll free, 1-877-444-6777; TDD 877-833-6777, www.recreation.gov, (Master, Visa, American Express & Discover cards).

HARLAN COUNTY LAKE (KC) 1

A 13,250 acre surface area lake located 1 mile south of Republican City off United States Route 136 in south-central Nebraska near the Kansas state line. Free sites in the off season may have reduced amenities. Operations Project Manager, Harlan County Lake, 70788 Corps Road A, Republican City, NE 68971-9742. (308) 799-2105.

CEDAR POINT/PATTERSON HARBOR CAMPGROUND

From Republican City/Junction United States Route 136, go 5 miles south on County Road A at dam on the south side. A picnic shelter and change house are available. 30 sites. From May 15th to September 15th, sites are $6. From September 16th to May 14th, some sites are available and are free. Open all year.

GREMLIN COVE CAMPGROUND

From Republican City/Junction United States Route 136, go 1.2 miles south on County Road A (Berrigan Road) to the dam on the north side. A picnic shelter and change house are available. 70 sites. From May 15th to September 15th, sites are $8. From September 16th to May 14th, some sites are available and are free. Open all year.

HUNTER COVE CAMPGROUND

From Republican City/Junction United States Route 136, go 1 mile south on Berrigan Road, 0.5 mile west on County Road B, on the north side. Boat storage and rentals are located at the North Shore Marina. Picnic shelters, an amphitheater, and a fish cleaning station are available, and off the road vehicles are prohibited. 150 sites, 84 with electric, 20 tent only site, 32 - 50 ampere, 19 pull through sites. During April, October and November, sites are

$6; From May 1st to September 30th, sites without electric hookups are $10; sites with electric hookups are $14; premium sites with electric hookups are $16. From December 1 to March 31st, some sites are available and are free, reduced facilities. Recreational vehicle maximum length is in excess of 65'. This campground requires a 3 night minimum stay on holiday weekends. Open all year. NRRS.

METHODIST COVE CAMPGROUND

From Alma/Junction United States Route 183, go 2.5 mi west on South Street. A fish cleaning station is available, and two group camping areas for up to 75 people and 16 vehicles, and a picnic shelter for up to 125 people and 41 vehicles is $50. 150 sites, 49 with electric. From May 15th to September 10th, sites without electric hookups are $10; sites with electric hookups are $14; from September 11th to May 14th, some sites are available and are free, no amenities. Recreational vehicle maximum length is in excess of 65'. This campground requires a 2 night minimum stay on weekends and a 3 night stay on holiday weekends. Open all year. NRRS.

NORTH OUTLET CAMPGROUND

From Republican City, go 2 miles south on County Road A, below dam, on the north side of the outlet. A picnic shelter is available. 30 sites. From May 15th to September 15th, sites are $6. From September 16th to May 14th, some sites are available and are free. Open all year.

SOUTH OUTLET CAMPGROUND

From Republican City, go 2 miles south on County Road A, 1 mile north on County Road 1, below the dam. 30 sites. From May 15th to September 15, sites are $6. From September 16th to May 14th, some sites are available and are free. Open all year.

LEWIS & CLARK LAKE (OM) 2

Located 4 miles west of Yankton, South Dakota on Highway 50 on the Nebraska state line. Seaplane usage. Plant tours are given daily from 10:00 a.m. to 6:00 p.m., from Memorial Day through Labor Day. Schedule special tours by contacting the office. Lake Manager, Gavins Point Project, P. O. Box 710, Yankton, SD 57078. (402) 667-7873. See SD listing.

COTTONWOOD CAMPGROUND

Located east of dam on the downstream side. A fish cleaning station and picnic shelter (call the office) are available. 77 sites with electric, 4 pull through sites, 1 handicap site. From April 19th to October 21st, sites with electric hookups are $14; premium sites with electric hookups are $16. From October 22nd to April 18th, some sites are available and are free. Recreational vehicle maximum length is in excess of 65'. This campground requires a 2 night minimum stay on weekends and a 3 night stay on holiday weekends. Open all year. NRRS (May 20th to September 5th).

NEBRASKA TAILWATERS CAMPGROUND

Located east of the dam on south side of the river off Route 121. A fish cleaning station and picnic shelters (call the office)are available. 43 sites, 32 with electric, 11 tent only sites, 1 handicap site. Tent only sites are $12; sites with electric hookups are $14. Recreational vehicle maximum length is in excess of 65'. This campground requires a 2 night minimum stay on weekends and a 3 night stay on holiday weekends. This campground requires a 2 night minimum stay on weekends and a 3 night stay on holiday weekends. Open from May 15th to October 13th. Closed for construction, call the office before going to ensure it is open. NRRS.

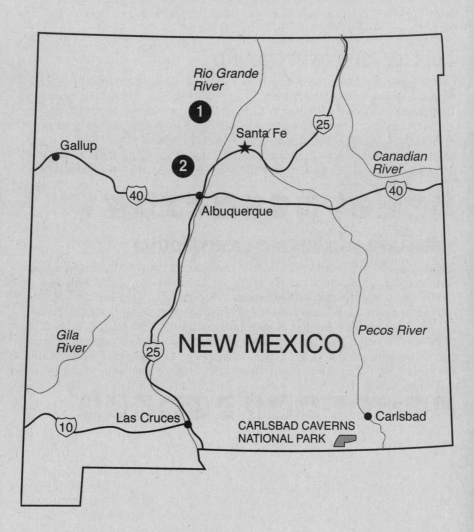

Rio Grande River

1

Santa Fe

25

Gallup

2

Canadian River

40

Albuquerque

40

Gila River

25

NEW MEXICO

Pecos River

10

Las Cruces

Carlsbad

CARLSBAD CAVERNS
NATIONAL PARK

NEW MEXICO

STATE CAPITAL:
Santa Fe
NICKNAME:
Land of Enchantment

47th State - 1912

Site reservation, National Recreation Reservation Service
(NRRS), toll free, 1-877-444-6777; TDD 877-833-6777,
www.recreation.gov, (Master, Visa, American Express
& Discover cards).

ABIQUIU RESERVOIR (AQ) 1

A 5,200 acre surface area lake located 7 miles northwest of Abiquiu off United
States Route 84, on State Road 96, 60 miles northwest of Santa Fe. This lake is
6400 feet above sea level. Swimming permitted except where prohibited by signs
and there is a visitor's center. Operations Manager, Abiquiu Dam, P. O. Box 290,
Abiquiu, NM 87510. (505) 685-4433.

RIANA CAMPGROUND

From Espanola, go 30 miles north on United States Route 84, 1 mile west
on State Road 96. A group camping area and an amphitheater are available,
and picnic shelters are $40 to $50. 54 sites, 15 tent only walk-in sites, 13 - 50
ampere, 2 pull through sites. From April 12th to October 12th, tent only sites
are $5; sites without electric hookups are $10; sites with electric hookups are
$14; from October 13th to April 11th, some sites are available and are free.
Recreational vehicle maximum length is in excess of 65'. Open all year. (505)
685-4561. NRRS.

COCHITI LAKE (AQ) 2

A 1,200 acre surface area lake located 50 miles northeast of Albuquerque,
northwest of I-25 on State Road 22, 35 miles southwest of Santa Fe. Visitor
center. There is a fee for additional vehicles. Ground fires and off the road
vehicles are prohibited. Swimming permitted except where prohibited by signs.
This lake is a no wake zone area. The favorite water activity is wind surfing.
Operations Manager, Cochiti Lake, 82 Dam Crest Road, Pena Blanca, NM 87041.
(505) 465-0307.

COCHITI CAMPGROUND

From Albuquerque, I-25 north, exit 259, go west on State Road 22 through Pena Blanca. A combination for the gate lock is provided registered campers for late entry and exit from the campground. Consists of Juniper (Loop A), 34 sites, Chamisa (Loop B), 21 sites and Apache Plume (Loop C) with 22 sites for overflow and group only camping. A picnic shelter is available and a group camping area for up to 28 people and 8 vehicles is $25. 76 sites, 34 with electric, 12 handicap sites (From tent only, electric, electric and water, water and 50 ampere, or 50 ampere pull through sites), , 8 - 50 ampere, 5 double sites, 18 pull through sites. Sites without electric hookups are $8; sites with electric hookups are $12. Recreational vehicle maximum length is in excess of 65'. This campground requires a 3 night minimum stay on holiday weekends. Open all year. NRRS.

TETILLA PEAK CAMPGROUND

From Albuquerque, I-25 north, exit 264, go west on State Road 16 to Tetilla Peak turnoff. Picnic shelters are available. Consists of Choll recreational vehicles, 36 sites with water and electric, and Coyote camp grounds, 10 sites, 7 tent only sites, 7 pull through sites, 35 handicap sites, 9 - 50 ampere. Sites without electric hookups are $8; sites with electric hookups are $12. Recreational vehicle maximum length in excess of 65'. This campground requires a 3 night minimum stay on holiday weekends. Open from April 1st to October 31st. NRRS.

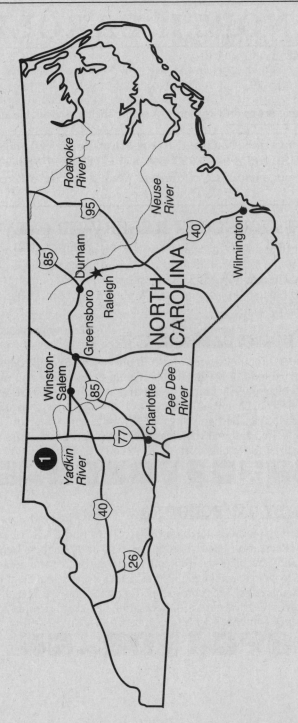

NORTH CAROLINA

STATE CAPITAL:
Raleigh
NICKNAME:
Tar Heel State

12th State - 1789

Site reservation, National Recreation Reservation Service
(NRRS), toll free, 1-877-444-6777; TDD 877-833-6777,
www.recreation.gov, (Master, Visa, American Express
& Discover cards).

W. KERR SCOTT RESERVOIR (WL) 1

A 1,470 acre surface area lake located 3 miles west of Wilkesboro, south of
United States Route 421 off State Road 268 in northwest North Carolina.
Visitors center, checkout time is 3 p.m., visitors to 10 p.m., and off the road
vehicles are prohibited. Project Manager, W. Kerr Scott Dam, P. O. Box 182,
Wilkesboro, NC 28697-0182. (336) 921-3390/3750.

BANDITS ROOST CAMPGROUND

From Wilkesboro/Junction United States Route 421, go 5.5 miles west on State
Road 268, go north on County Road 1141. Group camping area for up to 50
people and 2 vehicles is $60, amphitheater and a picnic shelter are available. 101
sites, 80 with electric, 21 tent only sites, 5 pull through sites, 2 handicap sites
with water and electric. Tent only sites are $16; sites with water and electric
hookups are $20. Recreational vehicle maximum length is in excess of 65'.
Open from April 1st to October 31st. (336) 921-3190. NRRS.

FORT HAMBY CAMPGROUND

From Wilkesboro, go 5 miles north on United States Route 421, 1.5 miles west
(left) on South Recreation Road. A group camping area, Robbers Den, for up
to 100 people and 32 vehicles is $125, and an amphitheater and horseshoe pits
are available. Alcohol is prohibited. 32 sites, 24 with water and 50 ampere, 11
handicap accessible sites, 8 tent only sites. Tent only sites are $14; sites with
water and 50 ampere service are $18. Recreation vehicle maximum length is in
excess of 65'. Open from April 15th to October 31st. (336) 973-0104. NRRS.

WARRIOR CREEK CAMPGROUND

From Wilkesboro, go 8 miles west on State Road 268 through Goshen, north on County Road 1180. Three group camping areas for up to 50 people and 2 vehicles are $60, and a picnic shelter is available. 71 sites, 42 with electric, 33 tent only sites, 1 handicap site with water and electric. Tent only sites without electric are $16; tent only sites with water and electric and sites with water and electric hookups are $20. Recreational vehicle maximum length is in excess of 65'. Open from April 15th to October 15th. (336) 921-2177. NRRS.

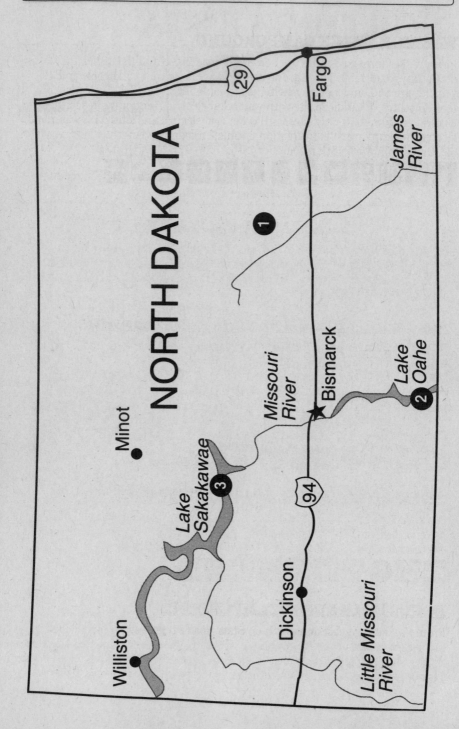

NORTH DAKOTA

STATE CAPITAL:
Bismarck
NICKNAME:
Sioux State

39th State - 1889

Site reservation, National Recreation Reservation Service
(NRRS), toll free, 1-877-444-6777; TDD 877-833-6777,
www.recreation.gov, (Master, Visa, American Express
& Discover cards).

LAKE ASHTABULA (SP) 1

A 5,234 acre surface area lake located 11 miles northwest of Valley City, exit
69 on I-94, in east-central North Dakota, northwest of Fargo. Snow mobiling.
Resource Manager, Lake Ashtabula, 2630 - 114th Avenue SE, Valley City, ND
58072-9795. (701) 845-2970.

ASHTABULA CROSSING EAST CAMPGROUND

From Valley City/I-94, exit 292, go 14 miles north on County Road 21 (signs).
A picnic shelter is available and alcohol is prohibited. 38 sites, 33 with electric,
1 double site, 5 tent only walk-in sites. Sites with electric hookups are $16;
a double site with electric hookups is $32. Recreational vehicle maximum
length is in excess of 65'. This campground requires a 2 night minimum stay
on weekends and a 3 night stay on holiday weekends. Open from May 1st to
September 30th. (701) 845-2970. NRRS.

ASHTABULA CROSSING WEST CAMPGROUND

From Valley City/I-94, exit 292, go 14 miles north on County Road 21 (signs).
A picnic shelter and a fish cleaning station are available. 41 sites. Sites with
electric hookups are $16. Open from May 1st to October 31st.

EGGERT'S LANDING CAMPGROUND

From the dam, go east and north on State Road 21, go west. A picnic shelter,
fish cleaning station and firewood are available. There are restaurants located
nearby. 41 sites, 35 with electric, 4 tent only sites, 2 handicap sites with electric.
Tent only sites and sites without electric hookups are $14; sites with electric

hookups are $16. Recreational vehicle maximum length is in excess of 65'. This campground requires a 3 night minimum stay on holiday weekends. Open from May 1st to September 30th. NRRS.

MEL RIEMAN CAMPGROUND

From Valley City/I-94, exit 292, go under the railroad bridge, 12 miles on County Road 19. A picnic shelter, group camping area, fish cleaning station and horseshoe pits are available, and a concessionaire is nearby. 27 sites, 15 with electric, 9 tent only sites (7 walk-in), 3 pull through sites, 1 handicap site. Tent only sites and sites without electric hookups are $12; sites with electric hookups are $14. Recreational vehicle maximum length is in excess of 65'. Open from May 1st to September 30th. NRRS.

LAKE OAHE (OM) 2

The lake has 2,250 miles of shoreline and is located 6 miles north of Pierre, South Dakota on State Road 1804. Powerhouse tours are provided daily during the summer. For large groups and for off season tours, call (605) 224-5862. Park Manager, Lake Oahe, 28563 Powerhouse Road, Room 105, Pierre, SD 57501-6174. (605) 224-5862/(701) 255-0015.

BADGER BAY CAMPGROUND

From Linton, go 13 miles west on State Road 13, 17 miles north on State Road 1804, go west. Nearest dump station is 23 miles. 6 primitive sites. All sites are free.

BEAVER CREEK EAST & WEST CAMPGROUND

From Linton, go 16 miles west on State Road 13, 1 mile west & 2 miles south on State Road 1804. A picnic shelter and fish cleaning station are available. 84 sites, 46 electric, 18 primitive sites, some pull through sites. Sites are from $8 to $12. Open from early May to mid September. (701) 255-0015.

CATTAIL BAY CAMPGROUND

From Strasburg, go 21 miles west on gravel road, 93rd Street. Nearest dump station is 15 miles. 6 primitive sites. All sites are free.

HAZELTON CAMPGROUND

From Hazelton, go 13 miles west on gravel road, 64th Street to 63rd Street. Fish cleaning station, and the nearest dump station is 25 miles. 12 primitive sites. All sites are free. Recreational vehicle maximum length is 30'. Open from April 1st to October 31st.

LAKE SAKAKAWEA (OM) 3

A 368,000 acre surface area lake located at Riverdale on State Road 200, 75 miles north of Bismarck west of United States Route 83. Powerplant tours are provided daily during summer (in the off season, call office). There is an off the road vehicle area and a national fish hatchery. Lake Manager, Lake Sakakawea, Box 527, Riverdale, ND 58565-0527. (701) 654-7411.

DEEPWATER CAMPGROUND

From junction United States Route 83, west on State Road 37. A picnic shelter is available. 17 primitive sites. All sites are free.

DOUGLAS CREEK CAMPGROUND

From junction United States Route 83, go 9 miles west of Garrison on State Road 37, 7 miles south on gravel road. 17 primitive sites. All sites are free. Recreational vehicle maximum length 25'. Open all year.

DOWNSTREAM CAMPGROUND

Located below the dam on the west side of the spillway. Interpretive programs, an amphitheater, fish cleaning station, horseshoe pits and a picnic shelter are available. For equestrian facilities, contact the office. 116 sites, 101 with electric, 2 double sites, 17 primitive tent only sites, 4 - 50 ampre, 2 handicap sites with electric. Tent sites are $10; sites with electric hookups are $14; double sites with electric hookups are $28. In the tenst site loop, providing space is

available, recreational vehicles may park on the asphalt road and walk into an
available tent site using the table and fire ring. Recreational vehicle maximum
length is in excess of 65'. This campground requires a 2 night minimum stay
on weekends and a 3 night stay on holiday weekends. Open from May 5th to
September 30. (701) 654-7440. NRRS.

EAST TOTTEN TRAIL CAMPGROUND

From Coleharbor, go north on United States Route 83 across lake bridge, 0.2
mile east. A fish cleaning station is available. 40 sites, 10 primitive sites. Sites
are from $6 to $10. Recreational vehicle maximum length 25'. Open from May
1st to September 30th.

WOLF CREEK CAMPGROUND

From project office, go 1 mile east, follow signs. A group camping area (contact
office), fish cleaning station, picnic shelter and horseshoe pits are available. 101
sites. All sites are $6. Open all year.

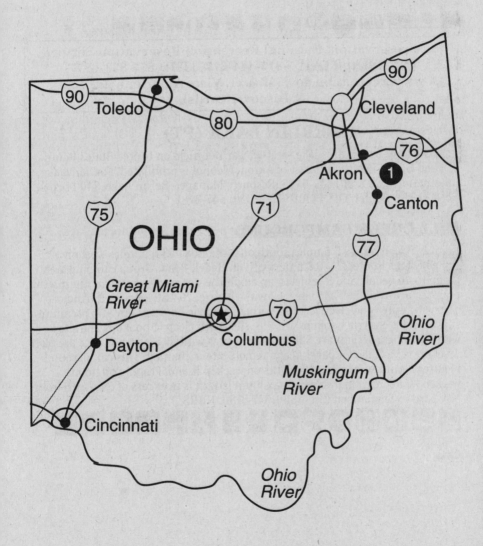

OHIO

STATE CAPITAL:
Columbus
NICKNAME:
Buckeye State

17th State - 1803

Site reservation, National Recreation Reservation Service
(NRRS), toll free, 1-877-444-6777; TDD 877-833-6777,
www.recreation.gov, (Master, Visa, American Express
& Discover cards).

BERLIN LAKE (PT) 1

A 3,590 acre surface area lake located near Deerfield on United States Route
224 and Bedell Road, southeast of Akron. Alcohol is prohibited. For daily lake
information, call (330) 547-5445. Resource Manager, Berlin Lake, 7400 Bedell
Road, Berlin Center, OH 44401-9707. (330) 547-3781.

MILL CREEK CAMPGROUND

From I 76, exit 54, go 5.5 miles south on State Road 534, 2 miles west on
United States Route 224, 0.8 mile south on Bedell Road. Group camping area
for up to 40 people and 8 vehicles, an amphitheater, pavilion and an interpretive
program are available. 348 sites, 62 with electric, 29 - 50 ampere, 2 handicap
sites with water and electric. Sites without electric hookups are $14; premium
sites without electric hookups are $18; sites with electric hookups and sites
with 50 ampere service are $20; premium sites with 50 ampere service are $24.
An extra vehicle fee for parking at a remote site is charged. This campground
requires a minimum stay of 2 nights on weekends and 3 nights on holiday
weekends. Recreational vehicle maximum length is in excess of 65'. Open from
May 23rd to September 15th. (330)547-8180. NRRS.

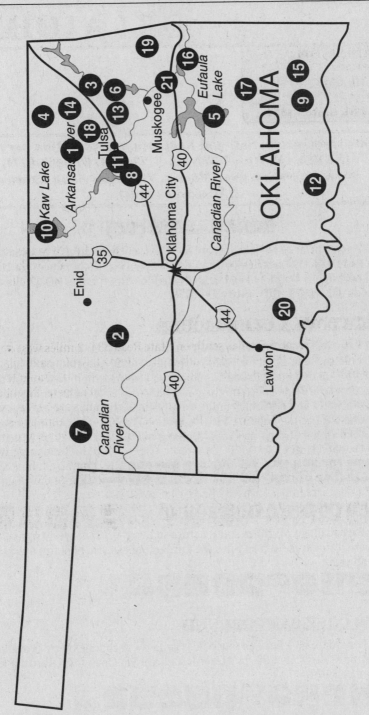

OKLAHOMA

STATE CAPITAL:
Oklahoma City
NICKNAME:
Sooner State

46th State - 1907

Site reservation, National Recreation Reservation Service (NRRS), toll free, 1-877-444-6777; TDD 877-833-6777, www.recreation.gov, (Master, Visa, American Express & Discover cards).

BIRCH LAKE (TU) 1

A 1,137 acre surface area lake located 20 miles southwest of Bartlesville off State Road 123/11, 1.5 miles south of Barnsdall, 35 miles northwest of Tulsa. Checkout time is 4 p.m. Lake Manager, Skiatook/Birch Lake, HC 67, Box 135, Skiatook, OK 74070-9103. (918) 396-3170.

BIRCH COVE A CAMPGROUND

From Barnsdall, go 3.1 miles south across spillway, 0.7 mile west (signs). Two picnic shelters, Egret for up to 100 people and 21 vehicles is $80 and Fly Catcher for up to 60 people and 11 vehicles is $60. An amphitheater and a change house are available, and there is a handicap accessible fishing area. 87 sites with water and electric, 5 pull through sites, 3 handicap sites. Sites with water and electric hookups are $16. Recreational vehicle maximum length is in excess of 65'. Open from April 1st to October 30th. (918) 847-2220. NRRS (April 1st to October 31st).

BIRCH COVE B CAMPGROUND

From Barnsdall, go 3.1 miles south across spillway, 0.7 mile west (signs). 12 sites with water and electric. Sites with water and electric hookups are $14. Open all year.

TWIN COVE CAMPGROUND

From Barnsdall, go 1.5 miles south near spillway. A change house is available and picnic shelters are $50. 11 sites. All sites are $8. Open from April 1st to September 30th.

CANTON LAKE (TU) 2

A 7,910 acre surface area lake located 75 miles northwest of Oklahoma City, 2 miles north of Canton on State Road 58A. Lake Manager, Canton Lake, HC 65, Box 120, Canton, OK 73724-0069. (580) 886-2989.

BIG BEND A & B CAMPGROUND

From Canton, go 1.8 miles west on State Road 51, 4 miles north on secondary road. A picnic shelter for up to 100 people and 21 vehicles is $35. 104 sites with electric, 14 - 50 ampere, 1 pull through site. From April 1st to October 31st, sites with electric hookups are $12; sites with water and electric hookups are $17; sites with 50 ampere service are $18. November & March, some sites are available and are free, no services. Recreational vehicle maximum length is 45'. This campground requires a 3 night minimum stay on holiday weekends. Open from April 1st to October 31st. (580) 886-3576. NRRS (May 1st to September 30).

BLAINE CAMPGRUND

From Canton, go 0.7 mile west on State Road 51, 1.7 miles north on State Road 58A, below dam. 16 sites. From April 1st to October 31st, sites are $8. November & March, some sites are available and are free, no utilities. Open from March 1st to November 30th.

CANADIAN A & B CAMPGROUND

From Canton, go 0.7 mile west on State Road 51, 1.5 miles north on State Road 58A, 0.8 mile west on secondary road. Two group camping areas, Cheyenne for up to 110 people and 40 vehicles is $176 and Arapaho for up to 140 people and 40 vehicles is $224. An amphitheater is available and a picnic shelter for up to 100 people and 21 vehicles is $35. A restaurant is located nearby. 120 sites with electric, 10 - 50 ampere, 1 pull through site. For March and November, sites with no water are $12; From April 1st to October 31st, sites with electric hookups are $16; sites with water and electric hookups are $17; sites with water and 50 ampere service are $18. From December 1st to February 28th, some sites are available and are free, no services. Recreational vehicle maximum length is in excess of 65'. This campground requires a 2 night minimum stay on weekends from May 1st to September 30th and a 3 night minimum stay on holiday weekends. Open all year. (580) 886-3454. NRRS (May 1st to September 30th).

FAIRVIEW GROUP CAMPGROUND

From Longdale, go 0.5 mile north, 2.5 miles west on secondary road. A group camping area for up to 100 people and 45 vehicles, and 4 recreational vehicles with several tents, is $45. The key for the gate must be procured from the Canadian gatehouse keeper. Open from April 1st to September 30th. NRRS.

LONGDALE CAMPGROUND

From Longdale/Junction State Road 58, go 2 miles west on secondary road. A picnic shelter for up to 100 people and 21 vehicles is $35. 48 sites, 12 tent only primitive sites. From April 1st to October 31st, tent only primitive sites and sites without electric hookups are $8. From November 1st to March 31st, some sites are available and are free, no utilities. Recreational vehicle maximum length is 40'. This campground requires a 2 night minimum stay on weekends and a 3 night stay on holiday weekends. Open from April 1st to October 31st. (580) 274-3454. NRRS (April 1st to September 7th).

SANDY COVE CAMPGROUND

From Canton, go 0.7 mile west on State Road 51, 5 miles north on State Road 58A, 1.2 miles west on secondary road. A picnic shelter for up to 100 people and 21 vehicles is $35. 37 sites with electric, 1 pull through site. Sites with electric hookups are $15. Recreational vehicle maximum length is 40'. This campground requires a 3 night minimum stay on holiday weekends. Open from April 1st to October 31st. (580) 274-3576. NRRS (May 1st to September 10th).

CHOUTEAU LOCK & DAM NO. 17 (TU) 3

Located southeast of Tulsa, 4 miles northwest of Okay. Lake Manager, Ft. Gibson, Fort Gibson Lake, State Highway 251A, Ft. Gibson, OK 74434-0370. (918) 682-4314.

AFTON LANDING CAMPGROUND

From Wagnor/Junction United States Route 69, go 5 miles southwest on State Road 51, 2 miles southeast before bridge (signs). A picnic shelter is $50. 22 sites, 20 with electric. Sites without electric hookups are $10; sites with electric hookups are $15. Open all year.

COPAN LAKE (TU) 4

A 4,850 acre surface area lake west of Copan, located 2 miles west of junction United States Route 75 on State Road 10, north of Tulsa near the Kansas state line. Checkout time is 4 p.m. Lake Manager, HC 67, Box 135, Skiatook, OK 74070. (918) 396-3170.

POST OAK CAMPGROUND

From junction United States Route 75, west over dam, go 1.2 miles north on State Road 10, go east. 20 sites with water and electric, 3 full hookups, 2 handicap sites with full hookups. Sites with water and electric hookups and sites with water and electric, 2nd price, are $16; sites with full hookups are $18. Recreational vehicle maximum length is in excess of 65'. This campground requires a 2 night minimum stay on weekends and a 3 night stay on holiday weekends. Open from April 1st to October 31st. (918) 532-4334. NRRS.

WASHINGTON COVE A & B CAMPGROUND

From the northwest corner of Copan city, go 0.3 mile west, 0.5 mile north on secondary road (signs). A picnic shelter for up to 45 people and 20 vehicles is $25. 101 sites with water and electric hookups, 2 handicap sites. Sites with water and electric hookups are $16. Recreational vehicle maximum length is in excess of 65'. This campground requires a 2 night minimum stay on weekends and a 3 night stay on holidays. Open from April 1st to October 31st. (918) 532-4129. NRRS.

EUFAULA LAKE (TU) 5

A 102,200 acre surface area lake with 600 miles of shoreline located 12 miles east of Eufaula on State Road 71, 31 miles south of Muskogee. Powerhouse tours are by appointment only. Lake Manager, Eufaula Lake, Route 4, Box 5500, Stigler, OK 74462-9440. (918) 484-5135/799-5843/799-5843.

BELLE STAR SOUTH

From junction I-40 (south of Checotah), go 7 miles south on United States Route 69, 2 miles east on State Road 150, 2 miles south, on right. Two picnic shelters, PS1 for up to 100 people and 21 vehicles and PS2 for up to 75 people and 21 vehicles are $50, and a change house is available. 117 sites with water and electric, 10 - 50 ampere, 36 pull through sites, 2 handicap sites. Sites with water and electric hookups are $16; sites with water and 50 ampere service are $18. Recreational vehicle maximum length is in excess of 65'. Open from April 1st to September 30th. NRRS.

BROOKEN COVE NORTH CAMPGROUND

From the dam, east side, go 2 miles south on State Road 71, go northwest. Two group camping areas are $160 and two picnic shelters, PS1 for up to 75 people and 21 vehicles, and PS2 for up to 100 people and 21 vehicles are $50. 75 sites, 62 with electric, 7 - 50 ampere, 8 pull through sites, 1 handicap site. Sites without electric hookups are $11; sites with electric hookups are $16; sites with water and 50 ampere service are $18. Recreation vehicle maximum length is 60'. Open from April 1st to October 31st. NRRS (April 1st to September 30th).

DAM SITE EAST CAMPGROUND

Located on the northeast side, below dam. 10 sites with electric. From April 1st to October 31st, sites with electric hookups are $11. From November 1st to March 31st, some sites are available and are free, no utilities. Open all year.

DAM SITE SOUTH

Across dam from Dam Site East, go west. A picnic shelter with water and electric for up to 100 people and 21 vehicles is $50 and a change house is available. 57 sites, 43 with water and electric, 5 tent only site, 2 handicap sites. Sites without hookups are $10; tent only sites are $11; sites with water and electric hookups are $16. Recreational vehicle maximum length is 55'. Open from April 1st to September 30th. NRRS.

ELM POINT CAMPGROUND

From McAlester/Junction United States Route 69, go 12 miles northeast on State Road 31, go northwest. A picnic shelter is available. 17 sites. From April 1st to October 31st, sites without electric hookups are $7; sites with electric hookups are $11. From November 1st to February 28th, some sites are available and are free, no utilities. Open all year.

GAINES CREEK CAMPGROUND

From Oak Ridge Park, go east across lake bridge on State Road 9A, south on secondary road. Primitive area which is free. Open all year.

GENTRY CREEK COVE

From Checotah, go 9 miles west on United States Route 266, go south, signs. 32 sites, 15 with electric, 3 tent only sites, 3 pull through sites. Sites without hookups are $10; sites with water hookups are $11; sites with water and electric hookups are $14. Recreational vehicle maximum length is 50'. Open from April 1st to September 30th. NRRS.

HICKORY POINT CAMPGROUND

From McAlister/Junction United States Route 69, go 4 miles east on State Road 31, 6 miles east, go north before bridge. 10 sites. All sites are free. Open all year.

HIGHWAY 9 LANDING EAST, NORTH & SOUTH

From Eufaula/Junction United States Route 69, 9 miles southeast on State Road 9, go north. A picnic shelter for up to 100 people and 21 vehicles is $50. 73 sites, 61 with water and electric, 6 pull through sites, 4 handicap sites with water and electric. Sites without electric hookups are $10; sites with electric hookups are $16. Recreational vehicle maximum length is in excess of 65'. Open from April 1st to September 30th. NRRS.

HIGHWAY 31 LANDING GROUP CAMPGROUND

From McAlister/Junction United States Route 270, go 5 miles northeast on State Road 31, north side. Primitive group camping area, free.

HOLIDAY COVE CAMPGROUND

From Junction I-40, go 2 miles south on State Road 150, exit east. A picnic shelter is available. Primitive area, free. Open all year.

JUNIPER POINT CAMPGROUND

From McAlister/Junction United States Route 270, go 5 miles north on United States Route 69, 1 mile east, 3 miles north. A picnic shelter is available. 21 primitive sites. All sites are free. Open all year.

MILL CREEK BAY CAMPGROUND

From Eufaula, go 6 miles west on State Road 9, 2 miles south. A picnic shelter is available. 12 sites. All sites are $7. Open from April 1st to October 31st.

OAK RIDGE CAMPGROUND

From Eufaula/Junction United States Route 69, go 6 miles south, northeast on State Road 9A. 13 sites. From March 1st to October 31st, sites without electric hookups are $7; sites with electric hookups are $11. From November 1st to February 28, some sites are available and are free, no utilities. Open all year.

PORUM LANDING CAMPGROUND

From Porum, go 6 miles west on State Road 150. A picnic shelter for up to 100 people and 21 vehicles is $50. 52 sites, 48 with water and electric, 6 pull through sites, 2 handicap sites with water and electric. Sites without electric hookups are $11; sites with electric hookups are $16. Recreational vehicle maximum length is 60'. Open from April 1st to September 30th. NRRS.

FORT GIBSON LAKE (TU) 6

A 19,900 acre surface area lake located 5 miles northwest of Ft. Gibson, on State Road 251A from the Muskogee Turnpike. Free sites in the off season may have reduced amenities. Lake Manager, Fort Gibson Lake, 8568 State Highway 251A, Ft. Gibson, OK 74434-0370. (918) 682-4314/6618.

BLUE BILL POINT CAMPGROUND

From Wagoner/Junction State Road 51, go 6 miles north on United States Route 69, 3 miles east northeast (signs). A picnic shelter for up to 100 people and 20 vehicles is $50. 43 sites, 40 with water and electric, 8 handicap sites with water and 50 ampere service. Sites without electric hookups are $11; sites with electric hookups are $16; sites with water and 50 ampere service are $17. Recreational vehicle maximum length is in excess of 65'. Open from March 13th to September 30th. (918) 476-6638. NRRS (April 1st to September 30th).

DAMSITE CAMPGROUND

From Okay, go 6 miles east on State Road 251A, below dam, west side of outlet. Two picnic shelters for up to 100 people and 20 vehicles are $50. There is a cafe nearby. 47 sites with electric. Sites with electric hookups are $15. Recreational vehicle maximum length is in excess of 65'. Open from March 13th to September 30th. NRRS (April 1st to September 30).

FLAT ROCK CREEK CAMPGROUND

From Maize, go 3 miles south on United States Route 69, 5 miles east and south. A picnic shelter for up to 100 people and 20 vehicles is $50. 38 sites, 36 sites with electric. Sites without electric hookups are $10; sites with electric hookups are $14; sites with water and electric hookups are $15. Recreational vehicle maximum length is in excess of 65'. Open from March 13th to September 30th. NRRS (April 1st to September 30th).

ROCKY POINT CAMPGROUND

From Wagoner/Junction State Road 51, go 5 miles north on United States Route 69, 1.8 miles east, 1 mile north, signs. A picnic shelter for up to 100 people and 20 vehicles is $50, and a change house is available. A convenience store and restaurants are nearby. 63 sites, 59 with electric, 2 handicap sites with full hookups. Sites without hookups are $11; sites with electric hookups are $15; sites with water and electric hookups are $16; handicap sites with full hookups are $17. Recreational vehicle maximum length is in excess of 65'. Open from March 13th to September 30th. NRRS (April 1st to September 30th).

TAYLOR FERRY SOUTH CAMPGROUND

From Wagoner/Junction United States Route 69, go 8 miles east on State Road 51, south before bridge. Picnic shelters are available. A convenience store and restaurants are located nearby. 99 sites, 95 with water and electric, 7 - 50 ampere. From March 13th to March 31st, sites without hookups are $11; sites with water and electric hookups are $16; from April 1st to September 30th, sites without hookups are $11; sites with water and electric are $16; sites with water and 50 ampere service are $17. Recreational vehicle maximum length is in excess of 65'. Open from March 13th to September 30th. (918) 485-4792. NRRS (April 1st to September 30th).

WILDWOOD CAMPGROUND

From Hulbert, go 4 miles west on State Road 80. A picnic shelter for up to 100 people and 20 vehicles is $50. 30 sites with water and electric, 9 pull through sites. Sites with water and electic hookups are $16. Recreational vehicle maximum length is in excess of 65'. Open from March 13th to September 30th. NRRS (April 1st to September 30th).

FORT SUPPLY LAKE (TU) 7

An 1,820 acre surface area lake located 15 miles northwest of Woodward on United States Route 183, 1 mile southeast of Fort Supply in northwest Oklahoma near the panhandle. Visitor center features exhibits of indian arrow heads, old camp supply artifacts and a wildlife display. Lake Manager, Fort Supply Lake, HC 65, Box 120, Canton, OK 73724. (580) 766-2701.

BEAVER POINT CAMPGROUND

Located near the dam. 16 sites. All sites are $8. Open all year.

SUPPLY NORTH & SOUTH CAMPGROUND

From Ft. Supply, go 1 mile south on the west side of the dam. A picnic shelter for up to 100 people and 21 vehicles is $35 and a group camping area is $136. There is a handicap accessible fishing area. 110 sites, 96 with water and electric, 2 - 50 ampere, 14 pull through sites. From March 1st to November 30th, sites without electric hookups are $12; sites with water and electric hookups are $17; sites with water and 50 ampere service are $18. Recreational vehicle maximum length is in excess of 65'. This campground requires a 2 night minimum stay on holidays. Open from March 1st to November 30th. (580) 755-2001. NRRS (April 1st to September 30th).

HEYBURN LAKE (TU) 8

A 920 acre surface area lake located 13 miles southwest of Sapulpa, 2 miles from United States Route 66, 26 miles southwest of Tulsa off I-44. Lake Manager, Heyburn Lake, 27349 West Heyburn Lake Road, Kellyville, OK 74039-9615. (918) 247-6391/6397.

HEYBURN CAMPGROUND

Across dam on west side. Group camping area for up to 200 people and 50 vehicles is $100, and a picnic shelter and change house are available. 46 sites with water and electric, 18 - 50 ampere, 10 pull through sites, 1 handicap site with water and electric. Sites with water and electric hookups are $14; sites with water and 50 ampere service are $15; premium sites with water and electric hookups are $16. This campground requires a 2 night minimum stay on weekends and a 3 night stay on holiday weekends. Open from April 1st to October 31st. (918) 247-6601. NRRS (April 1st to September 30th).

SHEPPARD POINT CAMPGROUND

Located on the north side of the lake. Two picnic shelters, 001 for up to 100 people and 50 vehicles is $50 and 002 for up to 50 people and 50 vehicles is $25. 38 sites, 21 with water and electric, 17 tent only sites, 1 handicap site with water and electric. Sites without electric hookups are $10; sites with water and electric hookups are $14; premium sites with water and electric hookups are $16. Recreational vehicle maximum length is in excess of 65'. This campground requires a 2 night minimum stay on weekends and a 3 night stay on holiday weekends. Open from April 1st to October 31st. (918) 247-4551. NRRS.

SUNSET BAY CAMPGROUND

Located on the northeast side of the dam. 14 sites. All sites are $7. Open all year.

HUGO LAKE (TU) 9

A 13,250 acre surface area lake located 6 miles east of Hugo on United States Route 70, 30 miles north of Paris, Texas, in southeast Oklahoma. Lake Manager, Hugo Lake, P. O. Box 99, Sawyer, OK 74756-0099. (580) 326-3345.

GROUP AREA CAMPGROUND

From Sawyer/Junction United States Route 70, go 3.5 miles north on State
Road 147, 1 mile west & 0.6 mile south (2.6 miles on County Road). Four picnic
shelters are $25 and a change house is available. Four group camping areas are
$75. Open from May 1st to September 30th.

KIAMICHI

From Hugo, go 6.8 miles east on United States Route 70, 1 mile north on
County Road (signs). Two picnic shelters are $25 and a change house is
available. 92 sites, 90 sites with electric, 5 full hookups. Sites without electric
hookups are $9; sites with electric hookups are $14; sites with water and
electric hookups are $15. Recreational vehicle maximum length is in excess of
65'. This campground requires a 2 night minimum stay on weekends and a 3
night stay on holiday weekends. Open from April 1st to September 30th. Some
camping is available during December through February. NRRS (April 1st to
September 30th).

RATTAN LANDING CAMPGROUND

From Rattan, go 4 miles west on State Road 3/7, go south. 13 sites with water
and electric. Sites with water and electric hookups are $12. Open all year.

VIRGIL POINT CAMPGROUND

From Sawyer/Junction United States Route 70, go 2.5 miles north on State
Road 147, go west. 51 sites with water and electric. Sites with water and
electric hookups are $15. Recreational vehicle maximum length is 55'. This
campground requires a 2 night minimum stay on weekends and a 3 night stay
on holiday weekends. Open from April 1st to September 30th. NRRS.

KAW LAKE (TU) 10

A 17,000 acre surface area lake located 8 miles east of Ponca City off United
States Route 60, 70 miles northeast of Enid. Checkout time is 4 p.m. Lake
Manager, Kaw Lake, 9400 Lake Road, Ponca City, OK 74604-9629. (580) 762-
7323.

BEAR CREEK COVE CAMPGROUND

From Newkirk, go 7 miles east on improved County Road, 3 miles south. A picnic shelter is available. 22 sites with water and electric. Sites with water and electric hookups are $13. Recreational vehicle maximum length is 40'. This campground requires a 2 night minimum stay on weekends and a 3 night stay on holiday weekends. Open from May 1st to September 30th. (580) 362-4189. NRRS (May 1st to September 10th).

COON CREEK COVE CAMPGROUND

From Ponca City, go 4 miles north, 6 miles east on State Road 11, 1 mile north & 2 miles east. 54 sites with water and electric. Sites with water and electric hookups are $16. Recreational vehicle maximum length is 55'. This campground requires a 2 night minimum stay on weekends and a 3 night stay on holidays. Open from March 1st to November 30th. (580) 362-2466. NRRS (April 1st to September 30th).

MCFADDEN COVE CAMPGROUND

From Ponca City, go 7 miles east, on north side. A picnic shelter and a marine dump station are available. 15 sites with electric. Sites with electric hookups are $12. Open from March 1st to November 30th.

OSAGE COVE CAMPGROUND

From Ponca City, go 9 miles east across dam, 2 miles north (signs). Three group camping areas for up to 40 people and 1 vehicle are $75, and a picnic shelter and an amphitheater are available. 94 sites with electric. Sites with electric hookups are $16. Recreational vehicle maximum length is 60'. This campground requires a 2 night minimum stay on weekends and a 3 night stay on holidays. Open from March 1st to November 30th. (580) 762-9408. NRRS (April 1st to September 30th).

SANDY CAMPGROUND

From Ponca City, go 9 miles east, 0.5 mile below the dam, east side. 12 sites. All sites are $12. Open from April 1st to October 31st.

SARGE CREEK COVE CAMPGROUND

From Kaw City, go 2.8 miles east on State Road 11 (signs). A group camping area for up to 60 people and 20 vehicles is $75, and a picnic shelter and an amphitheater are available. 51 sites with water and electric, 1 pull through site. Sites with water and electric hookups are $16. Recreational vehicle maximum length is 60'. This campground requires a 2 night minimum stay on weekends and a 3 night stay on holiday weekends. Open from March 1st to November 30th. (580) 269-2303. NRRS (April 1st to September 30th).

WASHUNGA BAY A CAMPGROUND

From Kaw City, go 2.6 miles east on State Road 11, 0.6 mile north, 4.5 miles west on improved road (signs). 22 with water and electric. From March 1st to April 30th and September 10th to November 30th, sites with water and electric hookups are $15; from May 1st to September 9th, sites with water and electric hookups are $16. Recreational vehicle maximum length is 60'. This campground requires a 2 night minimum stay on weekends and a 3 night stay on holiday weekends. Open from March 1st to November 30th. (580) 269-2220. NRRS (May 1st to September 9th).

KEYSTONE LAKE (TU) 11

A 26,000 acre surface area lake located 15 miles west of Tulsa on United States Route 412 and State Road 51. Powerhouse tours are by reservation. Lake Manager, Keystone Lake, 23115 West Wekiwa Road, Sand Springs, OK 74063-9312. (918) 865-2621.

APPALACHIA BAY CAMPGROUND

From Sand Springs, go 10.1 miles west on United States Route 64, go south, on west side of United States Route 64. 18 primitive sites. All sites are $8. (918) 243-7822. Open from April 1st to October 31st.

BRUSH CREEK CAMPGROUND

From Sand Springs, go 8 miles west on United States Route 64, below dam, north side of spillway. 20 sites with electric. Sites with electric hookups are $14. Open all year.

COWSKIN BAY SOUTH CAMPGROUND

Adjacent to northwest corner of Westport. 30 sites. All sites are free. Open all year.

SALT CREEK NORTH CAMPGROUND

From Mannford, go east across lake bridge on State Road 51, go north. Two picnic shelters, A75 for up to 40 people and 11 vehicles is $25 and B05 for up to 60 people and 21 vehicles is $50, and a change house is available. 126 sites, 113 with electric, 1 pull through site. Sites without electric hookups are $10; sites with electric hookups are $15; premium sites with electric hookups and sites with water and electric hookups are $16; premium sites with water and electric hookups are $17. Recreational vehicle maximum length is in excess of 65'. Open from April 1st to October 31st. (918) 865-2845). NRRS (April 1st to September 15th).

WASHINGTON IRVING SOUTH CAMPGROUND

From Sand Springs, go 10.1 miles west on United States Route 64, across lake bridge, go east. 41 sites, 39 with electric, 1 pull through site. Sites without electric hookups are $10; sites with electric hookups are $16; premium sites are $17. Recreational vehicle maximum length is in excess of 65'. This campground requires a 2 night minimum stay on weekends. Open from April 1st to October 31st. (918) 243-7673. NRRS (April 1st to September 9th).

LAKE TEXOMA (TU) 12

Located 5 miles north of Denison, Texas in south-central Oklahoma on the state line. Off the road vehicles are prohibited. Lake Manager, Lake Texoma, 351 Corps Road, Denison, TX 75020. (903) 465-4990. See TX listing.

BUNCOMBE CREEK CAMPGROUND

From Kingston, go 4 miles west on State Road 32, 7 miles south on State Road 99, 2 miles east (sign). A picnic shelter is available. 54 sites with water and electric, 1 handicap site. From September 16th to April 14th, sites are $10; from April 15th to September 15th, sites with water and electric hookups are $16. Recreational vehicle maximum length is 45'. Open all year. (580) 564-2901. NRRS (April 15th to September 15th).

BURNS RUN EAST CAMPGROUND

From Denison, TX, go 8 miles north on State Road 91 across dam, west side. A picnic shelter for up to 100 people and 20 vehicles is $50. Restaurants and a convenience store are nearby. 54 sites, 45 sites with water and electric. From September 16th to April 14th, walk in sites are $10; from April 15th to September 15th, sites with water hookups are $12; sites with water and electric hookups and sites with water and electric hookups, 2d price, are $20. Recreational vehicle maximum length is in excess of 65'. Open all year. (580) 965-4660. NRRS (April 15th to September 15th).

BURNS RUN WEST CAMPGROUND

From Denison, TX, go 8 miles north on State Road 91, across bridge, 3 miles west. Two picnic shelters, GS1 for up to 100 people and 20 vehicles and SRW for up to 100 people and 25 vehicles are $50, and five group camping areas for up to 50 people and 8 vehicles are $100. 115 sites, 103 with electric, 21 handicap full hookup pull through sites, 3 tent only site, 43 pull through sites. Tent only sites and sites without electric hookups are $12; sites with water and electric hookups, 3rd price, are $20; sites with full hookups are $22. Recreational vehicle maximum length is in excess of 65'. Open from April 15th to September 15th. (580) 965-4922. NRRS.

CANEY CREEK CAMPGROUND

From Kingston, go 3 miles south on Donahoo Street (Rock Creek Road), 2 miles east on Lassiter Road, 2 miles east & south. A picnic shelter for up to 100 people and 20 vehicles is $50. 52 sites, 42 with water and electric, 1 handicap site. From September 16th to March 31st, sites with electric hookups are $10; from April 1st to September 15th, sites without hookups are $10; sites with water and electric hookups are $18. Recreational vehicle maximum length is in excess of 65'. Open all year. (580) 564-2632. NRRS (April 15th to September 15th).

DAMSITE

At dam, Oklahoma side. 6 sites. All sites are $7. Open all year.

JOHNSON CREEK CAMPGROUND

From Durant, go 10 miles west on United States Route 70, north side of road at causeway. A picnic shelter for up to 50 people and 20 vehicles is $50, and there is a convenience store nearby. 53 sites with water and electric, 13 - 50 ampere, 1 double site, 1 handicap site. From September 16th to April 14th, some sites are available and are free, no services. From April 15th to September 15th, sites with water and electric hookups are $20; a double site is $36. Recreational vehicle maximum length is in excess of 65'. Open all year.(580) 924-7316. NRRS (April 15th to September 15th).

LAKESIDE CAMPGROUND

From Durant, go 9 miles west on United States Route 70, 4 miles south on Streetman Road. A picnic shelter for up to 100 people and 20 vehicles is $50, and there is a convenience store nearby. 139 sites, 135 with electric, 1 handicap site. From September 16th to April 14th, sites with electric hookups are $10; from April 15th to September 15th, sites without electric hookups are $12; sites with electric hookups, 2nd price and sites with electric hookups are $20. Reduced facilities in the off season. Recreational vehicle maximum length is in excess of 65'. Open all year. (580) 920-0176. NRRS (April 15th to September 15th).

PLATTER FLATS CAMPGROUND

From Colbert/Junction United States Route 69/75, north exit overpass, go 4 miles west (past 4 way stop sign), 3 miles west. Two picnic shelters, must be reserved, are $50. 83 sites, 44 with electric, 58 equestrian sites. From September 16th to April 14th, sites with electric are $10; from April 15th to September 15th, sites without hookups are $10; sites with water hookups and equestrian sites with water hookups are $12; sites with electric hookups and sites with water and electric hookups are $16. Recreational vehicle maximum length is in excess of 65'. Open all year. (580) 434-5864. NRRS (April 15th to September 15th).

NEWT GRAHAM L&D NO. 18 (TU) 13

Located 7 miles south of Inola, east of Tulsa. Lock Engineer, Route 2, Box 21, Gore, OK 74435-9404. (918) 775-4475.

BLUFF LANDING CAMPGROUND

From Wagnor, go 11 miles southeast on Muskogee Turnpike, east on 71st Street (signs). 21 sites with water and electric. From April 1st to October 31st, sites with water and electric hookups are $15; from November 1st to March 31st, sites are available at reduced rates. Open all year.

OOLOGAH LAKE (TU) 14

A 29,500 acre surface area lake located 2 miles southeast of Oologah on State Road 88, 25 miles northeast of Tulsa, northwest of I-44. Checkout time is 4 p.m. Project Officer, P. O. Box 700, Oologah, OK 74053-0700. (918) 443-2250.

BIG CREEK RAMP CAMPGROUND

From Nowata, 5.1 miles east on United States Route 60, 2 miles north. 16 sites. All sites are free. Open all year.

BLUE CREEK A & B CAMPGROUND

From Foyil, go 6 miles west on State Road 28A, 1.2 miles north, 1.5 miles west on gravel road (signs). A picnic shelter for up to 100 people and 20 vehicles is $50. 61 sites, 24 with electric, 2 handicap sites with electric. Sites without electric hookups are $12; sites with electric hookups are $16. Recreational vehicle maximum length is in excess of 65'. Open from April 1st to October 31st. (918) 341-4244. NRRS (April 1st to September 30th).

HAWTHORN BLUFF CAMPGROUND

From Oologah/Junction United States Route 169, go 1.5 miles east on State Road 93 (signs). Two Picnic shelters for up to 100 people and 50 vehicles are $50, and an amphitheater and change house are available. 93 sites, 68 with electric, 2 tent only sites, 2 handicap sites with electric. Tent only sites and sites without electric hookups are $14; sites with electric hookups are $18. Recreational vehicle maximum length is in excess of 65'. This campground requires a 2 night minimum stay on weekends and a 3 night stay on holiday weekends. Open April 1st to October 31st. (918) 443-2319. NRRS (April 1st to September 30th).

REDBUD BAY CAMPGROUND

From Oologah, go 3.2 miles east on State Road 88, east side of dam. A marine dump station and consessioniare services are available. 12 sites with electric. Sites with electric hookups are $14. Open from April 1st to October 31st.

SPENCER CREEK COVE CAMPGROUND

From Foyil, go 11 miles north on paved/gravel roads (signs). A picnic shelter is $50. 69 sites, 30 with electric, 2 handicap sites. Sites without electric hookups are $12; sites with electric hookups are $16. Recreational vehicle maximum length is in excess of 65'. This campground requires a 2 night minimum stay on weekends and a 3 night stay on holiday weekends. Open from April 1st to September 30th. (918) 341-3690. NRRS.

VERDIGRIS RIVER CAMPGROUND

From Oologah/Junction United States Route 169, go 3.1 miles east on State Road 88, below the dam. A picnic shelter is available. 7 sites. All sites are $10. Open all year.

PINE CREEK LAKE (TU) 15

A 3,800 acre surface area lake located 8 miles north of Valliant off State Road 98, in southeast Oklahoma near the Texas state line. Checkout time is 4. p.m. Lake Manager, Pine Creek Lake, Route 1, Box 400, Valliant, OK 74764-9615. (405) 933-4239.

LITTLE RIVER CAMPGROUND

From Wright City, go 6 miles north on State Road 98, 8.5 miles west on State Road 3, go southeast (signs). A group camping area for up to 100 people and 25 vehicles is $65 and a picnic shelter is available. 89 sites, 62 with water and electric, 12 - 50 ampere, 12 full hookups, 4 pull through sites. Sites without electric hookups are $10; sites with water and electric hookups are $15; sites with full hookups are $18. Overflow area. Recreational vehicle maximum length is in excess of 65'. This campground requires a 2 night minimum stay on weekends and a 3 night stay on holiday weekends. Open from April 1st to September 30th. (580) 876-3720. NRRS.

LOST RAPIDS CAMPGROUND

From Wright City, go 6 miles north on State Road 98, 6 miles west on State Road 3, go south (signs). A group camping area for up to 100 people and 25 vehicles is $65 and a picnic shelter is available. 30 sites, 16 with water and electric. Sites without electric hookups are $8; sites with water and electric hookups are $13. Recreational vehicle maximum length is in excess of 65'. This campground requires a 2 night minimum stay on weekends and a 3 night stay on holiday weekends. Open from april 1st to September 30th. (580) 876-3720. NRRS.

PINE CREEK COVE CAMPGROUND

From Valliant, go 8 miles north on Pine Creek Road (signs). A group camping area for up to 100 people and 25 vehicles is $65 and a picnic shelter is available. 41 sites, 40 with water and electric, 1 pull through site. A site without electric hookups is $10; sites with water and electric hookups are $15. Recreational vehicle maximum length is in excess of 65'. This campground requires a 2 night minimum stay on weekends and a 3 night stay on holiday weekends. Open from April 1st to September 30th. (580) 933-4214. NRRS.

TURKEY CREEK LANDING CAMPGROUND

From Little River Park/Junction State Road 3, go 0.5 mile west on State Road 3, 0.5 mile north to Burwell, 0.5 mile west, 2 miles north on secondary road, 1.5 miles east on secondary road (signs). A picnic shelter for up to 100 people and 25 vehicles is $40. 30 sites, 8 with water and electric, 2 pull through sites. Sites without electric hookups are $8; sites with water and electric hookups are $13. Recreational vehicle maximum length is in excess of 65'. This campground requires a 2 night minimum stay on weekends and a 3 night stay on holiday weekends. Open from April 1st to September 30th. (580) 876-3720. NRRS.

ROBERT S. KERR LAKE (TU) 16

A 42,000 acre surface area lake located 8 miles south of Sallisaw on United States Route 59, south of I-40 in east-central Oklahoma, 33 miles west of Ft. Smith, Arkansas. Project Engineer, Robert S. Kerr Project Office, HC 61, Box 238, Sallisaw, OK 74955-9945. (918) 775-4474/489-5541.

APPLEGATE COVE CAMPGROUND

From Sallisaw, go 8 miles south on United States Route 59, 2 miles west (signs). A picnic shelter for up to 50 people and 10 vehicles is $50. 27 sites with water and electric. Sites with water and electric hookups are $15. Recreational vehicle maximum length is 50'. This campground requires a 2 night minimum stay on weekends and a 3 night stay on holiday weekends. Open May 1st to September 30th. NRRS.

COWLINGTON POINT CAMPGROUND

From Star, go 2 miles east (signs). A picnic shelter for up to 50 people and 10 vehicles is $50. 38 sites, 23 with water and electric. Sites with electric hookups are $10; sites with water and electric hookups are $15. Recreational vehicle maximum length is 60'. This campground requires a 2 night minimum stay on weekends and a 3 night stay on holiday weekends. Open all year. NRRS (May 1st to September 30th).

SHORT MOUNTAIN COVE CAMPGROUND

From Cowlington, go 1 mile north (signs). A picnic shelter for up to 50 people and 10 vehicles is $50. 32 sites with water and electric. From April 1st to September 30th, sites with water and electric hookups are $15; from October 1st to March 31st, sites are $10. Recreational vehicle maximum length is 55'. This campground requires a 2 night minimum stay on weekends and a 3 night stay on holidays. Open all year. NRRS (May 1st to September 30th.

SARDIS LAKE (TU) 17

A 14,360 acre surface area lake located 3 miles north of Clayton on State Road 2/43, south of Wilborton & United States Route 270, in southeast Oklahoma. Do not bring firewood to the campground to help prevent spreading the Emeral Ash Borer insect. Lake Manager, Sardis Lake, HC 60, Box 175, Clayton, OK 74536-9727. (918) 569-4131.

POTATO HILLS CENTRAL CAMPGROUND

From junction United States Route 271, go 3.3 miles north on State Road 2. Two group camping areas, GCA for up to 64 people and 20 vehicles and GCB for up to 48 people and 10 vehicles with picnic shelters are $150. There is firewood available nearby. 94 sites with electric. Sites with electric hookups are $15.

Recreational vehicle maximum length is in excess of 65'. This campground requires a 2 night minimum stay on weekends and a 3 night stay on holiday weekends. Open from April 1st to September 13th. (918) 569-4146. NRRS.

POTATO HILLS SOUTH CAMPGROUND

From junction United States Route 271, go 2.5 miles north on State Road 2. Two picnic shelters for up to 100 people are $30, and a change house is available. 18 sites. All sites are $8. Recreational vehicle maximum length is in excess of 65'. This campground requires a 2 night minimum stay on weekends and a 3 night stay on holiday weekends. Open from April 1st to October 31st. (918) 569-4549. NRRS (April 1st to September 13th).

SARDIS COVE CAMPGROUND

From junction State Road 2, go 8.3 miles west on State Road 43. 45 sites, 22 with electric. Sites without electric hookups are $9; sites with electric hookups are $12. Open from April 1st to October 31st. (918) 569-4637.

SKIATOOK LAKE (TU) 18

Located 5 miles west of Skiatook on State Road 20, northwest of Tulsa. Checkout time is 4 p.m. Lake Manager, Skiatook Lake, HC 67, Box 135, Skiatook, OK 74070-9107. (918) 396-3170.

BULL CREEK PENINSULA CAMPGROUND

From dam, go 7.8 miles west on State Road 20, 3.7 miles northeast, access after second bridge crossing on the lake. 41 sites without electric. Sites without electric hookups are $8. Open all year. (918) 396-2444.

TALL CHIEF COVE CAMPGROUND

From dam, go 1.7 miles south, go west (signs). A picnic shelter for up to 200 people and 50 vehicles is $50 and an amphitheater is available. Tere is a handicap accessible swimming area. 55 sites with water and electric, 5 double sites with water and electric, 10 tent only overflow sites, 1 - 50 ampere, 2 handicap sites with water and electric. Tent only sites are $10; sites with water and electric hookups are $20; double sites with water and electric are $30. Recreational vehicle maximum length is in excess of 65'. This campground requires a 2 night minimum stay on weekends and a 3 night stay on holiday weekends. Open from April 1st to October 27th. (918) 288-6320. NRRS.

TWIN POINTS CAMPGROUND

From Skiatook, go 7 miles west, north of State Road 20 (signs). 54 sites with water and 50 ampere, 2 handicap sites. Sites with water and 50 ampere service are $20. Recreational vehicle maximum length is in excess of 65'. This campground requires a 2 night minimum stay on weekends and a 3 night stay on holiday weekends. Open from April 1st to October 28th. (918) 396-1376. NRRS.

TENKILLER FERRY LAKE (TU) 19

A 12,900 acre surface area lake located 7 miles northeast of Gore on State Road 100, 22 miles southeast of Muskogee. This lake may experience low water levels. Tenkiller Project Office, Route 1, Box 259, Gore, OK 74435-9547. (918) 487-5252.

CARTERS LANDING CAMPGROUND

From Tahlequah, go 4 miles southeast on United States Route 62, 6.6 miles south (left) on State Road 82, 2 miles northeast (left) on access road. A picnic shelter is $25 with a $10 reservation fee. 25 sites, 10 with water and electric. Sites without electric hookups are $7; sites with water and electric hookups are $11. Reduced fees in the winter. Open all year.

CHICKEN CREEK CAMPGROUND

From Tahlequah, go 4 miles southeast on United States Route 62, 16 miles south (left) on State Road 82, 2 miles west (right) on access road. Two picnic shelters for up to 50 people and 30 vehicles are $25. 102 sites with electric, 7 - 50 ampere, 1 handicap site. Sites with electric hookups are $14; sites with water and electric hookups are $15; sites with water and 50 ampere service are $18. Recreational vehicle maximum length is in excess of 65'. This campground requires a 2 night minimum stay on weekends and a 3 night stay on holidays. Open from January 1st to September 30th. NRRS (April 1st to September 30th).

COOKSON BEND CAMPGROUND

From Tahlequah, go 4 miles southeast on United States Route 62, 13 miles south (left) on State Road 82, 2 miles west (right) on access road. Two picnic shelters for up to 50 people and 21 vehicles are $25. 131 sites, 64 with electric, 7 - 50 ampere. Sites without electric hookups are $10; sites with electric hookups are $14; premium sites with electric hookups are $15; sites with water and 50 ampere service are $18. Recreational vehicle maximum length is in excess of 65'. This campground requires a 2 night minimum stay on weekends and a 3 night stay on holiday weekends. Open January 1st to September 30th. NRRS (April 1st to September 30th).

ELK CREEK LANDING CAMPGROUND

From Tahlequah, go 4 miles southeast on United States Route 62, 10 miles south (left) on State Road 82, turn right after crossing the Illinois River bridge. Two picnic shelters for up to 50 people and 11 vehicles are $10. 41 sites, 6 with electric. Sites without electric hookups are $10; sites with electric hookups are $15. Recreational vehicle maximum length is in excess of 65'. This campground requires a 2 night minimum stay on weekends and a 3 night stay on holiday weekends. Open from January 1st to September 30th. NRRS (April 1st to September 30th).

PETTIT BAY I & II CAMPGROUND

From Tahlequah, go 4 miles southeast on United States Route 62, 4.6 miles south (left) on State Road 82, 2 miles south (right) on Indian Road, 1 mile southeast (left) on access road. Three picnic shelters for up to 50 people and 11 vehicles are $10 to $25. 93 sites, 74 with electric, 5 - 50 ampere, 7 handicap sites with full hookups. Sites without electric hookups are $10; sites with electric hookups are $14; sites with full hookups are $18. Recreational vehicle maximum length is in excess of 65'. This campground requires a 2 night minimum stay on weekends and a 3 night stay on holiday weekends. Open from January 1st to September 30th. NRRS (April 1st to September 30th).

SIZEMORE LANDING CAMPGROUND

From Tahlequah, go 4 miles southeast on United States Route 62, 5 miles south (left) on State Road 82, 3.5 miles south (right)on Indian Road, 1 mile left at sign on access road. A picnic shelter is available. 32 sites. All sites are $5. Recreational vehicle maximum length 30'. Reduced fees in the winter. Open all year.

SNAKE CREEK COVE CAMPGROUND

From Interstate 40, Exit #297 Vian, OK. North on State Hwy. #82, 8.2 miles, then right at the T on State Hwy. #82 and 100, 3.3 miles, turn left at park entrance sign, proceed 1.2 miles to entrance gate. Three picnic shelters for up to 50 people and 21 vehicles are $25. 112 sites, 109 with electric, 5 - 50 ampere, 4 handicap sites with full hookups. Sites without electric hookups are $10; sites with electric hookups are $14; sites with full hookups are $18. Recreational vehicle maximum length is in excess of 65'. This campground requires a 2 night minimum stay on weekends and a 3 night stay on holiday weekends. Open from January 1st to September 30th. NRRS (April 1st to September 30th).

STRAYHORN LANDING CAMPGROUND

From Gore, go 7 miles northeast on State Road 100, 1.5 miles north on State Road 10A, 0.3 mile east (right) at sign on access road. Three picnic shelters, SO1 for up to 50 people and 16 vehicle, and SO2 & SO3 for up to 50 people and 11 vehicles are $25. 40 sites with electric, 2 handicap sites with full hookups. Sites with electric hookups are $15; sites with full hookups are $18. Recreational vehicle maximum length is in excess of 65'. This campground requires a 2 night minimum stay on weekends and a 3 night stay on holiday weekends. Open from January 1st to September 30th. NRRS (April 1st to September 30th).

WAURIKA LAKE (TU) 20

A 10,100 acre surface area lake located 6 miles northwest of Waurika on State Road 5, 25 miles northeast of Wichita Falls, Texas. Lake Manager, Waurika Lake, P. O. Box 29, Waurika, OK 73573-0029. (580) 963-2111.

CHISHOLM TRAIL RIDGE CAMPGROUND

From Hastings, go 5.2 miles east on State Road 5, merge onto gravel road, 3 miles north, 0.9 mile west. A change house is available and a night time exit is provided. There is a handicap accessible fishing area. 95 sites with electric, 14 pull through sites, 1 handicap site. Sites with electric hookups are $14; premium sites with water and electric hookups are $16. Recreational vehicle maximum length is 60'. Open May 1 to September 30th. (580) 439-8040. NRRS.

KIOWA I CAMPGROUND

From Hastings, go 1.2 miles east on State Road 5, 3 miles north. Two group camping areas for up to 64 people and 3 vehicles with a picnic shelter are $100, a picnic shelter and change house are available, and there is a handicap accessible fishing area. 180 sites with water and electric, 47 pull through sites, 1 handicap site with water and electric. Sites with water and electric hookups are $14; premium sites with water and electric hookups are $16. Recreational vehicle maximum length is 60'. This campground requires a 2 night minimum stay on weekends and a 3 night stay on holiday weekends for group camping. Open from March 1st to October 31st. (580) 963-9031. NRRS (May 1st to September 30th).

MONEKA NORTH CAMPGROUND

From Hastings, go 3.7 miles east on State Road 5, 0.8 mile north. A picnic shelter is available. 38 sites. All sites are $8. Open from March 1st to October 31st.

WICHITA RIDGE CAMPGROUND

From Hastings, go 1.2 miles east on State Road 5, 3 miles north, 1 mile west, 2.1 miles north. A picnic shelter is $20. 27 sites, 10 with electric. Sites without electric hookups are $8; sites with electric hookups are $12. Open all year.

WEBBERS FALLS L&D (TU) 21

A 10,900 acre surface area lake located 5 miles northwest of Webbers Falls (30 miles southeast of Muskogee). Project Manager, Route 2, Box 21, Gore, OK 74435-9404. (918) 489-5541.

BREWER BEND CAMPGROUND

From Webbers Falls, go 2 miles west on United States Route 64, 3 miles north & 2 miles northwest (signs). A picnic shelter is $50, and an amphitheater and change house are available. 42 sites, 34 with electric. From April 1st to October 31st, sites without electric hookups are $10; sites with electric hookups are $15; from November 1st to March 31st, sites are available at reduced rates. Open all year.

SPANIARD CREEK CAMPGROUND

From Muskogee/Junction Muskogee Turnpike with State Road 10, go 3 miles south on State Road 64 (signs). 36 sites with electric. From April 1st to October 31st, sites with electric hookups are $14; sites with water and electric hookups are $15; from November 1st to March 31st, sites are available at reduced rates. Open all year.

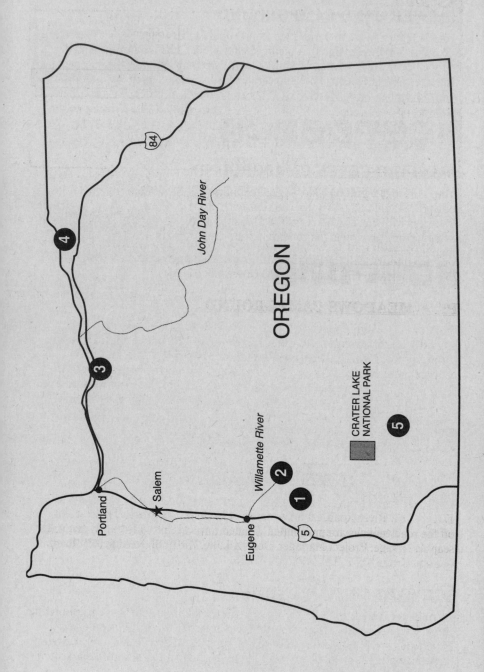

OREGON

STATE CAPITAL:
Salem
NICKNAME:
Beaver State

33rd State - 1859

Site reservation, National Recreation Reservation Service (NRRS), toll free, 1-877-444-6777; TDD 877-833-6777, www.recreation.gov, (Master, Visa, American Express & Discover cards).

COTTAGE GROVE LAKE (PORT) 1

An 1,100 acre surface area lake located 5 miles south of Cottage Grove off I-5 (exit 172) on London Road, 20 miles south of Eugene. Visitor hours to 10 p.m., and off the road vehicles are prohibited. Interpretive displays are available, and for guided tours, call (541) 942-5631. Project Manager, Cottage Grove Lake, 75819 Shortridge Hill Road, Cottage Grove, OR 97424.

PINE MEADOWS CAMPGROUND

From dam, go 1 mile southwest on Reservoir Road, north side. An amphitheater is available. 104 sites, 15 primitive, 4 handicap sites, 26 pull through sites. Primitive sites are $9; Standard sites are $15; a fee of $5 is charged for visitor/extra vehicles. Recreational vehicle maximum length is in excess of 65'. This campground requires a 2 night minimum stay on weekends and a 3 night stay on holidays. Open from May 18th to September 9th. (541) 942-8657. NRRS.

DORENA LAKE (PORT) 2

1,700 acre surface area lake located 6 miles east of Cottage Grove off I-5, exit 174, on Row River Road, 20 miles south of Eugene. Visitors to 10 p.m., and off the road vehicles are prohibited. Guided tours are provided upon request, seaplane usage. Project Manager, Dorena Lake, 75819 Shortridge Hill Road, Cottage Grove, OR 97424. (541) 942-5631.

SCHWARZ CAMPGROUND

From below dam/Junction Row River Road, go 0.2 mile southeast on Shoreline Drive, east near outlet. Six group camping areas for up to 100 people and 20 vehicles are $110 (Maximum 20 camping units & 20 extra vehicles), and horseshoe pits are available. 78 sites, 3 pull through sites, 9 double sites, 2 handicap sites. All sites are $13; double sites are $26. A $5 fee is charged for extra vehicle/visitors. Recreational vehicle maximum length is in excess of 65'. This campground requires a 2 night minimum stay on weekends and a 3 night stay on holiday weekends. Open from April 27th to September 23rd. (541) 942-1418. NRRS.

LAKE UMATILLA (PORT) 3

Located east of United States Route 97, exit 109 off I-84 on the Columbia River. Fish viewing window and self-guided tours are available. Resource Manager, Lake Umatilla, P. O. Box 564, The Dalles, OR 97058-9998. (541) 739-2713. See WA listing.

ALBERT PHILIPPI CAMPGROUND

Located on east side of the John Day River, 3.5 miles upstream from Le Page Park. Boat-in access only. Free.

GILES FRENCH CAMPGROUND

Below dam on Oregon side. Primitive camping, free.

LE PAGE CAMPGROUND

From John Day Dam, go 9 miles east on I-84, exit 114, go south. A fee is charged for use of the dump station by non campers and a $5 fee for extra vehicles, and off the road vehicles are prohibited. A fish cleaning station is available. Restaurants and a convenience store are located nearby. 27 sites, 22 with water and electric, 5 tent only sites available on weekends and holidays only, 8 pull through sites. Tent only sites are $12; sites with water and electric hookups are $17; sites with water and electric hookups, 2nd price, are $18. Recreational vehicle maximum length is 55'. This campground requires a 2 night minimum stay on weekends and a 3 night stay on holiday weekends. Open from April 1st to October 31st. NRRS.

QUESNEL

Located 3 miles east of Le Page Park. Primitive camping, free.

LAKE WALLULA (WW) 4

Located north of junction I-82/ United States 730, 1 mile north of Umatilla on I-82. Interpretive displays, fish viewing rooms. Resource Manager, Western Project, Monument Drive, Burbank, WA 99323. (541) 922-4388. See WA listing.

SAND STATION RECREATION AREA

From Umatilla, go 10.5 miles east on United States Route 730. 20 primitive sites, 15 tent only sites. All sites are free. Open all year.

LOST CREEK LAKE (PORT) 5

A 3,430 acre surface area lake located 30 miles northeast of Medford on State Route 62 and the Rogue River. Seaplane usage, call the office for powerhouse tours, free electrical cook stoves at group picnic sites and a visitor center at McGregor Park. The Cole M. Riven Fish Hatchery is just downstream from the dam. Park Manager, Rogue River Basin Projects, 100 Cole M. Rivers Drive, Trail, OR 97541-9607. (541) 878-2255.

FIRE GLEN CAMPGROUND

From junction Takelma Drive, go 3.6 miles northeast on State Route 62 across Peyton Bridge, 0.8 mile west on Lewis Road, go southwest. Hike-in/boat-in access only. Campsites restricted to 4 tents & 8 people. 4 sites. All sites are free. Open all year.

FOUR CORNERS CAMPGROUND

From junction State Route 62, go 1.4 miles north on Takelma Drive, 0.5 mile north on logging road, east side. Hike-in/boat-in access only. Campsites restricted to 4 tents & 8 people. 7 sites All sites are free. Open all year.

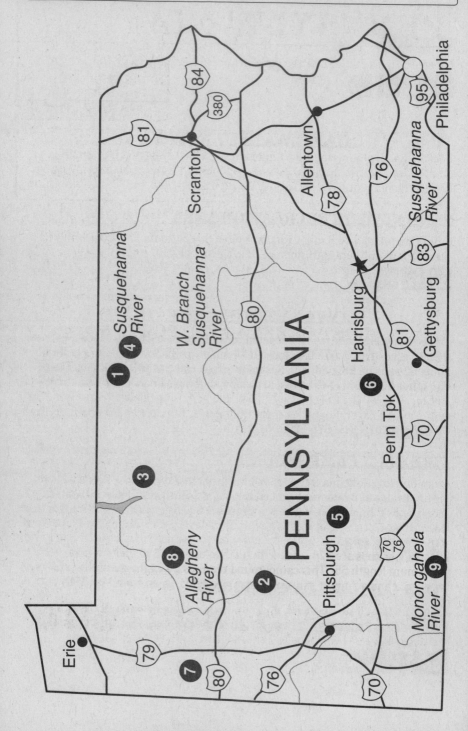

PENNSYLVANIA

STATE CAPITAL:
Harrisburg
NICKNAME:
Keystone State

2nd State - 1787

Site reservation, National Recreation Reservation Service
(NRRS), toll free, 1-877-444-6777; TDD 877-833-6777,
www.recreation.gov, (Master, Visa, American Express
& Discover cards).

**Pittsburgh District - Alcoholic beverages are prohibited at all
their projects. A Rent-A-Tent (RAT) program, includes 9'X12'
cabin tent (sleeps 5-6), 10'X 12' dining fly, 36 quart cooler,
sleeping pads, electric camp stove, camp light.**

COWANESQUE LAKE (BL) 1

A 1,085 acre surface area lake located 2.2 miles west of Lawrenceville on State
Road 49, north of Williamsport. Checkout time is 3 p.m., (a late fee applies),
an extra vehicle fee is $3 and visitors to 10 p.m. Operations Manager, Tioga-
Hammond/Cowanesque Lakes, RR 1, Box 65, Tioga, PA 16946-9733. (570) 835-
5281.

TOMPKINS CAMPGROUND

From Lawrenceville, go 5 miles west on Bliss Road, go south (west of the town
of Nelson). A group camping area with 7 sites is $126, 24 total sites at $16 for
each additional site, an amphitheater and fish cleaning station are available,
and there is a camp store and handicap accessible swimming area. 126 sites,
83 with electric, 40 - 50 ampere, 16 full hookups, 16 primitive tent only hike-in
sites, 1 handicap site without electric, 2 handicap sites with full hookups. Tent
only sites are $18; sites without electric hookups are $20; sites with water and
electric hookups are $24; sites with full hookups are $26. Recreational vehicle
maximum length 55'. This campground requires a 2 night minimum stay on
weekends and a 3 night stay on holiday weekends. Open from May 15th to
September 29th. (570) 827-2109. NRRS.

CROOKED CREEK LAKE (PT) 2

A 350 acre surface area lake located south of Kittanning and Ford City, on east side of State Road 66, 48 miles northeast of Pittsburgh. Winter activities include an ice rink, sled area and cross country skiing. For daily lake information, call (724) 763-2764. Resource Manager, Crooked Creek Lake, Road 3, Box 323A, Ford City, PA 16226-8815. (724) 763-3161.

CROOKED CREEK CAMPGROUND

From Ford City, go 5 miles south on State Road 66, 0.1 mile east on State Road 2019 to Park Managers Office. A group camping area (Memorial Day to Labor Day) and interpretive programs are available. 46 sites. All sites are $10. Open from May 12th September 10th.

CROOKED CREEK PRIMITIVE GROUP AREA

From Ford City, go 5 miles south on State Road 66, east on State Road 2019 to Park Managers Office, call or visit for information. A group camping area is $35 to $45 and a picnic shelter is available. Open from mid May September 30th.

EAST BRANCH CLARION RIVER (PT) 3

A 1,160 acre surface area lake located 36 miles north of De Bois off United States Route 219, 105 miles southeast of Erie, east of Allegheny National Forest. Winter activities include ice fishing. Daily lake information, (814) 965-4762. Resource Manager, 631 East Branch Dam Road, Wilcox, PA 15870-9709. (814) 965-5851.

EAST BRANCH CAMPGROUND

From Wilcox/Junction United States Route 219, go 5 miles southeast on Glen Hazel Road, exit east (left) past Resource Manager's Office to campground. Picnic shelter. 32 sites, 16 with electric, (9 tent only sites are being added), 7 pull through sites. Sites without electric hookups are $15; sites with electric hookups are $20. Open from April 13th to October 14th. (814) 965-2065.

HAMMOND LAKE (BL) 4

A 680 acre surface area lake located 5 miles south of Tioga on State Road 287 in north-central Pennsylvania, 72 miles west of Binghamton, New York. Display gardens, there is an extra vehicle fee of $3 and checkout time is 3 p.m., (late fee applies). Operations Manager, Tioga-Hammond/Cowanesque Lakes, RR 1, Box 65, Tioga, PA 16946-9733. (570) 835-5281.

IVES RUN CAMPGROUND

From Tioga, go 5 miles south on State Road 287, exit east (sign). A picnic shelter is $25 to $70, group camping area with 7 sites is $126 and $16 for each additional site. A fish cleaning station and an amphitheater are available, and there is a handicap accessible swimming area. 187 sites, 109 with water and electric, 45 full hookups, 1 handicap site without electric, 1 handicap site with full hookups, 2 handicap sites with water and electric, 5 pull through sites. Sites without electric hookups are $18; premium sites without electric hookups are $20; sites with water and electric hookups are $22; sites with full hookups are $24. Recreational vehicle maximum length is in excess of 65'. This campground requires a 2 night minimum stay on weekends and a 3 night stay on holiday weekends. Open from April 20th to October 30th. NRRS.

LOYALHANNA LAKE (PT) 5

A 400 acre surface area lake located south of Saltsburg and west of State Road 981, 32 miles east of Pittsburgh. For daily lake information, call (724) 639-3785. Resource Manager, Loyalhanna Lake, 440 Loyalhanna Dam Road, Saltsburg, PA 15681-9302. (724) 639-9013.

BUSH CAMPGROUND

From Saltsburg, go south on State Road 981 past the dam, 1 mile south on Bush Road. Interpretive programs, a picnic shelter is $40 and coin operated showers are available. 49 sites, 10 sites with water and electric. Sites without electric hookups are $14; sites with water and electric hookups are $20; Open from mid May to mid October.

KISKI GROUP CAMPING AREA

From Bush RA, go 0.3 mile north on Bush Road. Priitive group camping area for organized groups only. Call office. Open from mid May to the fall.

RAYSTOWN LAKE (BL) 6

An 8,300 acre surface area lake located just southwest of Huntingdon, east of Johnstown, north of the Pennsylvania Turnpike and east of United States Route 220. Facilities for the handicap include special fishing at Aitch and Shy Beaver Recreational Area. Checkout time is 4 p.m. Resource Manager, Raystown Lake, Road 1, Box 222, Hesston, PA 16647. (814) 658-3405. Raystown.

NANCY'S CAMP

From Marklesburg, go 1.5 miles southwest on State Road 26, go 1 mile southeast & north to trail. By boat-in or hike-in only. 50 sites. All sites are $9. Open all year.

SEVEN POINTS CAMPGROUND

From McConnelstown, go 1.2 miles southwest on State Road 26, 2 miles southeast past Hesston & south of the administration building. A picnic shelter is $50, group camping area is $60 to $80. There is an amphitheater and 6 camping loops available,. There is a convenience store and grocery store nearby. 265 sites, 264 with electric, 6 tent only sites, 15 double sites, 35 - 50 ampere, 2 pull through sites, 1 handicap site with electric. Tent only sites are $19; sites with electric hookups are $20; premium sites with electric hookups and sites with 50 ampere service are $22; buddy sites with electric hookups are $42. Recreational vehicle maximum length is 40'. This campground requires a 2 night minimum stay on weekends and a 3 night stay on holiday weekends. Open from March 30th to October 29th. NRRS (June 1st to July 31st).

SUSQUEHANNOCK CAMPGROUND

From Seven Points camp ground, go 1 mile northeast past the administration building, go southeast. There is a convenience store nearby. 62 sites, 17 tent only sites. All sites are $10. Recreational vehicle maximum length is in excess of 65'. This campground requires a 2 night minimum stay on weekends and a 3 night stay on holiday weekends. Open from May 3rd to September 10th. (814) 658-6806. NRRS.

SHENANGO RIVER LAKE (PT) 7

A 3,560 acre surface area lake located 2 miles north of Hermitage and United States Route 62, off State Road 18 and 518, 6 miles north of I-80, 21 miles northeast of Youngstown, Ohio. A fee is charged for non camper use of the dump station, checkout time is 4 p.m, alcohol is prohibited, visitors to 10 p.m., (a fee may be charged) and there is a 250 acre off the road vehicle area. For daily lake information call (724) 962-4384. Resource Manager, Shenango River Lake, 2442 Kelly Road, Hermitage, PA 16150-9703. (724) 962-7746.

SHENANGO CAMPGROUND

From Hermitage/Junction United States Route 62, go 4.6 miles north on State Road 18, 0.8 mile west on West Lake Road, go south. A picnic shelter is $40, interpretive programs, firewood for a fee, and an amphitheater and horseshoe pits are available. There is a grocery store located nearby. 326 sites, 110 with electric, 15 - 50 ampere, 5 Rent-A-Tent (RAT) only sites, 1 double site, 4 pull through sites, 3 handicap sites with electric. Sites without electric hookups are $15; premium sites without electric hookups are $17; sites with electric hookups are $20; a multiple site is $27, RAT sites are $30. Recreational vehicle maximum length is in excess of 65'. This campground requires a 2 night minimum stay on weekends and a 3 night stay on holiday weekends. Open from May 4th to September 23rd. (724) 646-1115/1118. NRRS (May 4th to September 4th).

TIONESTA LAKE (PT) 8

A 480 acre surface area lake southeast of Tionesta on State Road 36, 60 miles southeast of Erie near the southwest corner of the Allegheny National Forest. Resource Manager, 1 Tionesta Lake, Tionesta, PA 16353. (814) 755-3512.

LACKEY FLATS CAMPGROUND

By boat-in only. 17 primitive sites. All sites are free. Open alll year.

GLASNER RUN CAMPGROUND

By boat-in only. 10 primitive sites. All sites are free. Open all year.

KELLETTVILLE

From Kellettville, Junction State Road 666, southwest across bridge on Forest Road 127. 20 sites. From April 13th to September 22nd, sites are $10. From September 23rd to December 11th, some sites are available and are free. Open from April 13th to December 11th.

OUTFLOW CAMPING AREA

From Tionesta, go 0.5 mile south on State Road 36. A picnic shelter and fishing access for handicap are available. 39 sites. From April 13th to May 20th, sites are $7; from May 21st to September 22nd sites are $10; from September 23rd to April 12th, some sites are available and are free. Open all year.

TIONESTA RECREATION AREA

From Tionesta, go 0.5 mile south on State Road 36 (signs), below the dam. Group camping area for organized youth, scout or chruch groups with prior approval for up to 50 people and 2 vehicles is $24, firewood for a fee, pontoon boat rentals and a convenience store are nearby. 124 sites with full hookups, 62 - 50 ampere. Sites with full hookups are $25. Recreational vehicle maximum length is in excess of 65'. May 21st to September 23rd. NRRS (May 21st to September 3rd).

YOUGHIOGHENY RIVER LAKE (PT) 9

A 2,840 acre surface area lake located south of Confluence off State Road 281 and north of United States Route 40, in southwest Pennsylvania spanning the Mason-Dixon Line between Pennsylvania and Maryland. Trout stockings (April-September), and for lake/recreation information call (814) 395-3166. Resource Manager, Youghiogheny River Lake, R.D. 497 Flanigan Road, Confluence, PA 15424-1932. (814) 395-3242. See MD listing.

OUTFLOW CAMPGROUND

From Confluence, go 0.7 mile southwest on State Road 281. A picnic shelter and an amphitheater are available, bike rentals and firewood are located nearby. Two group camping areas, 1A with water and electric hookups for up to 40 people and 2A for up to 150 people are $30 to $110 (contact office). There is a convenience store and restaurant located nearby. Trout stocking occur from April to September. 63 sites, 32 with electric, 10 tent only sites, 4 full hookup, 9 - 50 ampere, 2 handicap sites without electric. From May 19th to September 10th, sites without electric hookups and tent only sites are $18; sites with electric hookups are $22; sites with full hookups are $38; from mid April to May 18th and September 11th to mid October, sites are at reduced rates; from mid October to mid April, some sites are avaiable and are free. Recreational vehicle maximum length is 60'. Open all year. NRRS (May 18th to September 9th).

TUB RUN CAMPGROUND

From Confluence, go 7 miles southwest on State Road 281, 1.5 miles south on Tub Run Road. An amphitheater is available and there is a convenience store and restaurant located nearby. 101 sites, 32 with electric, 12 tent only walk-in sites, 2 - 50 ampere, 2 handicap sites. Tent only sites and sites without electric hookups are $18; premium sites without electric hookups are $19; premium sites with electric hookups and sites with 50 ampere service are $22. Recreational vehicle maximum length is 55'. Open from May 18th to September 3rd. NRRS.

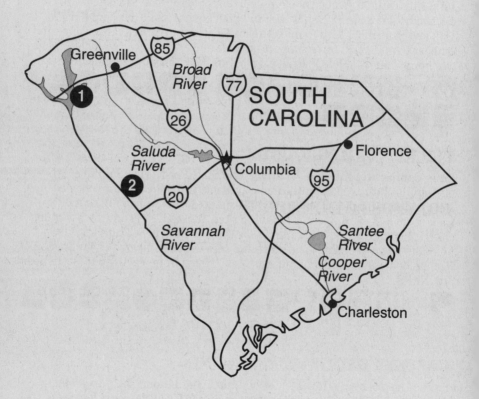

SOUTH CAROLINA

STATE CAPITAL:
Columbia
NICKNAME:
Palmetto State

8th State - 1788

Site reservation, National Recreation Reservation Service
(NRRS), toll free, 1-877-444-6777; TDD 877-833-6777,
www.recreation.gov, (Master, Visa, American Express
& Discover cards).

HARTWELL LAKE (SV) 1

A 56,000 acre surface area lake with 962 miles of shoreline located 5 miles
north of Hartwell, Georgia on United States Route 29, southwest of Greenville
on the state line. Guided tours of dam and power plant are available. Public
use of alcohol is prohibited in campgrounds. Golf carts, off the road vehicles,
motorized scooters, etc., are prohibited. Project Manager, Hartwell Lake and
Powerplant, P. O. Box 278, Hartwell, GA 30643-0278. (706) 856-0300/(888)
893-0678. See GA listing.

CONEROSS CAMPGROUND

From Townville, go 1.5 miles north on State Road 24, east on Coneross Creek
Road, signs. 106 sites, 94 with water and 50 ampere service, 36 pull through
sites, 1 handicap site. Sites without electric hookups are $12; sites with water
and 50 ampere service are $18; premium sites with water and 50 ampere
service are $20; a double site is $42. Open from May 1st to September 29th.
Recreational vehicle maximum length in excess of 65'. NRRS.

CRESENT GROUP CAMPGROUND

From Anderson, go 14 miles south on United States Route 29. Two group
camping areas, Loop A for up to 100 people and 30 vehicles with 10 sites is
$120, and Loop B for up to 100 people and 66 vehicles with 22 sites having
water and 50 ampere service is $120, from 101 to 150 people is $160; from 151
to 200 people is $200; from 201 to 300 people is $260, and with a picnic shelter
for up to 100 people. Open from April 1st to October 30th. Recreational vehicle
maximum length is 40'. NRRS.

OCONEE POINT CAMPGROUND

From Townville, go 1.5 miles north on State Road 24, 2.5 miles east on Coneross Creek Road, 3 miles south on Friendship Road, signs. this campground is suitable for tents and popup campers only. 70 sites with 50 ampere service, 15 overflow without hookups, 16 pull through sites, 1 handicap site. Sites with 50 ampere service are $20; double sites with 50 ampere service are $42; overflow sites without electric hookups are $12. Recreational vehicle maximum length is 25'. Open from May 1st to October 30th. NRRS.

SPRINGFIELD CAMPGROUND

From Anderson, go 4.5 miles west on State Road 24, 4 miles south on State Road 187, follow signs. Limited to tents and pop up campers only. Trailers and motor homes are not permitted, 79 sites with water and 50 ampere service, 28 pull through sites, 4 double sites, 1 handicap site. Sites with water and 50 ampere service are $20; double sites with water and 50 ampere service are $42. Open from April 1st to Ocdtober 30th. Recreational vehicle maximum length is 40'. NRRS.

TWIN LAKES CAMPGROUND

From Clemson, go 5.5 miles southeast on Highway 76, 3 miles southwest on County Road 56, follow signs. Two picnic shelters, GS1 for up to 75 people and 1 vehicle and GS2 for up to 150 people and 1 vehicle. 102 sites with water and 50 ampere service, 26 pull through sites, 2 double sites, 1 handicap site. From April 1st to September 29th, sites with water and 50 ampere service are $18; premium sites with water and 50 ampere service are $20; double sites with water and 50 ampere service are $42. For March and from September 30th to November 29th, sites with water and 50 ampere service are $16; premium sites with water and 50 ampere service are $18; double sites with water and 50 ampere service are $40. Open from March 1st to November 29th. Recreational vehicle maximum length is 60'. NRRS.

J. STROM THURMOND (SV) 2

A 70,000 acre surface area lake with 1200 miles of shoreline located adjacent to the west side of Clarks Hill, southwest of Greenville on United States Route 221 and the Georgia state line. Exhibits at visitor center, checkout time is 2 p.m., public use of alcohol is prohibited in campgrounds and an extra vehicle fee is $3. For current lake conditions, call 1 (800) 333-3478, ext. 1147. Resource Manager, J. Strom Thurmond Lake, Rt. 1, Box 12, Clarks Hill, SC 29821-9701. (864) 333-1100/(800) 533-3478. See GA listing.

HAWE CREEK CAMPGROUND

From McCormick/Junction United States Route 221, go 0.5 mile southwest on United States Route 378 past junction State Road 439, 4 miles south on Park Road. Shopping and restaurants are located nearby. 34 sites with water and electric, 24 - 50 ampere, 6 pull through sites. Sites with water and electric hookups are $18; sites with water and 50 ampere service are $20. Recreational vehicle maximum length is 45'. This campground requires a 2 night minimum stay on weekends and a 3 night stay on holiday weekends. Open from April 1st to September 30th. (864) 443-5441. NRRS.

LEROYS FERRY CAMPGROUND

From Willington, go 4 miles southwest. 10 primitive sites. All sites are $6. Open all year.

MODOC CAMPGROUND

From Modoc, go 1 mile south on United States Route 221, go east. A picnic shelter is available. 70 sites, 69 with water and electric, 29 pull through sites, 54 - 50 ampere, 1 double site. A site without electric hookups is $14; sites with water and electric hookups are $16; premium sites with water and electric hookups and a site with water and 50 ampere service are $18; premium sites with water and 50 ampere service are $20; from April 1st to October 31st, a double site with water and electric hookups is $40. From November 1st to November 30th, a double site with water and electric hookups is $32. Recreational vehicle maximum length is 45'. This campground requires a 2 night minimum stay on weekends and a 3 night stay on holiday weekends. Open from April 1st to November 30th. (864) 333-2272. NRRS.

MOUNT CARMEL CAMPGROUND

From Mount Carmel, go 4.3 miles southwest. A picnic shelter and a fish cleaning station are available. 44 sites, 39 with water and 50 ampere, 12 pull through sites. Sites with out electric hookups are $16; sites with water and 50 ampere service are $18; premium sites with water and 50 ampere service are $20. Recreational vehicle maximum length is 40'. This campground requires a 2 night minimum stay on weekends and a 3 night stay on holiday weekends. Open from April 1st to September 2nd. (864) 391-2711. NRRS.

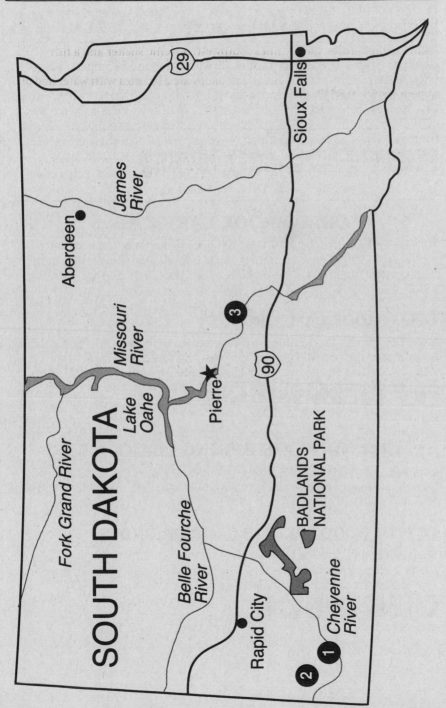

SOUTH DAKOTA

STATE CAPITAL:
Pierre
NICKNAME:
Mount Rushmore State
40th State - 1889

Site reservation, National Recreation Reservation Service
(NRRS), toll free, 1-877-444-6777; TDD 877-833-6777,
www.recreation.gov, (Master, Visa, American Express
& Discover cards).

COLD BROOK LAKE (OM) 1

Located 1 mile northwest of Hot Springs off United States Route 385 in
southwest South Dakota. An archery range is located on the east side of the
lake. Corps of Engineers, Cold Brook Lake & Cottonwood Springs, P. O. Box
664, Hot Springs, SD 57747. (605) 745-5476.

COLD BROOK CAMPGROUND

From Hot Springs, go 0.5 mile north. A group camping area and picnic shelters
are available. 13 sites. All sites are $5. From mid September to mid May, some
sites are available and are free, may have reduced amenities. Open all year.

COTTONWOOD SPRINGS LAKE (OM) 2

Located 5 miles west of Hot Springs in southwest South Dakota. Corps of
Engineers, Cold Brook Lake & Cottonwood Springs, P. O. Box 664, Hot Springs,
SD 57747. (605) 745-5476.

COTTONWOOD SPRINGS CAMPGROUND

From Hot Springs, go 5 miles west on State Road 18, 2 miles north on County
Road 17. Picnic shelters are available. 18 sites. All sites are $5. Open from May
15th to September 15th. Recreational vehicle maximum length is 30'.

LAKE SHARPE (OM) 3

Located 2 miles southwest of Fort Thompson, 60 miles southeast of Pierre. Power house tours daily during the summer and during the off season by appointment, and exhibit and artifact displays. Lake Manager, Lake Sharpe, HC 69, Box 74, Chamberlain, SD 57325-9407. (605) 245-2255.

OLD FORT THOMPSON CAMPGROUND

Located below the dam on the east side of the spillway. A picnic shelter is available. 13 primitive sites. All sites are free. Open all year.

NORTH SHORE CAMPGROUND

From dam/Junction State Road 47, go northwest past the project office. A fish cleaning station and picnic shelter are available. 24 primitive sites, 2 handicap sites. All sites are free. Open all year.

LEFT TAILRACE CAMPGROUND

Located below dam on the south side of the spillway. A picnic shelter, fish cleaning station, an amphitheater and horseshoe pits are available. 81 sites, 2 handicap sites, 35 pull through sites. All sites are $14. Recreational vehicle maximum length is 35'. Open from early May to late September.

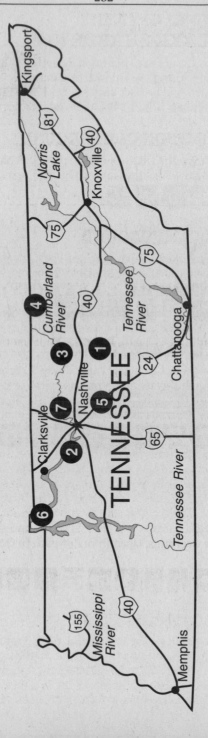

TENNESSEE

STATE CAPITAL:
Nashville
NICKNAME:
Volunteer State

16th State - 1796

Site reservation, National Recreation Reservation Service (NRRS), toll free, 1-877-444-6777; TDD 877-833-6777, www.recreation.gov, (Master, Visa, American Express & Discover cards).

Nashville District - Fees may be higher on weekends. A day time visitor fee may be charged.

CENTER HILL LAKE (NV) 1

An 18,220 acre surface area lake located south of I-40 on State Road 96 northwest Smithville, 64 miles east of Nashville. Wildlife exhibit, alcohol is prohibited and checkout time is 3 p.m. Resource Manager, Center Hill Lake, 158 Resource Lane, Lancaster, TN 38569-9410. (931) 858-3125/(615) 548-4521.

FLOATING MILL CAMPGROUND

From I 40, exit 273, go 5 miles south on Floating Mill Road, right at store (signs). An amphitheater and a fish cleaning station are available, and a picnic shelter for up to 100 people is $50. 118 sites, 27 - 50 ampere, 4 pull through sites, 13 handicap sites with water and 50 ampere service. Tent only sites are $14; sites without hookups are $16; premium tent only sites and sites with water and electric hookups are $18; premium tent only sites with water and electric are $20; premium sites with water and electric hookups and sites with water and 50 ampere service are $24. Recreational vehicle maximum length is 60'. This campground requires a 2 night minimum stay on weekends and a 3 night stay on holiday weekends. Open from April 9th to October 21st. (931) 858-4845. NRRS.

LONG BRANCH CAMPGROUND

From I-40, exit 268, go 5 miles west on State Road 96, 2 miles west on Center Hill Dam Road, 1 mile north on State Road 141, on right (signs). A picnic shelter for up to 125 people is $50 and a fish cleaning station is available. 60 sites with water and electric, 39 - 50 ampere, 3 full hookups, 3 handicap sites. Sites with water and electric hookups and sites with water and 50 ampere service are $20; sites with full hookups are $22; premium sites with water and 50 ampere service are $24. Recreational vehicle maximum length is in excess of 65'. This campground requires a 2 night minimum stay on weekends and a 3 night stay on holiday weekends. Open from March 30th to October 30th. (615) 548-8002. NRRS.

RAGLAND BOTTOM CAMPGROUND

From Smithville, go 8 miles northeast on United States Route 70 across Lake Bridge, left on Ragland Bottom Road (signs). A picnic shelter for up to 125 people is $50. 56 sites, 30 - 50 ampere, 8 pull through sites, 10 handicap sites with full hookups, 26 tent only sites. Tent only sites without electric are $14; premium tent only sites with water and electric and sites with water and 50 ampere service are $20; sites with full hookups and 50 ampere service are $22; premium sites with water and 50 ampere service are $24. Recreational vehicle maximum length is in excess of 65'. This campground requires a 2 night minimum stay on weekends and a 3 night stay on holiday weekends. Open from April 16th to October 14th. (931) 761-3616. NRRS.

CHEATHAM LAKE (NV) 2

A 7,450 acre surface area lake located 12 miles northwest of Ashland City off State Road 12 northwest of Nashville. Resource Manager, Cheatham Lake, 1798 Cheatham Dam Road, Ashland City, TN 37015-9805. (615) 254-3734/792-5697.

HARPETH RIVER BRIDGE CAMPGROUND

From Ashland City, go 6 miles west on State Road 49 to Harpeth River Bridge. 15 sites. Sites are $7 to $9; a visitor fee of $3 may be charged. Open from April 7th to October 31st. (615) 792-4195.

LOCK A CAMPGROUND

From Ashland City, go 8 miles west on State Road 12 to Cheap Hill, 4 miles southwest (left) on Cheatham Dam Road. A fish cleaning station, horseshoe pits and a picnic shelter are available, and there is a handicap accessible fishing area. 45 sites with water and 50 ampere, 7 tent only sites, 2 handicap sites. Tent only sites with water and electric and sites with water and electric hookups are $19; premium sites with water and electric hookups are $23. Recreational vehicle maximum length is 40'. This campground requires a 2 night minimum stay on weekends and a 3 night stay on holiday weekends. Open from April 1st to October 31st. (615) 792-3715. NRRS (April 1st to September 4th).

CORDELL HULL LAKE (NV) 3

An 11,960 acre surface area lake located 2.5 miles northeast of Carthage off State Road 263, 49 miles east of Nashville. Wildlife exhibit at visitor center. Golf carts, off the road vehicles, electic schooters, etc., are prohibited and a visitor fee of $3 per car is assessed. Campgrounds may charge $1 per day extra on weekends and holiday weekends. Resource Manager, Cordell Hull Lake, 71 Corps Lane, Carthage, TN 37030-9710. (615) 735-1034.

DEFEATED CREEK CAMPGROUND

From Carthage, go 4 miles west on State Road 25, north on United States Route 80, east on State Road 85, go south. Two picnic shelters, P001 for up to 100 people and 1 vehicle is $50 and C002 for up to 250 people and 1 vehicle is $100. 6 mile Bearwaller Gap Trail is available. 155 sites with water and electric, 63 full hookups, 35 pull through sites. Sites with water and electric hookups are $15; sites with water and electric hookups, 3rd and 4th price, are $18; sites with water and electric hookups, 2nd price, and sites with full hookups are $22; premium sites with water and electtric are $24; premium sites with full hookups are $25. A $1 per night additional fee on weekends and holidays. Recreational vehicle maximum length is in excess of 65'. This campground requires a 2 night minimum stay on weekends and a 3 night stay on holiday weekends. Open from April 5th to October 28th. (615) 774-3141. NRRS.

SALT LICK CREEK CAMPGROUND

From Carthage, go 4 miles west on State Road 27, north on United States Route 80, east on State Road 85, right on Smith Bend Road (signs). A picnic shelter for up to 100 people and 1 vehicle is $50, and there is a convenience store is located nearby. 150 sites with water and electric, 31 full hookups, 15 pull through sites. Sites with water and electric hookups, 4th price, are $15; premium sites with water and electric hookups, sites with water and electric hookups, 5th price, and sites with full hookups, 3rd price, are $18; a site with water and electric hookups is $20; sites with water and electric hookups, 2nd price, are $22; sites with full hookups, 2nd price, sites with full hookups and premium sites with full hookups are $25. Recreational vehicle maximum length is in excess of 65'.

This campground requires a 2 night minimum stay on weekends and a 3 night stay on holiday weekends. Open from May 10th to September 3rd. (931) 678-4718. NRRS.

DALE HOLLOW LAKE (NV) 4

A 27,700 acre surface area lake located 4 miles east of Celina, northeast of Nashville, on both sides of the Kentucky/Tennessee state lines. A National Fish Hachery is nearby. Alcohol is prohibited. Resource Manager, Dale Hollow Lake, 5050 Dale Hollow Dam Road, Celina, TN 38551-9708. (931) 243-3136.

DALE HOLLOW DAM CAMPGROUND

From Celina, go 2 miles northwest on State Road 32, 1.5 miles northeast (right) on State Road 53 (Dale Hollow Road, signs), go south, below spillway. A picnic shelter for up to 50 people is $50, from 51 to 100 people is $100, from 101 to 150 people is $150, from 151 to 200 people is $200, from 201 to 250 people is $250. An amphitheater and fish cleaning station are available, and there is a handicap accessible fishing area. 79 sites with water and 50 ampere service, 16 pull through sites, 2 handicap site. Sites with water and 50 ampere service, 2nd price, are $17; sites with water and 50 ampere service are $20; premium sites with water and 50 ampere service are $24. Recreational vehicle maximum length is 60'. This campground requires a 2 night minimum stay on weekends and a 3 night stay on holiday weekends. Open March 30th to October 28th. (931) 243-3554. NRRS.

LILLYDALE CAMPGROUND

From Highway 111, go 13.3 miles north on State Road 294 (Willow Grove Road). A picnic shelter for up to 100 people is $40. 111 sites, 82 with electric, 35 - 50 ampere, 29 tent only sites, 15 primitive sites (island camping), 3 pull through sites, 1 handicap site. Tent only sites, 2nd price, are $10; tent only sites and sites without electric hookups are $15; premium tent only sites, a tent only site with water and electric, premium sites without electric hookups, sites with water and electric hookups and sites with water and 50 ampere service are $20; premium sites with water and electric hookups and premium sites with water and 50 ampere service are $24. Recreational vehicle maximum length is 40'. This campground requires a 2 night minimum stay on weekends and a 3 night stay on holiday weekends. Open from April 27th to September 3rd. (931) 823-4155. NRRS.

OBEY RIVER CAMPGROUND

From Livingston, go 15 miles northeast on State Road 111 (signs), go west before lake bridge. Two picnic shelters, L1 with handicap facilities for up to 150 people, and S2 with handicap facilities for up to 50 people are $40. 132 sites, 89 with electric, 19 - 50 ampere, 26 tent only sites, 28 pull through sites. A tent only site, tent only sites, 2nd price, and sites without hookups, 2nd price, are $12; sites without hookups, 3rd price, are $15; sites without hookups, sites with water and electric hookups, 3rd price, and 1 site with water and 50 ampere service are $18; premium tent sites, premium sites without hookups, sites with water and electric hookups, sites with water and sites with water and 50 ampere service are $20; premium tent only sites with water and 50 ampere and premium sites with water and 50 ampere are $24. Recreational vehicle maximum length is 55'. This campground requires a 2 night minimum stay on weekends and a 3 night stay on holiday weekends. Open from April 13th to October 14th. (931) 864-6388. NRRS.

WILLOW GROVE CAMPGROUND

From Oakley, go 0.7 mile northeast on State Road 2260, 10 miles north & west on State Road 294. A picnic shelter for up to 50 people is $50, from 51 to 100 people is $100, from 101 to 150 people is $150, from 151 to 200 people is $200. An amphitheater is available, and scuba diving is permitted. 83 sites, 62 with water and 50 ampere service, 21 tent only sites, 1 handicap site with water and 50 ampere. Tent only sites are $12; a premium tent only site is $15; sites with water and 50 ampere service, 2nd price, are $17; sites with water and 50 ampere service are $20; premium sites with water and 50 ampere service are $24. Recreational vehicle maximum length is 45'. This campground requires a 2 night minimum stay on weekends and a 3 night stay on holiday weekends. Open from May 18th to September 3rd. (931) 823-4285. NRRS.

J. PERCY PRIEST LAKE (NV) 5

A 14,200 acre surface acre lake located 10 miles east of Nashville off I-40. Alcohol and off the road vehicles are prohibited in day use areas, exhibits and checkout time is 2 p.m., and a visitor fee may be charged at the campground. Resource Manager, J. Percy Priest Lake, 3737 Bell Road, Nashville, TN 37214-2660. (615) 889-1975.

ANDERSON ROAD CAMPGROUND

From Nashville, go 5 miles east on I-40, exit 219, 5 miles south on Bell Road, 1 mile east on Smith Spring Road, 1 mile north on Anderson Road. Two picnic shelters with handicap facilities for up to 160 people and 60 vehicles are available from April 1st to October 29th and require a $40 reservation fee and all users must pay a day use fee. 37 sites, 15 pull through sites. Sites without hookups are $12; premium sites without hookups are $14. Recreational vehicle maximum length is in excess of 65'. This campground requires a 2 night minimum stay on weekends and a 3 night stay on holiday weekends. May 2nd to October 30th. (615) 361-1980. NRRS.

POOLE KNOBS CAMPGROUND

From Lavergne, southeast on United States Route 41, go 2 miles north on Fergus Road, 4 miles northeast on Jones Mill Road. Group camping area for up to 40 people and 12 vehicles is $50. 87 sites, 6 tent only sites, 55 - 50 ampere, 56 pull through sites, 4 handicap sites. Tent only sites are $10; sites without hookups are $14; premium sites without hookups are $16; sites with water and 50 ampere service are $18; premium sites with water and 50 ampere service are $24. Recreational vehicle maximum length is in excess of 65'. This campground requires a 2 night minimum stay on weekends and a 3 night stay on holiday weekends. Open from April 30th to September 30th. (615) 459-6948. NRRS.

SEVEN POINTS CAMPGROUND

I-40, exit 221B, south (right) on Old Hickory Blvd. (sign), go east (left) on Bell Road, 1 mile south (right) on New Hope Road, 1 mile east (left) on Stewarts Ferry Pike (signs). Two picnic shelters, SP1 for up to 50 people and 45 vehicles is $40, and up to 100 people is $80, and SP2 for up to 150 people and 65 vehicles are is $120. 60 sites with water and electric, 1 full hookup, 45 - 50 ampere, 4 pull through sites, 6 handicap sites. Sites with water and electric hookups are $20; premium sites with water and electric hookups are $24. Recreational vehicle maximum length is in excess of 65'. This campground requires a 2 night minimum stay on weekends and a 3 night stay on holiday weekends. Open from April 2nd to October 30th. (615) 889-5198. NRRS.

LAKE BARKLEY (NV) 6

A 57,920 acre surface area lake located south of Junction I-24/United States Route 62, east of Paducah, Kentucky. Various exhibits. Resource Manager, Lake Barkley, Box 218, Highway 62, Grand River, KY 42045-0218. (502) 362-4236. See KY listing.

BUMPUS MILLS CAMPGROUND

From Clarksville, go 20 miles west on United States Route 79, 10 miles northwest on State Road 120 through Bumpus Mills, west on Tobaccoport Road, (sign), 1 mile of gravel road (continue straight at "Y" and sign, down hill). A convenience store is located nearby. 15 sites, with water and electric, 2 pull through sites. Sites with water and electric hookups are $16; premium sites with water and electric hookups are $17. Recreational vehicle maximum length is 65'. This campground requires a 2 night minimum stay on weekends and a 3 night stay on holiday weekends. Open from May 4th to September 3rd. (931) 232-8831. NRRS.

OLD HICKORY LAKE (NV) 7

A 22,500 acre surface area lake located 2 miles west of Hendersonville, south of United States Route 31E, 10 miles northeast of Nashville. Displays, exhibits and video programs, and an extra day use fee per vehicle may be charged at the campgrounds. Resource Manager, Old Hickory Lake, No. 5 Power Plant Road, Hendersonville, TN 37075-3465. (615) 822-4848/847-2395.

CAGES BEND CAMPGROUND

From Hendersonville, go 5.5 miles northeast on State Road 31E, southeast on Benders Ferry Road (signs). A convenience store is located nearby. 43 sites with water and electric, 1 pull through site, 2 handicap sites. Sites with water and electric hookups are $19; premium sites with water and electric hookups are $23. Recreational vehicle maximum length is in excess of 65'. This campground requires a 2 night minimum stay on weekends and a 3 night stay on holiday weekends. Open from March 30th to October 31st. (615) 824-4989. NRRS.

CEDAR CREEK CAMPGROUND

From junction County Road 109, go 6 miles west on United States Route 70, go north. A picnic shelter for up to 50 people is $35, and a convenience store is located nearby. 59 sites with water and electric. Sites with water and electric hookups are $19; premium sites with water and electric hookups are $23. Recreational vehicle maximum length is in excess of 65'. This campground requires a 2 night minimum stay on weekends and a 3 night stay on holiday weekends. Open from March 30th to October 31st. (615) 754-4947. NRRS.

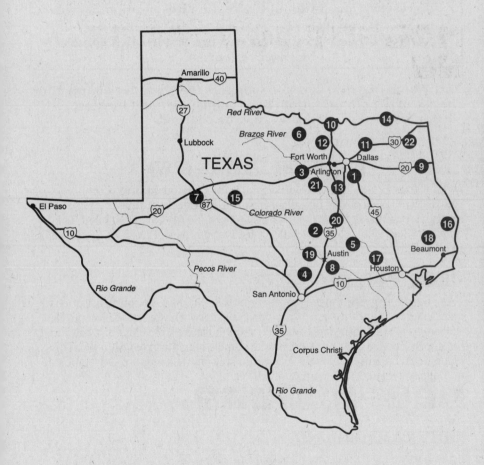

TEXAS

STATE CAPITAL:
Austin
NICKNAME:
Lone Star State

28th State - 1845

Site reservation, National Recreation Reservation Service
(NRRS), toll free, 1-877-444-6777; TDD 877-833-6777,
www.recreation.gov, (Master, Visa, American Express
& Discover cards).

**Fort Worth District - For non campers there is a fee charged for
the use of the dump station, boat launching and for showers.
Visitor's to 10 p.m., and a fee may be charged.**

BARDWELL LAKE (FW) 1

A 3,500 acre surface area lake with 25 miles of shoreline located south of
Ennis, 35 miles southeast of Dallas, west of I-45. Checkout time is 2 p.m., night
emergency exits at gated campgrounds and ground fires are prohibited. Lake
Manager, Bardwell Lake Office, 4000 Observation Drive, Ennis, TX 75119-9563.
(972) 875-5711.

HIGHVIEW CAMPGROUND

From Bardwell, go 1.7 miles northeast on State Road 34, go southeast prior to
lake bridge. A night time exit is provided. 39 sites with water and electric, 21
- 50 ampere. Sites with water and elctric hookups are $14; sites with water and
50 ampere service are $16. Recreational vehicle maximum length is 65'. This
campground requires a 2 night minimum stay on weekends and a 3 night stay
on holiday weekends. Open all year. NRRS.

MOTT CAMPGROUND

From Bardwell, go 1 mile northeast on State Road 34, go southeast. A picnic
shelter for up to 100 people and 4 vehicles is $80, and a group camping area for
up to 100 people and 31 vehicles is $80, and a night time exit is provided. 40
sites, 33 with water and electric, 14 pull through sites. Sites without electric
hookups are $14; sites with water and electric hookups are $16. Recreational

vehicle maximum length is 65'. This campground requires a 2 night minimum stay on weekends and a 3 night stay on holiday weekends. Open from April 1st to September 29th. NRRS.

WAXAHACHIE CREEK CAMPGROUND

From Bardwell, go 1.2 miles northeast on State Road 24, go northwest. A picnic shelter for up to 200 people and 100 vehicles is $120, group camping area is $110, boat rentals are located nearby, and a night time exit is provided. 76 sites, 73 with water and electric, 14 pull through sites, 1 tent only site, 4 horse sites with water and electric. A tent only site and sites without electric hookups are $14; horse sites and sites with water and electric hookups are $16; premium sites with water and electric hookups are $18. Recreational vehicle maximum length is 65'. This campground requires a 2 night minimum stay on weekends and a 3 night stay on holiday weekends. Open all year. NRRS.

BELTON LAKE (FW) 2

A 12,300 acre surface area lake located 5 miles northwest of Belton on Farm to Market Road 2271, adjacent to Fort Hood Army Base, north of Austin. Checkout time is 1 p.m. Resource Manager, Little River Project Office, 3110 Farm to Market Road Road 2271, Belton, TX 76513-6522. (254) 939-2461.

CEDAR RIDGE CAMPGROUND

From junction State Road 317 north of Belton, go 2 miles northwest on State Road 36, 1 mile southwest on Cedar Ridge Park Road. Two picnic shelters, Coveside for up to 80 people and 40 vehicles and Sunset for up to 100 people and 40 vehicles are $40, and Turkey Roost group camping area (see listing below). Park access codes are provided to registered campers for late entry and there is a handicap accessible swimming area. 68 sites with water and electric, 2 pull through sites, 37 - 50 ampere, 49 handicap sites, 1 double site, 8 screened shelters. Tent only sites and sites with water and electric hookups, 2nd, 3rd, and 5th price are $16; sites with water and 50 ampere service, 1st and 4th price are $18; 1 double site with water and electric hookups is $32, 8 screen shelters are $30. Recreational vehicle maximum length is in excess of 65'. This campground requires a 2 night minimum stay on weekends and a 3 night stay on holiday weekends. Open all year. NRRS.

IRON BRIDGE CAMPGROUND

From junction Farm to Market Road 2909/State Road 317, go 9 miles west on S.R. 36, go north on Iron Bridge Road. 5 sites. All sites are free. Open all year.

LIVE OAK RIDGE CAMPGROUND

From junction State Road 317, go 1.7 miles northwest on Farm to Market Road 2305, on right. An amphitheater is available. 48 sites with water and electric, 14 handicap sites, 11 - 50 ampere. Sites with water and electric hookups are $16; sites with water and 50 ampere service are $18. Recreational vehicle maximum length is in excess of 65'. This campground requires a 2 night minimum stay on weekends and a 3 night stay on holiday weekends. Open all year. NRRS.

OWL CREEK CAMPGROUND

From junction State Road 317, go 6.5 miles northwest on State Road 36, across lake bridge, 1 mile west at "Y", go south. 10 sites. All sites are free. Open all year.

TURKEY ROOST GROUP CAMPGROUND

Located at Cedar Ridge Park. Horseshoe pits, picnic shelter, group camping only. Must be by reservation made in person at the Little River Project Office. Contact the office for maximum number of recreational vehicles and tents permitted. 6 sites, 2 double sites with 50 ampere service. Friday-Sunday nights are $175; Monday-Thursday nights are $100. Open all year. NRRS.

WESTCLIFF CAMPGROUND

From junction State Road 317 north of Belton, go 3.7 miles northwest on Farm to Market Road 439, 0.2 mile northwest, go northeast on Westcliff Park road. A picnic shelter is available and there is a handicap accessible swimming area. 31 sites, 27 with water and electric, 4 tent only sites, 20 pull through sites, 4 handicap sites without electric, 8 handicap sites with water and electric. Tent only sites without electric are $10; tent only sites with water and electric and sites with water and electric hookups are $16. Recreational vehicle maximum length is in excess of 65'. This campground requires a 2 night minimum stay on weekends and a 3 night stay on holiday weekends. Open all year. NRRS.

WHITE FLINT CAMPGROUND

From junction State Road 317, go 5.5 miles northwest on State Road 36, across bridge, north side. Access codes are provided to registered campers for late night entry. 13 sites with 50 ampere, 6 handicap sites, 12 screened sites. Sites with 50 ampere service are $18; screened sites are $30. Recreational vehicle maximum length is 60'. This campground requires a 2 night minimum stay on weekends. Open all year. NRRS.

WINKLER CAMPGROUND

From junction State Road 317, go 5.5 miles northwest on State Road 36, exit right (northeast) 2 miles past White Flint Park. 15 sites, 11 tent only sites. All sites are $8. Recreational vehicle maximum length is 35'. Open all year.

BENBROOK LAKE (FW) 3

3,770-acre lake 12 miles southwest of Forth Worth, on the south side of Benbrook. Checkout time is 2 p.m. Resource Manager, Benbrook Lake, P. O. Box 26619, Ft. Worth, TX 76126-0619. (817) 292-2400.

HOLIDAY CAMPGROUND

From Benbrook & I-20, exit 429A, go 5.7 miles southwest on United States Route 377, 1.7 miles east on Farm to Market Road 1187 (Park Road). Horse rentals are located nearby. 105 sites, 70 with water and electric, 51 handicap accessible sites, 35 - 50 ampere, 1 horse site, 40 pull through sites, 5 screened shelters. Sites with electric hookups are $10; sites with water and electric hookups are $20; screened shelters are $30. Recreational vehicle maximum length is in excess of 65'. This campground requires a 2 night minimum stay on weekends and a 3 night stay on holiday weekends. Open all year. NRRS.

MUSTANG - BEAR CREEK CAMPGROUND

From Benbrook & I-20, go 6.4 miles southwest on United States Route 377, 1.4 miles southeast on Farm to Market Road 1187, 1.7 miles north on County Road 1042. Group camping area with 6 sites is $100 and a picnic shelter for up to 50 people and 11 vehicles is available. There is a night time exit. 46 sites with water and electric, 25 accessible handicap sites, 6 - 50 ampere, 2 full hookups, 10 pull through sites. Sites with water and electric hookups are $20; sites with full hookups are $22. Recreational vehicle maximum length is in excess of 65'. This campground requires a 2 night minimum stay on weekends and a 3 night stay on holiday weekends. Open all year. NRRS.

MUSTANG - POINT

Adjacent to Mustang Park - Bear. No designated sites, primitive area. Fees are $10. Open from April 1st to September 30th.

ROCKY CREEK CAMPGROUND

From Benbrook, south on United States Route 377, go 7 miles southeast on Farm to Market Road 1187, 3.6 miles north on County Road 1089, at Junction County Road 1150, exit south to park. 11 sites. All sites are $10. Open all year.

CANYON LAKE (FW) 4

An 8,230 acre surface area lake with 80 miles of shoreline is located northeast of San Antonio, 16 miles northwest of New Braunfels off Farm to Market Road 306. Checkout time is 2 p.m. Resource Manager, Canyon Lake, 601 COE Road, Canyon Lake, TX 78133-4129. (830) 964-3341.

CANYON CAMPGROUND

From Canyon City, go 3.2 miles northwest on Farm to Market Road 306, go southwest. A picnic shelter is $35 from Monday through Thursday and $75 on Friday, Saturday, Sunday and Holidays, and boat rentals are located nearby. 150 primitive sites. Monday through Thursday sites are $8; Friday through Sunday sites are $12. Open from April 1st to September 30th.

CRANES MILLS CAMPGROUND

From Startzville, go 2.8 miles north. Boat rentals are located nearby. 46 primitive sites. Monday through Thursday sites are $8; Friday through Sunday sites are $12. There are a limited number of camping sites from October 1st to February 28th. Open all year.

NORTH CAMPGROUND

From Canyon City, go 1.2 miles northwest on Farm to Market Road 306, 1 mile southeast. Divers welcome. 19 primitive sites. Monday through Thursday sites are $8; Friday through Sunday sites are $12. Open March 1st to November 30th.

POTTER'S CREEK CAMPGROUND

From Canyon City, go 6.2 miles northwest on Farm to Market Road 306, 2 miles south. A picnic shelter is $50 Monday through Thursday and $100 Friday through Sunday. a convenience store and restaurants are nearby. 119 sites with water and electric, 17 tent only sites, 102 - 50 ampere, 1 double site, 4 triple sites, 7 screened shelters, 50 handicap sites. Tent only sites with water and electric hookups are $14; sites with water and 50 ampere service are $18; a double site with water and 50 ampere service is $36; triple sites with water and 50 ampere service are $54; screened shelters are $34. Recreational vehicle maximum length 60'. Open all year. NRRS (May 1st to September 12th).

GRANGER LAKE (FW) 5

A 4,400 acre surface area lake located 30 miles northeast of Austin off State Road 95, 6.5 miles east of Granger on Farm to Market Road Road 971, 1 mile south on local road. Resource Manager, Granger Lake, 3100 Granger Dam Road, Granger, TX 76530-5067. (512) 859-2668.

FOX BOTTOM CAMPING

Hike-in from West Trailhead on County Road 496 on the Comanche Bluff Hiking Trail which starts at the park and ends at Taylor park; or by boat-in from Taylor Park (Pay boat ramp fee for number of days prior to departure); or 0.5 mile down stream from Box 7 primitive boat launch via jon boat or canoe. 8 primitive sites. All sites are free. Information and register (reguired) by calling (512) 859-2668. Open all year except during Hunt Draw periods.

TAYLOR CAMPGROUND

From Circleville/Junction Highway 95, go 9 miles northeast on Farm to Market Road 1331, go northwest. The Comanche Bluff Hiking trail starts at the park. 48 sites with water and electric, 4 double sites. Sites with water and electric hookups are $12; double sites with water and electric hookups are $18.

Recreational vehicle maximum length 50'. This campground requires a 2 night minimum stay on weekends and a 3 night stay on holiday weekends. Open from March 1st to September 30th. NRRS.

WILLIS CREEK CAMPGROUND

From Granger/Junction Highway 95, go 0.8 mile east on Farm to Market Road 971, 4 miles southeast on County Road 348, northeast on County Road 346. A picnic shelter for up to 50 people and 20 vehicles is $35. 28 sites with water and electric, 4 full hookups, 10 horse and horse trailer sites across from trailer camping area at the 7 mile trail head (for trail information call 512) 859-2668); 1 handicap site. Horse sites are $8; sites with water and electric hookups are $14; sites with full hookups are $18; double sites are $26. Recreational vehicle maximum length is 50'. This campground requires a 2 night minimum stay on weekends and a 3 night stay on holiday weekends. Open all year. NRRS.

WILSON H. FOX CAMPGROUND

From Taylor Park, go 1 mile northeast on Farm to Market Road 1331, go northwest, adjacent to south side of dam. A picnic shelter is $40 and a fish cleaning station is available. 58 sites with water and electric, 6 - 50 ampere sites, 5 double sites, 5 screened shelters, 1 handicap site. Sites with water and electric hookups are $14; sites with water and 50 ampere service are $18; double sites with water and electric hookups are $30; screen shelters with sinks are $30. Recreational vehicle maximum length is 50'. This campground requires a 2 night minimum stay on weekends and a 3 night stay on holiday weekends. Open all year. NRRS.

GRAPEVINE LAKE (FW) 6

A 7,380 acre surface area lake located just northwest of Grapevine (Dallas - Fort Worth Airport) off State Road 26, 23 miles northeast of Fort Worth. A golf course is located below the dam, alcoholic beverages are prohibited, there is an off the road vehicle area and an equestrian trail available. Resource Manager, Grapevine Lake, 110 Fairway Drive, Grapevine, TX 76051-3495. (817) 481-4541.

MURRELL WEST CAMPGROUND

From Grapevine/Junction State Road 121, go 4.5 miles north on Farm to Market Road 2499, 0.2 mile west (sign) on Farm to Market Road 3040, 0.4 mile west on McKamey Creek Road, south on Simmons Road. Group camping area (some free for use by boy scouts, church groups, etc.). 36 sites. All sites are free. Open all year.

HORDS CREEK LAKE (FW) 7

A 510 acre surface area lake located 8.7 miles west of Coleman, 55 miles south of Abilene. Resource Manager, Hords Creek Lake, HCR 75, Box 33, Coleman, TX 76834-9320. (915) 625-2322.

FLAT ROCK I & II CAMPGROUND

From Coleman, go 8.7 miles west on Highway 153, go south across dam, west to park (signs). Two group areas with shelters, GS2 for up to 80 people and 16 recreational vehicles is $125, and GS4 for up to 80 people and 12 recreational vehicles is $100, and seven picnic shelters and a fish cleaning station are available. 55 sites with water and electric, 10 - 50 ampere, 2 double sites with water and electric, 5 double sites with full hookups, 10 screened cabins, 10 pull through sites. Sites with water and electric hookups are $16; premium sites with water and electric hookups and sites with full hooks are $22; double sites with water and electric hookups are $32; screen cabins are $18. Recreational vehicle maximum length is in excess of 65'. This campground requires a 2 night minimum stay on weekends and a 3 night stay on holiday weekends. Open from May 1st to September 30th. NRRS.

LAKESIDE I & II CAMPGROUND

From Coleman, go 8 miles west on Highway 153 past Friendship Park, go south (signs). Five group camping areas with shelter, GS1 for up to 80 people and 12 RV's is $100, GS3 for up to 80 people and 8 RV's is $120, GS5 for up to 80 pelple and 12 RV's is $150, GS6 for up to 80 people and 12 RV's is $120 and GS7 for up to 200 people and 28 RV's is $250. A fish cleaning station and horseshoe pits are available, and there is a handicap accessible fishing area. 67 sites with water and electric, 2 handicap sites with water and electric, 2 handicap sites with water and 50 ampere, 8 - 50 ampere, 16 full hookups, 9 pull through sites. Sites with water and electric hookups are $16; premium sites with water and electric hookups and sites with water and 50 ampere service are $20; premium sites with water and 50 ampere service and sites with full hookups are $22.

Recreational vehicle maximum length is in excess of 65'. This campground requires a 2 night minimum stay on weekends and a 3 night stay on holiday weekends. Open all year. NRRS.

LAKE GEORGETOWN (FW) 8

A 1,310 acre surface area lake located 25 miles north of Austin off I-35, 2 miles west of Georgetown on Farm to Market Road 2338. A fee at developed campgrounds is charged for extra vehicles. Checkout time is 2 p.m. Resource Manager, Lake Georgetown, 500 Cedar Breaks Road, Georgetown, TX 78268-4901. (512) 930-5253.

CEDAR BREAKS CAMPGROUND

Fr I-35, go 3.5 miles west on Farm to Market Road 2338, 2 miles south on Cedar Breaks Road (signs). There is a late night emergency exit. Two picnic shelters for up to 25 people are $25. 64 sites with water and electric. Sites with water and electric hookups are $18; double sites with water and electric hookups are $26. Recreational vehicle maximum length is 55'. Recreational vehicle maximum length is in excess of 65'. This campground requires a 2 night minimum stay on weekends and a 3 night stay on holiday weekends. Open all year. NRRS.

CEDAR HOLLOW CAMP

Access by boat-in or hike-n on the Good Water Hiking Trail. Primitive area, free. Open all year.

JIM HOGG CAMPGROUND

From the project office, go 2.5 miles northwest on Farm to Market Road 2338, 2 miles south on Jim Hogg Road. A night time exit is provided. 148 sites with water and electric, 10 double sites, 5 screened shelters with 4 beds, bunk type. Sites with water and electric hookups are $18; double sites with water and electric hookups are $26; screen shelters are $30. Recreational vehicle maximum length is 55'. This campground requires a 2 night minimum stay on weekends and a 3 night stay on holiday weekends. Open all year. (512) 819-9046). NRRS.

RUSSELL GROUP CAMPING

From project office, go 3 miles northwest on Farm to Market Road 2338 (past exit to Jim Hogg Park), 0.7 mile west on Farm to Market Road 3405, 1 mile south on Route 262. Five shelters, three overnight for up to 50 people are $75. Contact office, enter option 21. Open all year.

SAWYER CAMP

Access by boat-in or hike-in on the Good Water Hiking Trail. Primitive area, free. Open all year.

TEJAS CAMPGROUND

Located northwest of the project office at junction State Road 2338, go 5.5 miles west on Farm to Market Road 3405, southeast on County Road 258. A picnic shelter for up to 25 people is $15. 12 primitive tent only sites, 3 walk-in/boat-in sites. All sites are $6. Open all year.

WALNUT SPRINGS CAMP

Access by water or hike-in on the Good Water Hiking Trail. Primitive area, free. Open all year.

LAKE O' THE PINES (FW) 9

A 19,780 acre surface area lake located 9 miles west of Jefferson, 25 miles northwest of Marshall. Checkout time is 2 p.m., fee campgrounds have emergency exits, and operation of off the road vehicles, golf carts and motorized scooters are prohibited in parks unless properly licensed in the state. Resource Manager, Lake O' The Pines, 2669 Farm to Market Road 726, Jefferson, TX 75657. (903) 665-2336.

ALLEY CREEK CAMPGROUND

From Jefferson, go 4 miles northwest on State Road 49, 12 miles west on Farm to Market Road 729 past Junction Farm to Market Road 726, go south (sign). A group camping area for up to 200 people and 24 vehicles, 12 recreational vehicle sites with a pavilion is $75. There is a convenience store is located nearby. 64 sites, 49 with water and electric, 15 tent only sites, 1 double site, 1 pull through site, 30 - 50 ampere. Tent only sites are $12; premium sites with water and electric are $18; sites with water and 50 ampere service are $20; premium sites with water and 50 ampere service are $22; a double site with water and 50 ampere service is $36. Recreational vehicle maximum length is in excess of 65'. This campground requires a 2 night minimum stay on weekends and a 3 night stay on holiday weekends. Open from March 1st to September 30th. (903) 755-2637. NRRS.

BRUSHY CREEK CAMPGROUND

From Jefferson, go 4 miles northwest on State Road 49, 3.5 miles west on Farm to Market Road 729, 4.8 miles south on Farm to Market Road 726 past dam, on right (sign). A convenience store is nearby. 100 sites, 72 with water and electric, 37 tent only sites, 45 - 50 ampere, 13 pull through sites, 2 double sites. Tent only sites are $10; premium tent only sites are $12; tent only sites with water and electric are $14; sites with water and 50 ampere service and sites with water and electric hookups are $18; premium sites with water and 50 ampere service and premium sites with water and electric hookups are $20; standard sites with water and electric hookups and standard sites with water and 50 ampere service are $22; premium standard sites with water and electric hookups and premium standard sites with water and 50 ampere service are $24; a double site with water and electric hookups is $32; a premium double site with water and 50 ampere service is $34. Recreational vehicle maximum length is in excess of 65'. This campground requires a 2 night minimum stay on weekends and a 3 night stay on holiday weekends. Open from March 1st to November 30th. (903) 777-3491. NRRS.

BUCKHORN CREEK CAMPGROUND

From Jefferson, go 4 miles northwest on State Road 49, 3.5 miles west on Farm to Market Road 729, 2.4 miles south on Farm to Market Road 726, on right (sign) before the dam. A convenience store is located nearby. 96 sites, 58 with water and electric, 38 tent only sites, 41 - 50 ampere, 13 pull through sites, 2 double sites with water and 50 ampere. Tent only sites are $12; sites with water and electric hookups are $16; sites with water and 50 ampere service are $18; premium sites with water and 50 ampere service are $20; standard sites with water and 50 ampere service are $22; premium standard sites with water and electric hookups are $24; a double site with water and electric hookups is $34; a double site with water and 50 ampere service is $36. Recreational vehicle maximum length is in excess of 65'. This campground requires a 2 night minimum stay on weekends and a 3 night stay on holiday weekends. Open from March 1st to September 30th. (903) 665-8261. NRRS.

CEDAR SPRINGS CAMPGROUND

From Jefferson, go northwest on State Road 49, west on Farm to Market Road 729, south on State Road 155 (sign), across lake on left. 28 sites. All sites are free. Open all year.

HURRICANE CREEK CAMPGROUND

From Jefferson northwest on State Road 49, go 2.5 miles west on Farm to Market Road 729 past Farm to Market Road 726, go south (sign). 23 sites. All sites are free. Open all year.

JOHNSON CREEK CAMPGROUND

From Jefferson, go 4 miles northwest on State Road 49, 8.5 miles west on Farm to Market Road 729, on left. a fish cleaning station is available. A group camping area with 12 sites is $150, a picnic shelter for up to 200 people and 1 vehicle is $75 and an amphitheater is available. 85 sites, 73 with water and electric, 22 tent only sites, 23 - 50 ampere, 4 pull through sites. Tent only sites are $12; tent only sites with water and electric are $14; sites with water and electric hookups are $18; premium sites with water and electric hookups are $20; standard sites with water and electric hookups are $22; premium standard sites with water and electric hookups are $24. Recreational vehicle maximum length is in excess of 65'. This campground requires a 2 night minimum stay on weekends and a 3 night stay on holiday weekends. Open all year. (903) 755-2435. NRRS.

LAKE TEXOMA (TU) 10

An 89,000 acre surface area lake located 5 miles northwest of Denison on State Road 91, 88 miles north of Dallas/Ft. Worth, on the Oklahoma state line. Off the road vehicles are prohibited. Lake Manager, Texoma Lake, 351 Corps Road, Denison, TX 75020. (903) 465-4490. See OK listing.

DAM SITE CAMPGROUND

From Denison, go 5 miles north on State Road 91, on the south side of the dam. A picnic shelter is available, call (903) 463-6455. 27 sites, 20 with water and electric. Sites without electric hookups are $10; sites with water and electric hookups are $16. From November 1st to March 31st, some sites are available and are free, reduced facilities. Recreational vehicle maximum length is in excess of 65'. Open all year. NRRS (April 1st to October 31st).

JUNIPER POINT CAMPGROUND

From Madill, go 17 miles south on State Road 99, across lake bridge, go east. A picnic shelter for up to 100 people and 20 vehicles is $50, and there is a convenience store nearby. 70 sites, 44 with water and electric. Sites without electric hookups are $12; sites with water and electric hookups are $18. Recreational vehicle maximum length is 50'. From November 1st to March 31st, some sites are available and are free, reduced facilities. Open all year. (903) 523-4022. NRRS (April 15th to September 15th).

PRESTON BEND CAMPGROUND

From Pottsboro, go 9 miles north on State Road 120, on right. A picnic shelter is available. A convenience store is located nearby. 38 sites, 26 with water and electric. Sites without electric hookups are $12; sites with water and electric hookups are $16. Recreational vehicle maximum length is in excess of 65'. Open from April 1st to October 31st. (903) 786-8408. NRRS.

LAVON LAKE (FW) 11

A 21,400 acre surface area lake located 30 miles northeast of Dallas, 3 miles east of Wylie off State Road 78. Alcohol is prohibited. Resource Manager, Lavon Lake, 3375 Skyview Drive, Wylie, TX 75098-0429. (972) 442-3014/3141.

BROCKDALE GROUP CAMPGROUND

From Wiley, go 0.8 mile north on Farm to Market Road 2514, 6.2 miles north on Farm to Market Road 1378, 0.7 mile east on Farm to Market Road 3286, go south. A group camping area is $100. Open from April 1st to September 29th.

CLEAR LAKE CAMPGROUND

From Princeton, go 9 miles south on Farm to Market Road 982 (changes into County Road 735). A picnic shelter for up to 200 people and 1 vehicle is $100 and there is a handicap accessible fishing area. 23 sites with water and electric, 1 handicap site. Sites with water and electric hookups are $18. Recreational vehicle maximum length is in excess of 65'. This campground requires a 2 night minimum stay on weekends and a 3 night stay on holiday weekends. Open from April 1st to September 29th. NRRS.

EAST FORK CAMPGROUND

From Wylie, go east on State Road 98, north on Farm to Market Road 389, right at fork to camp. A group camping area with picnic shelter for up to 175 people and 1 vehicle is $110 (call the office to reserve). 62 sites, 50 with water and 50 ampere service, 12 tent only sites. Tent only sites are $10; sites with water and 50 ampere service are $18. Recreational vehicle maximum length is 55'. This campground requires a 2 night minimum stay on weekends and a 3 night stay on holiday weekends. Open all year. NRRS.

LAKELAND CAMPGROUND

From Princeton, go 6.8 miles east on United States Route 380, 4.1 mile south on State Road 78, access west. A picnic shelter is $100. 32 primitive tent only sites. All sites are $8. Open from April 1st to September 30th.

LAVONIA CAMPGROUND

From Wylie, go 7.5 miles east on State Road 78, go north & west on County Road 486 (Lake Road), on east side of dam. 53 sites, 38 with water and electric, 15 tent only sites. Tent only sites are $10; sites with water and electric hookups are $18. Recreational vehicle maximum length is 60'. This campground requires a 2 night minimum stay on weekends and a 3 night stay on holiday weekends. Open from February 14th to September 29th. NRRS.

LITTLE AVALON CAMPGROUND

Located at the dam on the west side. Group camping area with 13 tent only sites is $30. Open all year.

LEWISVILLE LAKE (FW) 12

A 28,980 acre surface area lake located just north and adjacent to Lewisville, east of Mill Street and I-35E, northwest of Dallas. Off the road vehicles are prohibited and checkout time is 2 p.m. Observation drive- through of fee parks is not permitted on weekends from Easter through Labor Day weekend. Resource Manager, Lewisville Lake, 1801 North Mill Street, Lewisville, TX 75067-1821. (469) 645-9100.

HICKORY CREEK CAMPGROUND

From Lewisville, go 4 miles north on I-35E across lake bridge, exit 457B (From the north, use exit 458) to Lake Dallas, take overpass west over I-35E, 0.2 mile west on Turbeville Road, 0.5 mile south on Pt. Vista Road, on right. A group camping area with 20 sites and up to 80 people, an amphitheater and a night time exit is available. Convenience stores are located nearby. 126 sites, 116 with water and electric, 10 primitive tent only sites, 49 - 50 ampere, 33 handicap sites, 10 pull through sites, 1 full hookup. Tent only sites are $10; sites with water electric hookups are $16; sites with water and 50 ampere service are $18; one site with full hookups is $20. Recreational vehicle maximum length is 65'. This campground requires a 2 night minimum stay on weekends and a 3 night stay on holiday weekends. Open all year. (940) 497-2902. NRRS.

NAVARRO MILLS LAKE (FW) 13

A 5,070 acre surface area lake located 71 miles south of Dallas, 11 miles southwest of Corsicana off State Road 31. Checkout time is 1 p.m., and off the road vehicles are prohibited. Resource Manager, Navarro Mills Lake, 1175 Farm to Market Road 677, Purdon, TX 76679. (254) 578-1058/1431.

BRUSHIE PRAIRIE CAMPGROUND

From Dawson/Junction State Road 31, go 4 miles north on Farm to Market Road 667, 2.5 miles west on Farm to Market Road 744, 2 miles south on Farm to Market Road 1578, left to park. 10 sites. All sites are free. Open all year.

LIBERTY HILL CAMPGROUND

From Dawson/Junction State Road 31, go 4 miles northwest on Farm to Market Road 709, on right. A picnic shelter for up to 125 people and 70 vehicles is $75. a convenience store is located nearby. 102 sites, 100 with water and electric, 6 full hookups, 3 double sites with water and electric, 3 screened shelters, 24 pull through sites. There is a handicap accessible fishing area. From March 1st to October 31st, sites without electric hookups are $14; sites with water and electric hookups are $20; sites with full hookups are $20; screened shelters are $24; double sites with water and electric hookups are $32; From November 1st to February 28th, sites without electric hookups are $10; sites with water and electric hookups are $12; sites with full hookups are $16; double sites with water and electric hookups are $24; screened shelters are $24. Recreational vehicle maximum length is in excess of 65'. This campground requires a 2 night minimum stay on weekends and a 3 night stay on holiday weekends. Open all year. NRRS.

![icons]

OAK CAMPGROUND

From Dawson, go 4.3 miles northeast on State Road 31, 1.5 miles north on Farm to Market Road 667, on left. A picnic shelter for up to 125 people and 70 vehicles is $75. 48 sites with water and electric, 6 full hookups, 1 pull through site. There is a handicap accessible fishing area and a convenience store is located nearby. From March 1st to October 31st, sites with water and electric hookups are $16; sites with full hookups are $20; from November 1st to February 28th, sites with water and electric hookups are $12; sites with full hookups are $16. Recreational vehicle maximum length is in excess of 65'. This campground requires a 2 night minimum stay on weekends and a 3 night stay on holiday weekends. Open all year. NRRS.

PECAN POINT CAMPGROUND

From Dawson, go 3.5 miles northeast on State Road 31, 3.2 miles north on Farm to Market Road 667, southwest on Farm to Market Road 744, southeast on Farm to Market Road 1578 to the Park. 35 sites, 5 sites with water and 50 ampere service, 11 pull through sites. There is a convenience store and restaurants are located nearby. Sites without electric hookups are $8; sites with water and 50 ampere service are $10. Recreational vehicle maximum length is in excess of 65'. Open from April 1st to September 30th. NRRS.

![icons]

WOLF CREEK CAMPGROUND

From junction Farm to Market Road 639, go 2.2 miles southwest on Farm to Market Road 744, 2 miles southeast on Farm to Market Road 1578. A picnic shelter for up to 125 people and 70 vehicles is $75. There is a handicap accessible fishing area and a convenience store is located nearby. 72 sites, 50 with water and electric, 12 pull through sites, 2 double sites. Sites without electric hookups and sites with water hookups are $12; sites with water and electric hookups are $14; double sites without electric hookups are $24. Recreational vehicle maximum length is in excess of 65'. This campground requires a 2 night minimum stay on weekends and a 3 night stay on holiday weekends. Open from April 1st to September 30th. NRRS.

PAT MAYSE LAKE (TU) 14

A 5,990 acre surface area lake located 1 mile south of Chicota off Farm to Market Road Road 197, 12 miles north of Paris in northeast Texas, 100 miles west of Texarkana. Off the road vehicles are prohibited and gated campgrounds provide an emergency late night exit. Lake Manager, Pat Mayse Lake, P. O. Box 129, Powderly, TX 75473-0129. (903) 732-3020.

LAMAR POINT CAMPGROUND

From junction Farm to Market Road 1499, go north on Farm to Market Road 1500. 9 sites. All sites are $7. Open all year.

PAT MAYSE EAST CAMPGROUND

From Chicota, go 0.8 mile west on Farm to Market Road 197, go south on County Road. 26 sites with water and electric. Sites with water and electric hookups are $13. Open all year.

PAT MAYSE WEST CAMPGROUND

From Chicota, go 2.3 miles west on Farm to Market Road 197, go south on County Road. A night time exit is provided. 88 sites, 83 with water and electric, 1 pull through site, 7 handicap sites. Sites without electric hookups are $10; sites with water and electric hookups are $15. Recreational vehicle maximum length is in excess of 65'. This campground requires a 2 night minimum stay on weekends and a 3 night stay on holidays. Open all year. (903) 732-4955. NRRS (April 1st to September 30th).

SANDERS COVE CAMPGROUND

From Chicota, go 3.2 miles east on Farm to Market Road 906, south on entrance road. A group camping area is $75 and a picnic shelter is $25, and a night time exit is provided. 89 sites, 85 with water and electric, 9 handicap sites. Sites without electric hookups are $10; sites with water and electric hookups are $15. Recreational vehicle maximum length is in excess of 65'. This campground requires a 2 night minimum stay on weekends and a 3 night stay on holidays. Open all year. (903) 732-4956. NRRS (April 1st to September 30th). .

PROCTOR LAKE (FW) 15

A 4,610 acre surface area lake located 8 miles northeast of Comanche off United States Route 67, on Farm to Market Road Road 1476, 97 miles southwest of Ft. Worth. Gated campgrounds provide an emergency late night exit, and an extra vehicle fee may be charged for each vehicle over two. Resource Manager, Proctor Lake, 2180 Farm to Market Road 2861, Comanche, TX 76442-7248. ((254) 879)2424.

COOPERAS CREEK CAMPGROUND

From Proctor/Junction Farm to Market Road 1476, go 5.5 miles south through Hasse on United States Route 377, 2.5 miles north on Farm to Market Road 2861. Two group camping areas for up to 100 people and 26 vehicles with a picnic shelter are GR1 - $100 and GR2 - $130. 66 sites with water and electric, 2 - 50 ampere, 7 full hookups, 4 double sites, 4 pull through sites. Sites with water and electric hookups are $16; sites with water and 50 ampere service and sites with full hookups are $20; double sites are $32. Recreational vehicle maximum length is in excess of 65'. From April 1st to September 30th this campground requires a 2 night minimum stay on weekends and a 3 night stay on holiday weekends. Open all year. (254) 879-2498. NRRS.

PROMONTORY CAMPGROUND

From Comanche/Junction United States Route 377, go 12 miles north on State Road 16, 5 miles east on Farm to Market Road 2318. Three group camping areas for up to 100 people and 26 vehicles with picnic shelter are GR1 - $90, GR3 - $130, and GR4 - $100. Groups must sign a group shelter policy form prior to arrival at the campground (Contact the office by phone for the form). 88 sites, 63 with electric, 5 - 50 ampere, 3 double sites, 1 quad site, 4 pull through sites, 5 screened shelters, call office for information. From March 16th to March 31st,

sites without electric hookups are $8; sites with water and electric hookups are
$16; premium sites with water and 50 ampere service are $20; premium double
sites with water and electric are $32; a screened shelter with electric hookups
is $20; screened shelters with water and electric hookups are $34; a quad site is
$50; from April 1st to September 30th, sites without electric hookups are $8;
sites with water and electric hookups are $16; premium sites with water and 50
ampere service are $20; premium double sites with water and electric hookups
are $32; a screened shelter with electric hookups is $22; screened shelters with
water and electric hookups are $38; a quad shelter with water and electric
hookups is $50. Recreational vehicle maximum length is in excess of 65'. This
campground requires a 2 night minimum stay on weekends and a 3 night stay
on holiday weekends. Open from March 16th to September 30th. (254) 893-
7545. (254) 893-7545. NRRS.

SOWELL CREEK CAMPGROUND

From Proctor/Junction United States Route 377, go 2 miles west on Farm to
Market Road 1476, go south before dam on recreation road. Two group camping
areas for up to 100 people and 26 vehicles with picnic shelter are GP1 with
water hookups at $90 and GP2 with water and electric hookups at $190, and
there is a handicap accessible fishing area. 61 sites with water and electric,
7 full hookups, 18 - 50 ampere, 5 double sites, 1 quad site, 2 handicap sites.
Sites with water and electric hookups are $16; sites with water and 50 ampere
service are $20; sites with full hookups are $26; double sites with water and
electric hookups are $32; a quad site with water and electric hookups is $50.
Recreational vehicle maximum length is in excess of 65'. This campground
requires a 2 night minimum stay on weekends and a 3 night stay on holiday
weekends. Open all year. (254) 879-2322. NRRS.

SAM RAYBURN LAKE (FW) 16

A 114,500 acre surface area lake located 15 miles north of Jasper on United
States Route 96 in east-central Texas, 89 miles north of Beaumont, 30 miles
west of the Louisiana state line. Equestrian trail, checkout time is 2. p.m.,
and a $3 extra vehicle fee may be charged. Resource Manager, Sam Rayburn
Reservoir, Route 3, Box 486, Jasper, TX 75951-9598. (409) 384-5716.

EBENEZER CAMPGROUND

From Jasper, go 12 miles north on United States Route 96, 8 miles west on
Route 255 across dam, go north. A picnic shelter, G1, is $200 and may be
reserved through the office, some equestrian camping sites are available

(all horses must have current negative Coggins certification), scuba diving is permitted and the nearest boat ramp is at Twin Dikes Park. A restaurant is located nearby. 30 sites, 10 with water and electric, 3 - 50 ampere. Sites without electric hookups are $9; sites with water and electric hookups are $15. Recreational vehicle maximum length is 50'. Open all year. NRRS.

HANKS CREEK CAMPGROUND

From Huntington, go 12 miles southeast on Farm to Market Road 3801, 2 miles northeast on Farm to Market Road 2801. A picnic shelter is $30 and a convenience store is located nearby. 44 sites with water and electric, 3 - 50 ampere, 4 pull through sites. Sites with water and electric are $16; sites with water and 50 ampere service are $18. Recreational vehicle maximum length is 60'. This campground requires a 2 night minimum stay on weekends and a 3 night stay on holiday weekends. Open all year. NRRS.

MILL CREEK CAMPGROUND

From Brookeland, go 2 miles west on Loop 149, 1 mile west on Spur 165. A picnic shelter for up to 50 people and 30 vehicles is $50, horseshoe pits are available, a convenience store is located nearby and a fee for extra vehicles may be collected. 110 sites with water and electric, 5 - 50 ampere. Sites with water and electric hookups are $16; premium sites with water and electric hookups are $18. Recreational vehicle maximum length is in excess of 65'. This campground requires a 2 night minimum stay on weekends and a 3 night stay on holiday weekends. Open all year. NRRS.

RAYBURN CAMPGROUND

From Pineland/Junction United States Route 96, go 10 miles north on Farm to Market Road 83, 11 miles south on Farm to Market Road 705, 1 mile west on Farm to Market Road 3127. A group campground area for up to 20 people and 4 vehicles is $20, and a convenience store and restaurants are located nearby. 75 sites, 24 with electric, 8 pull through sites with 50 ampere service. Tent only sites and sites without electric hookups are $11; sites with water and electric hookups are $16; premium sites with water and 50 ampere service are $18. Recreational vehicle maximum length is in excess of 65'. This campground requires a 2 night minimum stay on weekends and a 3 night stay on holiday weekends. Open all year. NRRS.

SAN AUGUSTINE CAMPGROUND

From Pineland/Junction United States Route 96, go 6 miles west on Farm to Market Road 83, 4 miles south on Farm to Market Road 1751. A picnic shelter for up to 50 people and 26 vehicles is $50, a fish cleaning station and horseshoe pits are available, a convenience store is located nearby and a fee for extra vehicles may be collected. 100 sites, 101 with water and electric, 5 tent only sites. Tent only sites and sites with water and electric hookups are $16; premium sites with water and electric hookups are $18. Recreational vehicle maximum length is in excess of 65'. This campground requires a 2 night minimum stay on weekends and a 3 night stay on holidays. Open all year. NRRS.

TWIN DIKES CAMPGROUND

From Jasper, go 13 miles north on United States Route 96, 5 miles west on Route 255, go north. A picnic shelter for up to 30 people and 16 vehicles is $30, and a fee for extra vehicles may be collected. a restaurant is located nearby. 44 sites, 16 with electric, 9 full hookups, 4 - 50 ampere, 3 screened shelters with full hookups. Sites without electric hookups are $12; sites with water and electric hookups are $16; sites with water and 50 ampere service and sites with full hookups are $18; screen shelters with full hookups are $30. Recreational vehicle maximum length is 60'. This campground requires a 2 night minimum stay on weekends and a 3 night stay on holiday weekends. Open all year. NRRS.

SOMERVILLE LAKE (FW) 17

An 11,460 acre surface area lake with 85 miles of shoreline located 1 mile west of Somerville on State Road 36 on Thornberry Avenue, 84 miles east of Austin. Resource Manager, Somerville Lake, P. O. Box 549, Somerville, TX 77879-0549. (409) 596-1622.1666.

ROCKY CREEK CAMPGROUND

From Somerville, go southeast on State Road 36, 4.5 miles west on Farm to Market Road 1948. A picnic shelter for up to 100 people and 20 vehicles, from October 1st to February 28th, is $100 and from March 1st to September 30th, is $125, and off the road vehicles are prohibited. A convenience store and restaurants are located nearby. 201 sites, 82 with water and electric, 46 primitive sites, 41 - 50 ampere, 8 handicap sites. From March 1st to September 30th, sites without electric hookups are $18; sites with water and electric hookups are $20; sites with water and 50 ampere service are $22; from October 1st to December 31st, sites without electric hookups are $16; sites with water and electric hookups are $18; sites with water and 50 ampere service are $20; from January 1st to February 28th, sites without electric hookups are $14; sites with water and electric hookups are $16; sites with water and 50 ampere service are $18. Recreational vehicle maximum length is in excess of 65'. This campground requires a 2 night minimum stay on weekends and a 3 night stay on holiday weekends. Open all year. NRRS.

YEGUA CREEK CAMPGROUND

From Somerville, go southeast on State Road 36, 2 miles west on Farm to Market Road 1948. 82 sites, 47 with water and electric. From March 1st to September 30th, sites with water hookups are $16; sites with water and electric hookups are $20; from October 1st to February 28th, sites with water hookups are $16; sites with water and electric hookups are $18. Recreational vehicle maximum length is in excess of 65'. This campground requires a 2 night minimum stay on weekends and a 3 night stay on holiday weekends. Open all year. NRRS.

B. A. STEINHAGEN LAKE (FW) 18

A 13,700 acre surface area lake located 15 miles southwest of Jasper off Farm to Market Road Road 1746 in east-central Texas, 75 miles north of Beaumont. Off the road vehicles are prohibited and gated campgrounds may charge an extra vehicle fee. Resource Manager, Town Bluff Dam & B. A. Steinhagen Lake, 890 Farm to Market Road Road 92, Woodville, TX 75979-9631. (409) 429-3491.

CAMPERS COVE CAMPGROUND

From Woodville, go 12.1 mile southeast on United States Route 190, 2.5 miles southeast on Farm to Market Road 92, go north. 25 sites. Open from April 1st to September 30th.

MAGNOLIA RIDGE CAMPGROUND

From Woodville, go 11 miles east on United States Route 190, 1.5 miles northwest on Farm to Market Road 92, go northeast. A picnic shelter for up to 200 people and 30 vehicles is $45, there is a children's fishing pond, a convenience store and restaurants are located nearby, a night time exit is provided and there is a handicap accessible fishing area. 41 sites, 34 with water and electric, 9 pull through sites, 1 screened shelter. From April 1st to

September 30th, sites without electric hookups are $12; sites with water and electric hookups are $18; a screened shelter is $25; from October 1st to March 31st, sites without electric hookups are $10; sites with water and electric hookups are $16; 1 screened shelter is $25. Recreational vehicle maximum length is in excess of 65'. This campground requires a 2 night minimum stay on weekends and a 3 night stay on holidays. Open all year. May be closed part of the year due to high water. (409) 283-5493. NRRS.

SANDY CREEK CAMPGROUND

From Woodville, go 14.1 mile northeast on United States Route 190 across lake, 1.4 miles south on Farm to Market Road 777, 2.5 miles southwest on County Road 155, gravel (signs). A picnic shelter is available and boat rentals and a convenience store are located nearby. 72 sites, 66 with water and electric, 7 - 50 ampere, 2 screened shelters, 12 pull through sites. Sites without electric hookups are $12; sites with water and electric hookups are $16; sites with water and 50 ampere service are $18; screen shelters are $25. Recreational vehicle maximum length is in excess of 65'. This campground requires a 2 night minimum stay on weekends and a 3 night stay on holidays. Open all year. (409) 384-6166. NRRS.

STILLHOUSE HOLLOW LAKE (FW) 19

A 6,430 acre surface area lake located 5 miles southwest of Belton on Farm to Market Road Road 1670, south of Fort Hood, 80 miles north of Austin. Checkout time is 2 p.m. Resource Manager, Stillhouse Hollow Lake, 3740 Farm to Market Road 1670, Belton, TX 7651. (254) 939-2461.

DANA PEAK CAMPGROUND

From junction United States Route 190, go 0.3 mile south on Simmons Road, 5 miles west on Farm to Market Road 2410, 5 miles south on Comanche Gap Road. A picnic shelter for up to 80 people and 40 vehicles is $40 and a change shelter is available. 34 sites, 25 with water and electric, 10 tent only sites, 18 handicap sites, 2 shelters, 2 pull through sites. Tent only sites without electric are $6; tent only sites with water and electric and standard sites with water and electric hookups are $16; 3 double sites with water and electric hookups are $26; shelters are $22. Recreational vehicle maximum length is in excess of 65'. This campground requires a 2 night minimum stay on weekends and a 3 night stay on holiday weekends. Open all year. NRRS.

UNION GROVE CAMPGROUND

From junction I-35, go 0.8 mile west on Farm to Market Road 1670, 5.3 miles west on Farm to Market Road 2484. 37 sites with water and electric, 7 tent only sites, 13 - 50 ampere, 24 handicap sites, 2 double sites, 3 screened shelters, 4 pull through sites. Tent only sites with water and electric and sites with water and electric hookups are $16; sites with water and 50 ampere service are $18; a double site with water and electric hookups is $26; screened shelters are $30; a double site with water and 50 ampere service is $32. Recreational vehicle maximum length is in excess of 65'. This campground requires a 2 night minimum stay on weekends and a 3 night stay on holiday weekends. Open all year. NRRS.

WACO LAKE (FW) 20

A 8,900 acre surface area lake located on the northwest side of Waco off Farm to Market Road Road 1637. Off the road vehicles are prohibited, wildlife viewing area, fossil pit, and gated campgrounds may charge an extra vehicle fee. Resource Manager, Waco Lake, Route 10, Box 173-G, Waco, TX 76708-9602. (254) 756-5359.

AIRPORT CAMPGROUND

From I-35, exit 339, go west on Industrial, at 2d light, right on Stienback Bend Drive, right at 4 way stop sign, 2 miles east on Skeet Leson Road (Just behind the regional airport). A picnic shelter for up to 100 people and 26 vehicles, and a floating restaurant is located at the marina. 82 sites, 54 with water and 50 ampere, 15 tent only sites, 29 full hookups, 6 handicap shelters, 50 handicap sites. Tent only sites are $12; sites with water and 50 ampere service are $20; sites with full hookups are $24. Recreational vehicle maximum length is in excess of 65'. This campground requires a 2 night minimum stay on weekends and a 3 night stay on holiday weekends. Open all year. NRRS.

MIDWAY CAMPGROUND

From Waco & I-35, exit 330, go 5 miles west on State Road 6, exit on Fish Pond Road and go under State Road 6, stay on access road. A convenience store and restaurants are located nearby. 38 sites, 33 with water and electric, 3 tent only sites, 11 full hookups, 6 - 50 ampere, 3 pull through sites, 4 double sites, 3 handicap sites. Tent only sites are $12; sites with water and electric hookups are $20; sites with full hookups are $22; double sites with water and electric hookups are $36. Recreational vehicle maximum length is in excess of 65'. This campground requires a 2 night minimum stay on weekends and a 3 night stay on holidays. Open all year. NRRS.

REYNOLDS CREEK CAMPGROUND

From Waco & I-35, exit 330, go 7 miles west on State Road 6 across lake, 1 mile northeast on Speegleville Road, go through 4 way stop sign, approximately 1 mile on right. An amphitheater and picnic shelter are available, and a group camping area, Bosque Bend Clubhous, and off the road vehicles are prohibited. A convenience store and restaurants are located nearby. Interpretive programs are presented on Saturday nights between Memorial Day and Labor Day. 57 sites, 51 with water and electric, 6 tent only sites, some pull through sites. Tent only sites are $12; sites with water and electric hookups are $20. This campground requires a 2 night minimum stay on weekends and a 3 night stay on holidays. Open all year. NRRS.

WHITNEY LAKE (FW) 21

A 23,560 acre surface area lake located 5.5 miles southwest of Whitney on State Road 22, 79 miles south of Fort Worth. Dam tours are available, checkout time is 2 p.m., and off the road vehicles are prohibited. Resource Manager, Whitney Lake, 285 County Road 3602, Clifton, TX 76634. (254) 694-3189.

CEDAR CREEK CAMPGROUND

From Whitney, go 5.5 miles northwest on Farm to Market Road 933, 2.2 miles southwest & southeast on Farm to Market Road 2604. A picnic shelter for up to 100 people and 1 vehicle is $30, and a convenience store is located nearby. 20 sites. All sites are free. Open all year.

CEDRON CREEK CAMPGROUND

From Whitney, go 2.4 miles northwest on Farm to Market Road 933, 6 miles southwest on Farm to Market Road 1713 across Katy Bridge on left, signs. A group camping area containing 8 sites with water and electric hookups is $140, horseshoe pits and a pinic shelter are available, a convenience store is located nearby and a night time exit is provided. 57 sites with water and electric, 11 - 50 ampere, 3 pull through sites. Sites with water and electric hookups are $16; sites with water and 50 ampere service are $20. Recreational vehicle maximum length is 45'. This campground requires a 2 night minimum stay on weekends and a 3 night stay on holiday weekends. Open from April 1st to September 29th. NRRS.

KIMBALL BEND CAMPGROUND

From Blum/Junction Farm to Market Road 933, go 6 miles southwest on State Road 174 across bridge, go northwest. 11 sites. All sites are free. Open all year.

LOFERS BEND EAST CAMPGROUND

From Whitney, go 5.7 miles south on State Road 22, go west. A group camping area for up to 75 people and 10 vehicles is $105 and a picnic shelter is $50, a convenience store is located nearby and a night time exit is provided. 68 sites, 62 with water and electric. From April 1st to September 30th, sites witout electric hookups are $12; sites with water and electric hookups are $16; from October 1st to March 31st, sites without electric hookups are $10; sites with water and electric hookups are $14. Recreational vehicle maximum length is 45'. This campground requires a 2 night minimum stay on weekends and a 3 night stay on holidays. Open all year. NRRS.

LOFERS BEND WEST CAMPGROUND

Adjacent to Loafer's Bend East. A group camping area for up to 75 people is $80 and a picnic shelter is $50, a convenience store is located nearby and a night time exit is provided. 68 sites with water and electric, 6 - 50 ampere, 5 pull through sites. Sites with water hookups are $12; sites with water and electric hookups are $16; sites with water and 50 ampere service are $20. Recreational vehicle maximum length is 45'. This campground requires a 2 night minimum stay on weekends and a 3 night stay on holiday weekends. From April 1st to September 29th. NRRS.

MCCOWN VALLEY CAMPGROUND

From Whitney, go 2.4 miles northwest on Farm to Market Road 933, 4 miles southwest on Farm to Market Road 1713. A picnic shelter for up to 150 people and 1 vehicle is $45, and horseshoe pits, a group camping area and an equestrian camping area are available. A convenience store is located nearby and a night time exit is provided. 104 sites, 94 with water and electric, 39 horse sites with water and 50 ampere service, 6 pull through sites and 7 handicap sites, 51 - 50 ampere, 12 handicap sites, 14 pull through sites. From April 1st to September 30th, sites with water hookups are $12; sites with water and electric hookups are $16; horse sites with water and 50 ampere service are $20; shelters with water and electric hookups are $24; shelters with water and 50 ampere service are $30; from October 1st to March 31st, sites with water hookups are $10; sites with water and electric hookups are $14; horse sites with water and 50 ampere service are $18; shelters with water and electric hookups are $24; shelters with water and 50 ampere service are $30. Recreational vehicle maximum length is 50'. This campground requires a 2 night minimum stay on weekends and a 3 night stay on holiday weekends. Open all year. NRRS.

PLOWMAN CREEK CAMPGROUND

From junction State Road 174, go 2.5 miles southeast on Farm to Market Road 56, 1 mile south of Kopper. A convenience store is located nearby and a night time exit is provided. 38 sites, 18 with water and electric, 10 equestrian sites. From April 1st to September 30th, sites without electric hookups are $12; sites with water and electric hookups are $16; from October 1st to March 31st, sites without electric hookups are $10; sites with water and electric hookups are $14. Recreational vehicle maximum length is 45'. This campground requires a 2 night minimum stay on weekends and a 3 night stay on holiday weekends. Open all year. NRRS.

SOLDIER BLUFF

Located on the west side of the dam south of the outlet. A picnic shelter is $30. 14 primitive sites. All sites are free. Open all year.

STEELE CREEK CAMPGROUND

From Junction Farm to Market Road 927, 1 mile southeast on Farm to Market Road 56, go northeast on gravel road. 21 sites. All sites are free. Open all year.

WALLING BEND

From Junction State Road 22, go 2 miles northwest on Farm to Market Road 56, northeast on Farm to Market Road 2841. A picnic shelter is $20. 6 sites. All sites are free. Open all year.

WRIGHT PATMAN LAKE (FW) 22

A 33,750 acre surface area lake located 9 miles southwest of Texarkana and junction United States Route 82, off United States Route 59. Visitor center, wildlife viewing area and checkout time is 2 p.m. Project Manager, Wright Patman Lake, P. O. Box 1817, Texarkana, TX 75504-1817. (903) 838-8781.

CLEAR SPRINGS CAMPGROUND

From Texarkana, go 9 miles south on United States Route 59, 0.5 miles west on State Road 2148, 2 miles west on park road. A picnic shelter is $60, horseshoe pits and a group camping area, 12 sites, with water and electric hookups. is $80 plus camp fee, and a combination lock is provided for late entry by registered campers. 102 sites, 87 with electric, 10 - 50 ampere, 15 tent only sites, 1 pull through sites, 1 handicap site without electric, 2 handicap sites with water and electric, 2 handicap sites with water and 50 ampere. Tent only sites are $10; sites with water and electric hookups are $16; sites with water and 50 ampere service are $18; premium sites with water and 50 ampere service are $20. Recreational vehicle maximum length is in excess of 65'. This campground requires a 2 night minimum stay on weekends and a 3 night stay on holiday weekends. Open all year. NRRS (January 1st to September 12th).

JACKSON CREEK CAMPGROUND

From Douglassville/Junction State Road 8, go 4.1 mile east on State Road 77, 1.5 miles north on Farm to Market Road 2791, go 3 miles north. 10 sites. All sites are free. Recreational vehicle maximum length is 25'. Open all year.

MALDEN LAKE CAMPGROUND

From Maud/Junction United States Route 67, go 8.4 miles south on State Road 8, before bridge, on left. Coded gate locks are provided for late entry by resitered campers. A restaurant is located nearby. 39 sites with water and electric, 10 - 50 ampere, 8 pull through sites, 2 handicap sites. Sites with water and electric hookups are $16; sites with water and 50 ampere service are $18; double sites with water and electric hookups are $28. Recreational vehicle maximum length is 55'. This campground requires a 2 night minimum stay on weekends and a 3 night stay on holiday weekends. Open all year. NRRS (January 1st to September 12th).

PINEY POINT CAMPGROUND

From Texarkana, go 12 miles south on United States Route 59, 1st right past Sulphur River bridge (signs). A picnic shelter for up to 75 people and 31 vehicles is $50, and a coded gate entrance is provided for registered campers. A convenience store is located nearby. 68 sites, 48 with water and electric, 20 tent only sites, 6 - 50 ampere, 1 pull through site, 4 handicap sites. Tent only sites and sites with water and electric hookups are $16; sites with water and 50 ampere service are $18. Recreational vehicle maximum length is 55'. This campground requires a 2 night minimum stay on weekends and a 3 night stay on holiday weekends. Open from March 1st to November 30th. NRRS.

ROCKY POINT CAMPGROUND

Just south of Piney Point camp ground, south of the dam. A picnic shelter for up to 60 people and 31 vehicles is $50, and a fish cleaning station and an amphitheater are available. A convenience store is located nearby. 124 sites with water and electric, 8 - 50 ampere, 15 full hookups, 1 handicap site with water and 50 ampere service, 6 pull through sites. Sites with water and electric hookups are $16; sites with water and 50 ampere service and sites with full hookups are $18; sites with full hookups and 50 ampere service are $20. Recreational vehicle maximum length is in excess of 65'. This campground requires a 2 night minimum stay on weekends and a 3 night stay on holiday weekends. Open all year. NRRS (January 1st to September 12th.

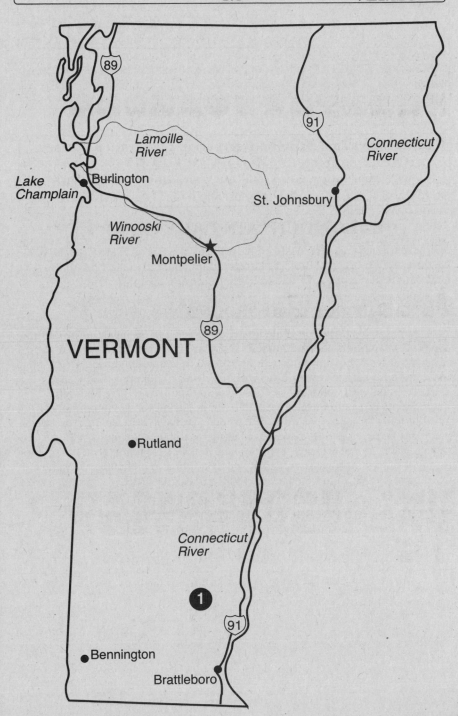

VERMONT

STATE CAPITAL:
Montpelier
NICKNAME:
Green Mountain State

14th State - 1791

Site reservation, National Recreation Reservation Service
(NRRS), toll free, 1-877-444-6777; TDD 877-833-6777,
www.recreation.gov, (Master, Visa, American Express
& Discover cards).

BALL MOUNTAIN LAKE (NAE) 1

A 75 acre surface area lake located northwest of Jamaica off State Road 30/100,
northwest of Brattleboro. Project Manager, Ball Mountain Lake, 88 Ball
Mountain Road, Jamaica, VT 05343-9713. (802) 874-4881.

WINHALL BROOK CAMPGROUND

From Jamaica, northwest off State Road 30/100, go 5 miles north of the dam
& office. An amphitheater and horseshoe pits are available, and there is a
handicap accessible swimming area. 111 sites, 25 with water and electric,
14 Leanto's, 21 handicap sites. Sites without electric hookups are $16; sites,
2nd price, sites with water and electric hookups and Leanto's are $20; Site
limit, 2 tents or 1 hard wheeled unit and 1 tent. 2 adults and children under
18. Additional fee for more adults. Fire wood is available for a fee. Interpretive
programs and visitors to 10 p.m., fee of $1 per person or maximum of $4 per
vehicle. Recreational vehicle maximum length is 60'. This campground requires
a 2 night minimum stay on weekends and a 3 night stay on holiday weekends.
Open from April 20th to October 8th. (802) 824-4570. NRRS.

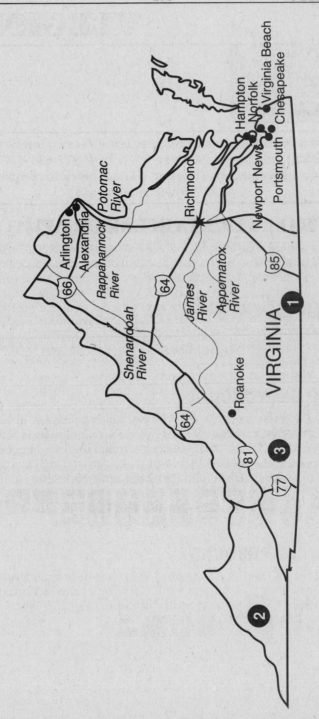

VIRGINIA

STATE CAPITAL:
Richmond
NICKNAME:
The Old Dominion

10th State - 1788

Site reservation, National Recreation Reservation Service
(NRRS), toll free, 1-877-444-6777; TDD 877-833-6777,
www.recreation.gov, (Master, Visa, American Express
& Discover cards).

JOHN H. KERR RESERVOIR (WL) 1

A 50,000 acre surface area lake with 900 miles of shoreline located on the
Virginia/North Carolina state line near Boydton, 20 miles west of Spring Hill
on I-85 and 20 miles north of Henderson, NC on I-85. Power house tours are
conducted daily from June through August. Alcoholic beverages, dirt bikes and
off the road vehicles are prohibited, checkout time is 4 p.m., and visitors to 10
p.m. The gated campgrounds may charge a $4 fee for extra/visitor vehicles.
For lake level information, call (434) 738-6371. John H. Kerr Reservoir
Management Center, 1930 Mays Chapel Road, Boydton, VA 23917-9725. (434)
738-6143/6144.

BUFFALO CAMPGROUND

From Clarksville, go 8 miles west on US 58 past junction State Road 49 across
bridge, go 3 miles north on County Road 732, east on County Road 869. 19
sites. All sites are $15. Recreational vehicle maximum length is in excess of 65'.
This campground requires a 2 night minimum stay on weekends and a 3 night
stay on holiday weekends. Open from May 1st to September 29th. (434) 374-
2063. NRRS.

IVY HILL CAMPGROUND

From Townsville, NC, north on State Road 39 to VA state line, north on County
Road 825. 25 primitive sites. All sites are $10. Recreational vehicle maximum
length is 32'. Open from May 1st to September 30th. (434) 252-0903.

LONGWOOD CAMPGROUND

From Clarksville/Junction United States Route 58/15, go 5 miles south on United States Route 15, on the west side. A picnic shelter is available. 66 sites, 25 with water and electric, 3 handicap sites without electric, 9 handicap sites with water and electric, 1 double site, 2 pull through sites. Sites without electric hookups are $15; sites with water and electric hookups are $20; a double site is $30. Recreational vehicle maximum length is in excess of 65'. This campground requires a 2 night minimum stay on weekends and a 3 night stay on holiday weekends. Open from April 1st to October 30th. (434) 374-2711. NRRS.

NORTH BEND CAMPGROUND

From Boydton, go 5 miles east on United States Route 58, 6 miles south on State Road 4 (Buggs Island Road). Three group camping areas and an amphitheater are available, a convenience store is located nearby and there is a handicap accessible fishing area. 244 sites, 94 with water and electric, 7 pull through sites, 2 handicap sites with water and electric. Sites without hookups are $15; sites with water and electric hookups are $20. Recreational vehicle maximum length is in excess of 65'. This campground requires a 2 night minimum stay on weekends and a 3 night stay on holiday weekends. Open April 1st to October 31st. NRRS.

RUDDS CREEK CAMPGROUND

From Boydton, 3 miles west on United States 58, on the south side of road before lake bridge. A picnic shelter and an amphitheater are available, and a convenience store is located nearby. 99 sites, 70 with water and 50 ampere, 24 primitive sites, 3 double sites without electric, 5 double sites with water and 50 ampere, 3 pull through sites. Sites without electric hookups are $15; sites with water and electric hookups are $20; double sites without electric hookups are $30; premium double sites with water and electric are $40. Recreational vehicle maximum length is in excess of 65'. This campground requires a 2 night minimum stay on weekends and a 3 night stay on holiday weekends. Open from April 1st to October 31st. (434) 738-6827. NRRS.

JOHN W. FLANNAGAN LAKE (HU) 2

A 1,145 acre surface area lake with almost 40 miles of shoreline is located near the Kentucky state line, northwest of Haysi on State Road 63, northwest of Bristol. Resource Manager, John W. Flannagan Dam & Reservoir, Route 1, Box 268, Haysi, VA 24256-9736. (276) 835-9544.

CRANESNEST #1 & #2 CAMPGROUND

From Clintwood, go 2 miles southeast on State Road 83, go north. A picnic shelter and an amphitheater are available. 24 sites. Sites are from $10 to $12. Open from Memorial Day through Labor Day.

CRANESNEST #3 CAMPGROUND

From Cranesnest #1 & #2, go 1 mile northeast. 11 sites. All sites are $10. Open from Memorial Day through Labor Day.

LOWER TWIN CAMPGROUND

From State Road 739, go 3 miles west on State Road 611, exit southeast on State Road 683. An amphitheater is available. 33 sites, 15 with electric. Sites without electric hookups are $10; sites with electric hookups are $12. Open from Memorial Day through Labor Day.

POUND RIVER CAMPGROUND

From Clintwood, go 0.2 mile west on State Road 83, 2 miles north on State Road 631, 1.2 miles east on State Road 754. 27 sites, some pull through sites. Sites are from $12 to $14. Open from Memorial Day through Labor Day.

PHILPOTT LAKE (WL) 3

A 2,880 acre surface area lake with 100 miles of shoreline is located northwest of Martinsburg off United States Route 220, State Road 57 and Philpott Dam Road. Visitor center, visitors to 10 p.m., checkout time is 4 p.m., alcoholic beverages are prohibited, and a $4 fee may be charged for extra/visitor vehicles. A free loan of fishing rod and tackle is provided at the visitor center and parks. Project Manager, Philpott Lake, 1058 Philpott Dam Road, Basset, VA 24055-8618. (276) 629-2703/7385.

DEER ISLAND CAMPGROUND

Access by boat-in only, south of Salthouse on Deer Island, 2 miles north of the dam. 21 primitive sites. All sites are $18. Contact office for information. Open from April 1st to October 31st.

GOOSE POINT CAMPGROUND

From Martinsville, north on United States Route 220, go 11 miles north on State Road 57, access on County Road 822 (winding access roads). An amphitheater and picnic shelter are available. 63 sites, 53 with water and 50 ampere service, 2 handicap sites with water and 50 ampere, 28 pull through sites. Sites without electric hookups are $18; sites with water and 50 ampere service are $21. Recreational vehicle maximum length is 60'. This campground requires a 2 night minimum stay on weekends. Open from March 29th to October 30th. (276) 629-1847. NRRS.

HORSESHOE POINT CAMPGROUND

From Martinsville, north on United States Route 220, go 6.2 miles west on County Road 605 through Henry, 2.3 miles southwest on County Road 903, 1 mile west on County Road 934. A picnic shelter is available. 49 sites, 15 with water and electric, 36 pull through sites. Sites without electric hookups are $18; premium sites without electric hookups and sites with water and electric hookups are $21. Recreational vehicle maximum length is 40'. This campground requires a 2 night minimum stay on weekends. Open from May 1st to September 29th. (276) 365-7385. NRRS.

JAMISON MILL CAMPGROUND

From Henry/Junction County Road 606, go 5 miles northwest on County Road 605, 2 miles south on County Road 778. 9 sites, 5 with water and electric, some pull through sites. Sites without electric hookups are $18; sites with water and electric hookups are $21; 4 overflow sites are $18. Open from April 1st to October 31st.

PHILPOTT

Near dam, south side. Group camping area by permit only. Contact the office. A picnic shelter is $75. Open from April 1st to late October.

RYANS BRANCH CAMPGROUND

From Ferrum, go 7 miles southwest on County Road 623, access before the bridge. 8 primitive sites. Primitive sites are $16. Recreational vehicle maximum length is 32'. Open from April 1st to October 31st.

SALTHOUSE BRANCH CAMPGROUND

From Henry, go 3 miles west on County Road 605, 1.4 miles southwest on County Road 798, go south on County Road 603. An amphitheater is available, and a picnic shelter for up to 100 people is $75. 93 sites, 26 with water and electric, 25 - 50 ampere, 32 tent only sites, 17 pull through sites, 1 handicap site with water and 50 ampere. Tent only sites and sites without electric hookups are $18; sites with water and electric hookups and sites with water and 50 ampere service are $21. Recreational vehicle maximum length is 50'. This campground requires a 2 night minimum stay on weekends. Open from March 29th to October 30th. (276) 365-7005. NRRS.

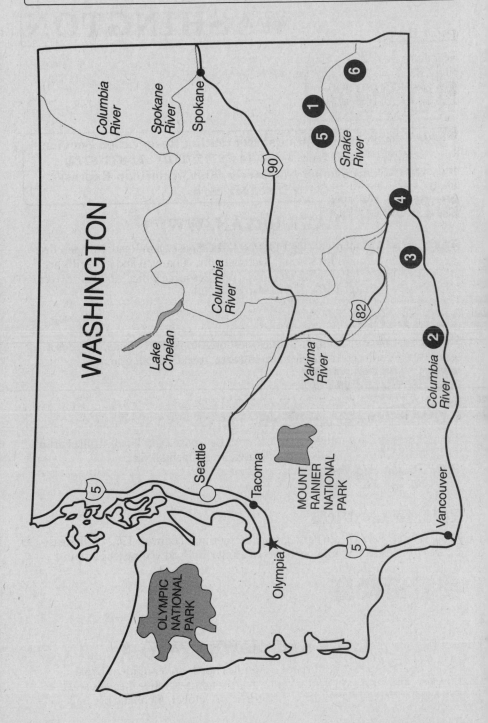

WASHINGTON

STATE CAPITAL:
Olympia
NICKNAME:
Evergreen State

42nd State - 1889

Site reservation, National Recreation Reservation Service (NRRS), toll free, 1-877-444-6777; TDD 877-833-6777, www.recreation.gov, (Master, Visa, American Express & Discover cards).

LAKE BRYAN (WW) 1

From Starbuck, go 9 miles northeast on Little Goose Dam Road. No open fires permitted from June 10th through October 10th (Charcoal and gas grills are permitted). Park Manager, Clarkston Natural Resource Office, 100 Fair Street, Clarkston, WA 99403-1943. (509) 751-0240/0250.

ILLIA LANDING

From Lower Granite Dam, go 3 miles west on Almota Ferry Road. There is a grocery store nearby. Primitive camping area, free. Open all year.

LITTLE GOOSE LANDING

From Starbuck, go 9 miles northeast on Little Goose Dam Road, 1 mile east of Little Goose Dam. Primitive camping area, free. Open all year.

WILLOW LANDING

From Central Ferry State Park, go 1 mile south on Highway 127, 4 miles east on Deadman Road, 5 miles north on Hasting Hill Road. Primitive camping area, free. Open all year.

LAKE SACAJAWEA (WW) 2

Located 5.5 miles east of Burbank, 2.4 miles north on Monument Drive. Checkout time is 2 p.m. Visitor center featuring interpretive displays and a fish viewing room is open daily April through October. Alcoholic beverages are prohibited by state law. Self guided tours of the powerhouse/navigation lock during day light hours. Resource Manager, Ice Harbor Project, 1215 East Ainsworth, Pasco, WA 99301. (509) 547-2048/543-6060.

CHARBONNEAU CAMPGROUND

From Burbank, go 8.3 miles east on Highway 124, 1.5 miles north on Sun Harbor Drive, left on Charbonneau Road. A picnic shelter is $75 (contact office), and a marine dump station is available, and a convenience store and marina store are nearby. 54 sites with water and electric, 18 pull through sites, 15 full hookups, 1 handicap site with full hookups. Sites with water and electric hookups are $18; Premium sites with water and electric hookups are $20; sites with full hookups are $22; overflow area and boat camping sites are $8. Recreational vehicle maximum length is 60'. This campground requires a 2 night minimum stay on weekends and a 3 night stay on holiday weekends. Open from April 1st to September 30th. (509) 547-9252. NRRS.

FISHHOOK

From Burbank, go 18 miles east on Highway 124, 4 miles north on Fishhook Park Road. A picnic shelter is $75 and a convenience store is nearby. 61 sites, 41 with water and electric, 20 tent only sites, 2 double tent only sites, 8 pull through sites, 1 handicap site with water and electric. Tent only sites are $14; double tent only sites are $22; a site without electric hookups is $16; sites with water and electric hookups are $20; premium sites with water and electric hookups are $22; boat camping is $8. Recreational vehicle maximum length is 45'. This campground requires a 2 night minimum stay on weekends and a 3 night stay on holiday weekends. Open from May 1st to September 9th. NRRS.

WINDUST CAMPGROUND

From Kahlotus, go 4 miles southwest on Pasco/Kahlotus Road, 5.2 miles southeast on Burr Canyon Road. Covered sun shelters and a picnic shelter are available. 24 primitive sites, 2 tent only sites. All sites are $12, boat camping is $8. Recreational vehicle maximum length is 40'. This campground requires a 2 night minimum stay on weekends and a 3 night stay on holiday weekends. Open from April 1st to September 30th. NRRS.

LAKE UMATILLA (PORT) 3

Located on the Columbia River off State Road 14 near Rufus, Oregon, 25 miles east of The Dalles, Oregon. Resource Manager, Lake Umatilla, P. O. Box 564, The Dalles, OR 97058-9998. (503) 296-1181. See OR listing.

CLIFFS

Located near the dam on the north of United States Route 97, Washington side. Free camping area.

PLYMOUTH CAMPGROUND

From McNary Dam, on State Road 14, go 1.2 miles west below the dam on the north side. Alcohol is prohibited. A convenience store is nearby. 32 sites with water and electric, 17 full hookups, 29 pull through sites. Sites with water and electric hookups are $18; sites with full hookups are $20; overflow tent camping available on weekends and holidays is $12. There is a fee each extra vehicle and a dump fee for non campers. Recreational vehicle maximum length 40'. This campground requires a 2 night minimum stay on weekends and a 3 night stay on holiday weekends. Open from April 1st to October 31st. (509) 783-1270. NRRS.

LAKE WALLULA (WW) 4

A 38,800 acre surface area lake with 242 miles of shoreline located north of junction I-82/United States Route 730, 1 mile north of Umatilla. Interpretive displays and fish viewing rooms are available, and alcohol is prohibited by state law. Park Manager, Western Project, 2339 Ice Harbor Drive, Burbank, WA 99323. (541) 922-2268/4388. See OR listing.

HOOD CAMPGROUND

From Pasco, go 3 miles south on United States Route 12/395 at junction of Highway 124, east of Burbank. A picnic shelter is $100, reservation fee required, an amphitheater and horseshoe pits are available, and checkout time is 2 p.m. The campground is located near shopping malls. 69 sites with electric, 50 - 50 ampere, 25 pull through sites, 1 handicap site with 50 ampere. Sites with electric hookups are $18; premium sites with electric hookups are $20; boat camping and overflow sites are $8. Recreational vehicle maximum length is 65'.

This campground requires a 2 night minimum stay on weekends and a 3 night stay on holiday weekends. Open from April 1st to September 30th. 509-547-7781. NRRS.

LAKE WEST (WW) 5

Located off United States Route 260 south of Kahlotus on the Snake River. Resource Manager, Ice Harbor Project, 1215 East Ainsworth, Pasco, WA 99301. (509) 547-2048/543-6060.

AYER BOAT BASIN

From Burbank, go 26 miles east on State Road 124, 24 miles north through Clyde & Pleasant View to Ayers. A picnic shelter is available. Primitive camping area, free. Recreational vehicle maximum length is 40'. Open all year.

DEVILS BENCH

From Kahlotus, go 6 miles south on State Road 263. Primitive camping area, free. Open all year.

RIPARIA

From Little Goose Dam, go 3 miles west on North Shore Road. Primitive camping area, free. Recreational vehicle maximum length is 40'. Open all year.

LOWER GRANITE LAKE (WW) 6

From Lewiston, Idaho/Clarkston, WA, go 19 miles west on United States Route 12, 2 miles north on Ledgerwood Spur Road, 16 miles north on Kirby Mayview Road, 12 miles east on Casey Creek Road. No open fires permitted from June 10th through October 10th (Charcoal and gas grills are permitted). Park Manager, Clarkston Natural Resource Office, 100 Fair Street, Clarkston, WA 99403-1943. (509) 751-0240/0250.

BLYTON LANDING

From Lewiston, Idaho, go 20 miles west on County Road 9000 (North Shore Snake River Road). Primitive camping area, free. Open all year.

NISQUALLY JOHN LANDING

From Lewiston, Idaho, go 15 miles west on County Road 9000 (North Shore Snake River Road). Primitive camping area, free. Open all year.

WAWAWAI LANDING

From Lewiston, Idaho, go 28 miles west on County Road 9000 (North Shore Snake River Road), or 19 miles southwest of Pullman on Wawawai road. Primitive camping area, free. Open all year.

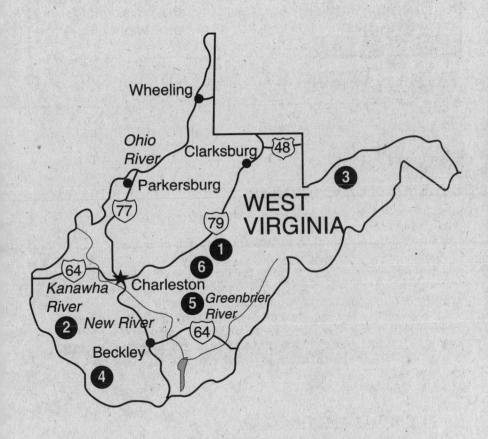

Wheeling

Ohio
River

Clarksburg

48

3

Parkersburg

WEST
VIRGINIA

77

79

1

6

64

Kanawha
River

Charleston

5

Greenbrier
River

2

New River

64

Beckley

4

WEST VIRGINIA

STATE CAPITAL:
Charleston
NICKNAME:
Mountain State

35th State - 1863

Site reservation, National Recreation Reservation Service (NRRS), toll free, 1-877-444-6777; TDD 877-833-6777, www.recreation.gov, (Master, Visa, American Express & Discover cards).

BURNSVILLE LAKE (HU) 1

A 968 acre surface area lake located east of Burnsville and I-79, on State Road 5, in central West Virginia. Checkout time is 5 p.m., visitors until 10 p.m. A Civil War site is nearby, reenactment every two years, call (304) 853-2371. Resource Manager, HC 10, Box 24, Burnsville, WV 26335. (304) 853-2371/8170. Lake information, (304) 853-2398.

BULLTOWN CAMPGROUND

From I-79 at Flatwoods, exit 67, go 10 miles north on United States Route 19 through Flatwoods & Napier, across lake bridge, on left, signs. A picnic shelter and horseshoe pits are available, and a convenience store is located nearby. No pets permitted in Loops E and F. 204 sites, 196 with electric, 12 - 50 ampere, 8 primitive tent only sites, 5 handicap sites with electric. Tent only sites are $12; sites with electric hookups are $20; premium sites with electric hookups are $22. Recreational vehicle maximum length is in excess of 65'. This campground requires a 2 night minimum stay on weekends and a 3 night stay on holiday weekends. Open from May 18th to September 2nd. (304) 452-8006. NRRS.

RIFFLE RUN CAMPGROUND

From Burnsville/Junction I-79, exit 79, go 3 miles east on State Road 5. A picnic shelter is available. 60 sites, 49 with electric, 6 primitive tent only sites, 5 full hookups. Tent only sites are $6; sites with electric hookups are $14; sites with full hookups are $18. Open April 21st to November 26th. (304) 853-2583.

EAST LYNN LAKE (HU) 2

A 1,005 acre surface area lake located 12 miles south of Wayne on Twelvepole Creek off State Road 37, south-western West Virginia. Resource Manager, East Lynn Lake, East Lynn, WV 25512. Lake information, (304) 849-2355.

EAST FORK CAMPGROUND

Located 10 miles east of the dam on State Road 37. Horseshoe pits and an amphitheater are available and checkout is 5 p.m. 169 sites with electric, 26 handicap sites, 1 pull through site, 1 double site. Sites with electric hookups are $18; premium sites with electric hookups are $20; a double site with electric hookups is $30. Recreational vehicle maximum length is in excess of 65'. This campground requires a 3 night stay on holidays. Open from May 11th to October 7th. (304) 849-5000. NRRS.

JENNINGS RANDOLPH LAKE (BL) 3

A 952 acre surface area lake located 5 miles north of Elk Garden, east of Morgantown, west of Kyser, in north-eastern West Virginia. An excellent trout fishing river is nearby and checkout time is noon. Resource Manager, Jennings Randolph lake, P. O. Box 247, Elk Garden, WV 26717. (301) 359-3861/(304) 355-2346.

ROBERT W. CRAIG CAMPGROUND

From Elk Garden, go 5 miles northeast on State Road 46, exit north at sign. A picnic shelter, horseshoe pits and an amphitheater are available. A camp store is nearby. 82 sites, 70 with electric, 9 - 50 ampere, 12 tent only sites, 9 - 50 ampere. Tent only sites are $18; sites with electric hookups are $22. Recreational vehicle maximum length is 55'. This campground requires a 3 night stay on holidays. Open from April 30th to September 30th. NRRS.

R. D. BAILEY LAKE (HU) 4

A 630 acre surface area lake located near Justice, 4 miles east of Gilbert on United States Route 52 and State Road 97. For 24-hour lake information call (304) 664-9587. Off the road vehicles are prohibited. Resource Manager, R. D. Bailey Lake, P. O. Drawer 70, Justice, WV 24851-0070. (304) 664-3220/3229.

GUYANDOTTE CAMPGROUND

From the Dam, go 1.1 miles to United States Route 52, 2.2 miles south on United States Route 52, 5.8 miles south on State Road 97. This campground is located in 4 areas. A picnic shelter is $50, plus a vehicle fee, horseshoe pits are available, and concession services are nearby. 94 sites, 163 with electric. Sites without electric hookups are $12; sites with electric hookups are $14. Open from Memorial Day through Labor Day. A primitive area, free, is open during archery hunting season only, October-December.

SUMMERSVILLE LAKE (HU) 5

A 2,790 acre surface area lake located south of Summersville off United States Route 19, 69 miles east of Charleston, west of Mt. Nebo on State Road 129, in south-central West Virginia. Visitors to 10 p.m., for a fee, picnic shelters and checkout time is 5 p.m. A Civil War site is nearby. Whitewater rafting below dam - Class V River during fall draw down. There is a 3000' airport at lake. Trout stocking below dam in spring and fall. Resource Manager, Summersville Lake, Route 2, Box 470, Summersville, WV 26651-9802. (304) 872-3412/5809.

BATTLE RUN CAMPGROUND

Located south of Summersville/Junction United States Route 19, 3.4 miles west on State Road 129 across dam, go north (right) at sign. Pets and off the road vehicles are prohibited. Horseshoe pits are available. There is a handicap accessible swimming pier with submerged ramp for wheel chairs and a handicap accessible fishing area. A convenience store and restaurant are located nearby. 117 sites, 110 with electric hookups, 7 tent only sites, 3 handicap sites, 24 pull through sites. Tent only sites are $14; sites with electric hookups are $18. Recreational vehicle maximum length is in excess of 65'. This campground requires a 2 night minimum stay on weekends and a 3 night stay on holidays. Open from May 1st to October 14th. (304) 872-3459. NRRS (May 26th to September 4th).

SUTTON LAKE (HU) 6

A 1,440 acre surface area lake located 1 mile east of Sutton off United States Route 19, northeast of Charleston in central West Virginia. Lake information, (304) 765-2816. Resource Manager, Sutton Lake, P. O. Box 426, Sutton, WV 26601. (304) 765-2816.

BEE RUN CAMPGROUND

From Sutton/Junction I-79, exit 67, go 1 mile east on State Road 4, 1.2 miles east on State Road 15, turn right. 12 primitive pull through sites. All sites are $8. Recreational vehicle maximum length 20'. Open all year.

BAKER'S RUN - MILL CREEK CAMPGROUND

From Sutton/Junction I-79, exit 62, go 2 miles to Sutton, 4 miles south on old United States Route 19 (County Road 19/40) 12 miles east on County Road 17. 77 sites, some pull through sites. Sites are from $16 to $18. Open from May 19th to September 5th. (304) 765-5631.

GERALD R. FREEMAN

From Sutton/Junction I 79, exit 67, 1 mile south on State Road 4, 12 miles east on State Road 15. Horseshoe pits are available and off the road vehicles are prohibited. 158 sites, 77 with electric, 1 pull through site, 1 handicap site. Sites without electric hookups are $16; sites with electric hookups are $18; premium sites with electric hookups are $20. This campground requires a 2 night minimum stay on weekends and a 3 night stay on holiday weekends. Open from May 11th to October 22nd. (304) 765-7756. NRRS (May 19th to September 4th).

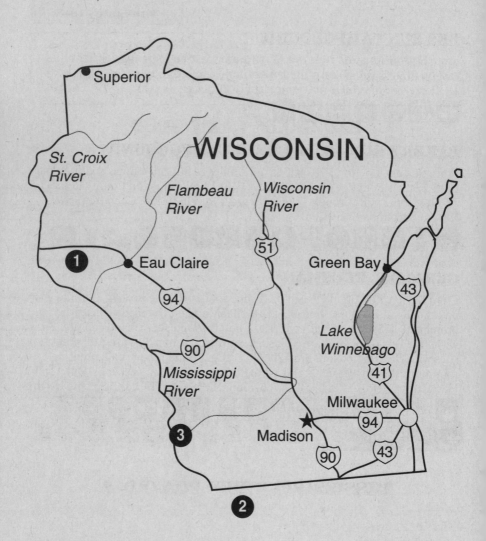

WISCONSIN

STATE CAPITAL:
Madison
NICKNAME:
Badger State

30th State - 1848

Site reservation, National Recreation Reservation Service
(NRRS), toll free, 1-877-444-6777; TDD 877-833-6777,
www.recreation.gov, (Master, Visa, American Express
& Discover cards).

EAU GALLE LAKE (SP) 1

An 150 acre surface area lake located 45 miles southeast of St. Paul off I-94, exit 24 south, 2 miles south on County Road B, 2 miles north on County Road N, 2 miles south on County Road NN, 0.5 mile north of Spring Valley, 40 miles west of Eau Galle. Electric motors only are permitted on the lake. Park Manager, Eau Galle Lake, P. O. Box 190, Spring Valley, WI 54767-0190. (715) 778-5562.

HIGHLAND RIDGE CAMPGROUND

From I-95, exit 24, go 2 miles south on County Road B, 2 miles east on County Road N, 2 miles south on County Road NN. Horseshoe pits, a picnic shelter, a group camping area, firewood and ice machines are available. Free movies or interpretive programs provided on weekends. Electric motors only are permitted on the lake. A shower fee is charged. Call for information on horse camping. 45 sites, 35 with electric, 7 tent only walk-in sites, 1 handicap site with electric. Tent only sites are $14; sites without electric hookups are $16; sites with electric hookups are $18. Recreational vehicle maximum length is in excess if 65'. This campground requires a 2 night minimum stay on weekends and a 3 night stay on holiday weekends. Open from April 1st to October 22nd. (715) 778-5562. NRRS (April 30th to September 30th).

MISSISSIPPI RIVER PUA (RI) 2

For information, contact Park Ranger, L&D #11, Dubuque, IA 52001, (319) 582-0881. See IL, IA & MO listings.

GRANT RIVER CAMPGROUND

From Dubuque, IA, go east across river, north on United States Route
61, 2 miles west on State Road 133 (signs). A picnic shelter is $25 and an
amphitheater is available. 73 sites, 10 tent only sites, 63 - 50 ampere. Tent
only sites are $10; sites with 50 ampere service are $16; premium sites with
50 ampere service are $18. Recreational vehicle maximum length is 55'. This
campground requires a 2 night minimum stay on weekends and a 3 night stay
on holiday weekends. Open from April 13th to October 28th. (608) 763-2140, 1-
800-645-0248. NRRS.

POOL 9 MISSISSIPPI RIVER (SP) 3

Located 30 miles south of La Crosse off State Road 35 on County Road B1.
Resource Manager, Blackhawk Park, East 590 County Road B1, DeSoto, WI
54624. (608) 648-3314.

BLACKHAWK CAMPGROUND

From DeSoto, go 3 miles north on State Road 35, go southwest on County Road
B1. Picnic shelters are $30, interpretive programs, fish cleaning station and
horseshoe pits are available, and there is a handicap accessible fishing area.
Off the road vehicles and other unlicensed motorized vehicles are prohibited.
Free movies are provided on weekends. Checkout time is 2 p.m., and a shower
fee is charged. 150 sites, 51 with electric, 14 - 50 ampere, 5 pull through sites.
Sites without electric hookups are $14; sites with electric hookups are $20.
Recreational vehicle maximum length is in excess if 65'. This campground
requires a 2 night minimum stay on weekends and a 3 night stay on holidays.
Open from April 1st to October 31st. (608) 648-3314. NRRS (June 1st to
October 31st).

— ABBREVIATIONS —

AQ	Albuquerque district
BL	Baltimore district
CR	County route
E	East
Fr	From
FW	Fort Worth district
HU	Huntington district
JX	Jacksonville district
JCT	Junction
KC	Kansas City district
LD	Labor Day
LR	Little Rock district
MB	Mobile district
MD	Memorial Day
N	North
NE	New England district
NRRS	National Recreation Reservation Service
NV	Nashville district
OM	Omaha district
POR	Portland district
PRIM	Primitive
PT	Pittsburgh district
PT's	Pull Throughs (preceded by a number)
Resv	Reservation
RV	Recreational Vehicle
SAC	Sacramento district
SEA	Seattle district
SF	San Francisco district
SL	St. Louis district
SP	St. Paul district
SPT	Some pull throughs
SR	State route
S	South
SV	Savannah district
TU	Tulsa district
TO	Tents only
US	United States route
VK	Vicksburg district
W	West
WL	Wilmington district
WW	Walla Walla district

— ADDRESSES —

NATIONAL

Headquarters, U. S. Army Corps of Engineers, 20 Massachusetts Avenue, N.W., Washington, D. C. 20314-1000, Attn: Public Affairs, CEPA-I. www.usace.army.mil

DISTRICTS

Start all addresses with "U. S. Army Corps of Engineers."

Albuquerque Dist., POB 1580, Albuquerque, NM 87103-1580
(505) 342-3464. (AQ). **www.spa.usace.army.mil**

Baltimore Dist., POB 1715, Baltimore, MD 21203-1715
(410) 962-3693. (BL). **www.nab.usace.army.mil**

Ft. Worth Dist., P. O. Box 17300, Ft. Worth, TX 76102-0300
(978) 334-4910. (FW). **www.swf.usace.army.mil**

Huntington Dist., 502-8th St., Huntington, WV 25701-2070
(304) 529-5608. (HU). **www.1rh.usace.army.mil**

Jacksonville Dist., POB 4970, Jacksonville, FL 32232-0019
(904) 791-2235. (JX). **www.saj.usace.army.mil**

Kansas City Dist., 700 Fed. Bldg., 601 E-12th St., Kansas City, MO 64106-2896 (816) 426-6816. (KC). **www.nwk.usace.army.mil**

Little Rock Dist., Attn: PAO (CESWL-PA), POB 867, Little Rock, AR 72203-0867 (501) 324-5551. (LR). **www.swl.usace.army.mil**

Louisville Dist., POB 59, Louisville, KY 40201-0059
(502) 582-5736. (L0). **www.lrl.usace.army.mil**

Mobile Dist., POB 2288 (Attn: OP-TR), Mobile, AL 36628-0001
(334) 690-2505). (MB). **www.sam.usace.army.mil**

Nashville Dist., POB 1070, Nashville, TN 37202-1070
(615) 736-5115. (NV). **www.lrn.usace.army.mil**

New England Dist., 696 Virginia Road, Concord, MA 01742-2751
(978) 318-8238. (NE). **www.nae.usace.army.mil**

Omaha Dist., 215 N. 17th St., Omaha, NE 63102-4978
(402) 221-4175. (OM). **www.nwo.usace.army.mil**

Pittsburgh Dist., Wm S. Moorehead Fed. Bldg., 1000 Liberty Ave.,
Pittsburgh, PA 15222-4186 (412) 644-6924. (PT).
www.lrp.usace.army.mil

Portland Dist., POB 2946, Portland, OR 97208-2946
(503) 326-6868/6021. (PORT). **www.nwp.usace.army.mil**

Rock Island Dist., POB 2004, Rock Island, IL 61204-2004
(309) 794-5561. (RI). **www.mvr.usace.army.mil**

Sacramento Dist., 1325 J St., Sacramento, CA 95814-2922
(916) 557-5279. (SAC). **www.spk.usace.army.mil**

San Francisco Dist., 211 Main St., San Francisco, CA 94105-1905
(415) 332-3871. (SF). **www.spn.usace.army.mil**

Savannah Dist., POB 889, Savannah, GA 31402-0889
(912) 944-5297. (SV). **www.sas.usace.army.mil**

Seattle Dist., POB C-3755, Seattle, WA 98124-2255
(206) 764-3440/3750. (SEA). **www.nws.usace.army.mil**

St. Louis Dist., 1222 Spruce St., St. Louis, MO 63103-2833
(314) 331-8622. (SL). **www.mvs.usace.army.mil**

St. Paul Dist., 190 5th Street East, St. Paul, MN 55101-1628
(612) 290-5200, (612) 290-5676. (SP). **www.mvp.usace.army.mil**

Tulsa Dist., POB 61, Tulsa, OK 74121-0061
(918) 581-7346. (TU). **www.swt.usace.army.mil**

Vicksburg Dist., 4155 Clay Street, Vicksburg, MS 39183-3435
(601) 631-5300. (VK). **www.mvk.usace.army.mil**

Walla Walla Dist., Walla Walla, WA 99362-9265
(502) 522-6717. (WW). **www.nww.usace.army.mil**

Wilmington Dist., POB 1890, Wilmington, NC 28402-1890
(919) 251-4192. (WL). **www.saw.usace.army.mil**

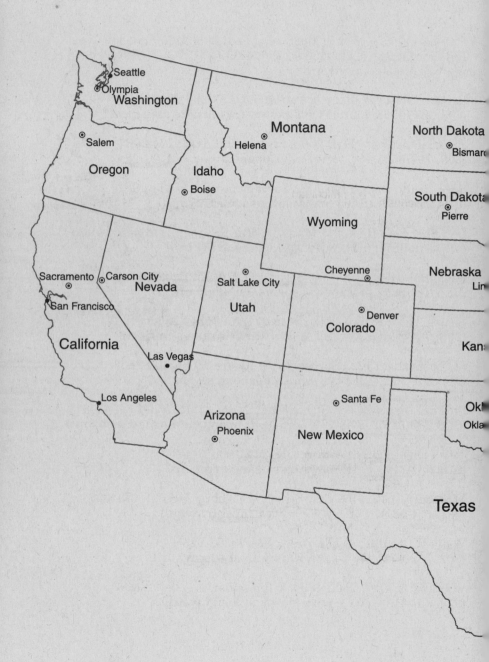